THE STREET OF
WONDERFUL POSSIBILITIES

The STREET *of* WONDERFUL POSSIBILITIES

WHISTLER, WILDE & SARGENT *in* TITE STREET

DEVON COX

FRANCES LINCOLN LIMITED
PUBLISHERS

Frances Lincoln Limited
74–77 White Lion Street
London N1 9PF
www.franceslincoln.com

FRONTISPIECE *The Acheson Sisters* by John Singer Sargent, 1902
PAGE 6 *A View of Tite Street* by Joseph Pennell, 1889

CONTENTS

INTRODUCTION

Alongside this artistic squalor we have the curious contrast of artistic splendour in a blazing, brand-new quarter, of which the sacred centre is Tite Street. Here, amid much that is good and genuine in our modern manner, there is an aggressive affectation of antiquity shown by the little houses and studios obtruding on the street, by the grandiose piles of mansions towering on the embankment: all in raging red brick, and in the so-called Queen Anne style. This is a quarter, however, much in vogue; mighty swells dwell here, and here pose some famous farceurs in art and literature.
– Benjamin Ellis, *Old Chelsea*, 1889

On a grey morning in 1889, a carriage arrived at 33 Tite Street. The renowned actress Ellen Terry, then starring as Lady Macbeth in Henry Irving's production at the Lyceum, emerged on to the pavement draped in a costume of sparkling emerald robes and floor-length magenta hair. Terry swept gracefully into the studio building where a young John Singer Sargent was eagerly waiting to paint her portrait. From the window of his library at 34 Tite Street, Oscar Wilde watched the scene unfold with fascination. 'The street that on a wet and dreary morning has vouchsafed the vision of Lady Macbeth in full regalia, can never again be as other streets,' he dreamily professed. 'It must always be full of wonderful possibilities.'[1] And so it would be.

Over a century later, in the summer of 1994, the 'wonderful possibilities' of Tite Street were still alive. It was not a dreary morning, but a fresh summer afternoon, and it was not a carriage, but a green Audi parked in front of No. 33. A woman emerged, not a flame-haired Lady Macbeth, but a blonde princess. The American artist Nelson Shanks was using a studio in the Tite Street building where such legendary artistic giants as James Abbott McNeill Whistler, John Singer Sargent and Augustus John had all lived and worked. In the light and airy studio, Diana, Princess of Wales sat for a portrait. Posed in a cream-coloured silk blouse and emerald-green taffeta skirt, hands folded, face tilted downwards, Diana was entertained by the artist and his wife, talking and laughing, as the strains of the outside world melted away.

Diana was not the only woman sitting for a portrait in Tite Street that summer. Margaret Thatcher was an altogether different figure from the Princess. Shanks had been commissioned by the former Prime Minister with the portrait intended as a gift for the National Portrait Gallery. While Diana's sittings were free and casual, Thatcher was more organised, her sittings fitted into a rigid schedule, with a security entourage lingering in the dark corners of the studio. Unsurprisingly she retained her poise and dignity throughout the entire ordeal. At breaks, when most sitters would relax on a sofa, the Iron Lady held her pose, merely moving a hand to reach for a cup of tea.

Nelson Shanks and his portraits *H.R.H. The Princess of Wales* and *Lady Margaret Thatcher* stand at the end of a dramatic 120-year history of Tite Street – a colourful history of art and intrigue, bankruptcies and prosecutions, madness and suicide. From approximately 1877 until the outbreak of the First World War, Tite Street sat at the heart of a thriving avant-garde community of artists, writers and bohemians in Chelsea. In a proximity of fewer than 200 yards lived some of the most influential artistic figures of the period – the bold, daring American artist James Abbott McNeill Whistler, the witty Irish playwright Oscar Wilde, and the celebrated portraitist John Singer Sargent. Just as the controversial legacies of Diana and Thatcher coloured the late twentieth century, so Whistler, Wilde and Sargent influenced the world of art and literature at a pivotal moment at the close of the Victorian era and the dawn of the twentieth century.

During its dynamic and turbulent history, Tite Street's 'smart bohemians' gave the street its unique flavour as a home to outsiders – not only in art and literature, but in nationality, sexuality and society. Unlike other artistic quarters, the demographic of Tite Street was almost entirely composed of foreign artists. Of all the nationalities in Tite Street there was a particular abundance of Americans, from Whistler and Sargent to Edwin Abbey, Anna Lea Merritt and later, Romaine Brooks.[2] In addition to the prevalence of Americans there was the Italian Carlo 'Ape' Pellegrini, the German-born Walter Sickert and the Australian Mortimer Menpes. Even within the British contingent, Edith Elizabeth Downing, Peter Warlock and Augustus John were all Welsh, and Oscar Wilde was Irish.

These artists often operated beyond the traditions and customs of those trained within the English establishment. Most of Tite Street's artists had trained in Paris. They were not inhibited by English tastes and social systems. Towards the end of his career, Whistler complained that the British were a people 'absolutely unfitted for [art]'[3] but in some cases this rejection of English norms had profound consequences. After all, the street that saw the creation of such modern masterpieces as *Harmony in Pink and Grey* or *The Picture of Dorian Gray*, also saw Whistler bankrupted and Wilde sent to prison.

Tite Street had its share of social scandal. This was a street where barmaids and dance-hall singers married millionaires, where flower girls became celebrated models overnight, where unwed mothers lived as mistresses, and where police were called to investigate fugitive paedophiles. Deviance in Tite Street took other forms as well. With camp Italian cartoonist, Carlo 'Ape' Pellegrini, Tite Street had been a haven for homosexuals – Oscar Wilde, Romaine Brooks, Edith Elizabeth Downing, Ellen Sparks, Radclyffe Hall, Gluck and Glyn Philpot to name a few, while questions remain over the sexual orientation of artists like Frank Miles and John Singer Sargent.

Tite Street's individuality was nowhere more apparent than in the very street itself. While most streets in the capital held symmetric terraces of identical buildings, Tite Street was largely composed of individual studio-houses, each with its own unique personality, usually identified by name rather than number such as the White House, Chelsea Lodge, Keats House and Canwell House. This was in part due to the individualistic nature of the artists designing and inhabiting them. By the mid-nineteenth century, studio-building had become a necessary facet to an artist's career. The studio was not only a place to work, it stood as a visible symbol of aesthetic taste and status – a calling card in bricks and mortar. In Tite Street, the architect E.W. Godwin, dubbed by Max Beerbohm as the 'greatest aesthete of them all', was designing studio-houses in a clean and simple style inspired by Japanese designs.

Throughout its turbulent existence, Tite Street has mirrored the world around it. From the aesthetes of the *fin de siècle* to the Edwardian struggle for women's suffrage, through the bombs of the Blitz in the 1940s to the bombs of the IRA in the 1970s, Tite Street remained home to innumerable artists and writers, socialites and suffragettes, musicians and madmen. Although some of its buildings have been demolished or converted, and billionaires have replaced bohemians, its colourful and important history remains.

NOTE TO THE READER

Throughout the 1880s and 1890s, the houses and studios of Tite Street were renumbered several times. The studio block that both Whistler and Sargent lived in was located at No. 13 Tite Street which today is No. 33. Frank Miles's Keats House was originally No. 1 Tite Street which today is No. 44. Oscar Wilde's House Beautiful was No. 16 which today is No. 34. Many of the houses and studios of Tite Street were commonly identified by name rather than number – the White House, Chelsea Lodge, Canwell House, More House, the Cottage – and in most cases, the author has chosen to use these names for consistency. Where possible, the author has used the numbers as they currently exist, but for clarification of location please consult the map on pages 248–9.

I.

VISIONARY
& UNREAL

Art alone remains the fact. All the rest is anecdote.
– James Abbott McNeill Whistler

22 July 1903 – the genteel Chelsea riverfront sat under a sky of heavy grey clouds. At 74 Cheyne Walk, a small crowd had gathered as a coffin draped in purple cloth passed out of the front door and into the attending funeral carriage. A ring of pallbearers accompanied the sombre procession as the coffin containing the body of James Abbott McNeill Whistler was solemnly marched to the nearby Old Church for a brief funeral service.

After the service, and under looming storm clouds, Whistler's coffin was conveyed to Chiswick Cemetery where the artist's beloved mother and his wife Beatrice were already buried beneath a wall of fragrant clematis, only a stone's throw from the former home and grave of Whistler's favourite British artist, William Hogarth. It was a simple plot adorned with flowers as Whistler had wished. Later, the family erected a bronze monument designed by the artist's stepson, Edward Godwin.

Police had arrived to control the crowds, but just a small group of mourners assembled from Whistler's once-thriving circle of friends – artists and aristocrats, collectors, new world millionaires, models and mistresses. Of this latter group Maud Franklin trembled and nearly fainted as she approached the coffin of the once vibrant, outspoken man who had fathered her children. Among the other familiar faces were Charles Freer, Theodore Duret, Sir John Lavery, George Vanderbilt and Sir Lawrence Alma-Tadema. But the list of people not present was far more revealing.

In his life Whistler made many friends, recruited countless followers, but had also mastered what he liked to call 'the gentle art of making enemies'. From this vast circle of artists, writers and bohemians only a handful of them were still on friendly terms, and out of that dwindling group only a few were still living. Oscar Wilde, who had revered Whistler in his youth, was already dead, and Walter Sickert, another devoted pupil, had abandoned

Chelsea for the northern suburb of Camden Town. Of all the absentees and apologies, however, there was one that stood out as particularly poignant. The United States Embassy in London had failed to send an emissary to commemorate the influential American who Wilde had applauded as 'the first British artist'.[1]

This was a disappointing dénouement for a man who prided himself on causing so much controversy during his lifetime. The hurricane of a life that was James Abbott McNeil Whistler's began in the small New England town of Lowell, Massachusetts. Childhood photographs of the artist show a prim-faced boy, smartly dressed and confidently poised with a head full of rich, coal-black curls and dark, mischievous eyes. As a young man Whistler demonstrated a precocious talent for drawing but his razor-sharp tongue and acutely insubordinate nature eventually saw him expelled from West Point Military Academy by Robert E. Lee, later to become General of the Confederate Army in the American Civil War.

After a brief flirtation with a military career, in late 1855 Whistler found himself in Paris. It was a pivotal moment, when the Parisian art world was the scene of a fierce war of aesthetics. Entrenched in the cafes and ateliers of the *Rive Gauche*, the Parisian avantgarde fought to breach the ramparts of the highly selective annual Salon. The twenty-one-year-old aspiring artist, sporting a beret and fashionable moustache, soon found himself in the company of artists like Henri Fantin-Latour swearing allegiance to Gustav Courbet.

A generation prior, the famous *Hernani* riots had signalled a rift in Paris between romantic bohemians and conservative classicists, a rift that was still festering when Whistler arrived. From this clash emerged the foundations of what, in Britain, would be called the aesthetic movement, and literary castles were being built upon it – Théophile Gautier's novel *Mademoiselle Maupin* and later Baudelaire's poems *Les Fleurs du Mal* are but two examples. 'L'art pour l'art' had already become the banner for a very different brand of Parisian artist. They inhabited a world of lead-based paints, absinthe and loose women, so colourfully brought to life in Murger's *Scenes de la Vie Bohème* and later in George du Maurier's *Trilby*. In this bohemian circle young Whistler cut his teeth as an artist.[2]

By the early 1860s, however, Whistler had migrated across the Channel where his sister, Deborah, and brother-in-law, Francis Seymour-Haden were living in Sloane Street, Knightsbridge. The London in which he arrived could not have been more different from the bohemian world of Paris. There was no café culture, no artistic quarter, no friendly exchange of ideas. In Paris, studios had been open as ateliers and salons where fellow artists were free to come and go at will, inspecting their work, and engaging in discussion. But in London artists 'locked themselves up in their studios' and only 'opened the doors on the chain'.[3] In matters of art, sentimental tableaus and historical narrative painting were the hot items of the day, and the century-old Royal Academy had the final word on British artistic taste.

In these early years, Whistler found himself on the right side of the British art establishment. For the first ten years or so in London his work garnered institutional attention, and he found a position at the fringes of critical acclaim at the Academy. One of his earliest paintings, *At the Piano*, had been rejected from the Paris Salon, but was warmly accepted by the Royal Academy in 1860, who placed it in a prime viewing position. Sir Charles Eastlake, President of the Royal Academy, was so enthusiastic about the picture he steered patrons like the Duchess of Sutherland to the painting, saying it was 'the finest piece' on show.[4] *At the Piano* was a reflection of Whistler's early tendency towards realism, but it does demonstrate a promising eye for colour with its bold but well-balanced palate of mid-tones and form that would develop and sharpen in the years to come. Even eminent Academicians like John Everett Millais conceded it was 'the finest piece of colour that has been on the walls of the Royal Academy for years.'[5]

However, the Academy was not prepared to accept a complete departure from tradition. There were certain boundaries that could not be crossed. So it came as little surprise when *Symphony in White, No. 1: The White Girl*, submitted for the 1862 exhibition, was rejected. The painting featured the first of several lovers who would double as Whistler's model and live-in secretary. In this case the soft Celtic face was that of Joanna Hifferman, or Jo, a pale skinned, auburn-haired model dressed in a flowing white muslin dress, standing in front of a slightly off-white curtain.

Whistler's funeral procession, Cheyne Walk, London, 1903

LEFT *Symphony in White,
No. 1: The White Girl* by
James Abbott McNeill
Whistler, 1862
RIGHT *Symphony in White,
No. 2: The Little White Girl*
by James Abbott McNeill
Whistler, 1864

Painted in full-length, the seven-foot tall *White Girl* demonstrates a mastery of colour manipulation, with subtle tonalities and inflections – the use of varying shades of white-on-white was difficult to achieve effectively and required a sensitive eye. While *At the Piano* burst with reds, blacks and yellows, *The White Girl* looked almost sickly with the pale, virginal Jo standing upon a ruggedly masculine wolf skin, with its fierce teeth projecting out of the frame. To some contemporaries, the lines were rough and the painting looked incomplete. 'He is a sort of Wagner in painting,' one critic later wrote, 'a Wagner who is always composing beautiful themes, exquisite conceptions of harmony, and leaving them unfinished.'[6]

With *The White Girl*, Whistler took his first decisive step out of the orbit of the Royal Academy circle and began to align himself with the somewhat fragmented English avant-garde, formerly represented by the short-lived but highly influential Pre-Raphaelite Brotherhood. Founded in 1848 by a group of young painters including John Everett Millais, Dante Gabriel Rossetti and William Holman Hunt, the early Pre-Raphaelites relished the purity and simplicity of medieval art. The perceived radicalism of these early Victorian avant-garde artists lay 'in a refusal to accept the conventions revered by their teachers and society at large'.[7]

Within a decade of its inception, the young fraternity, based in Gower Street, had fizzled out with each artist pursuing his own independent aims. But in 1859 Dante Gabriel Rossetti re-emerged onto the art scene with *Bocca Baciata*, a half-length portrait of his new model, mistress and muse, Fanny Cornforth. The painting is dedicated, in both composition and style, to the celebration of beauty as an end in itself.[8] The poet Algernon Swinburne considered the painting to be 'more stunning than can be decently expressed'[9] while fellow Pre-Raphaelite artist William Holman Hunt found it 'remarkable for gross sensuality of a revolting kind'.[10] Whether stunning or revolting, *Bocca Baciata* raised more than a few eyebrows as the meaty figure of its subject fills the frame, leaving the eye no choice but to dwell upon her warm skin, thick lips and liquid eyes in a manner that was far from decent in a high-Victorian art gallery.

After his wife died from a laudanum overdose in 1862, Rossetti relocated to Tudor House, a comfortable if eccentric Georgian dwelling on Cheyne Walk on the rustic Chelsea riverfront. The lease was taken along with Algernon Swinburne and, for a time, the poet and novelist George Meredith rented rooms, as did Rossetti's brother William. The calm, placid figure of Meredith was contrasted by the petite, hyperactive Swinburne. A highly excitable alcoholic, prone to bouts of extreme depression, Swinburne proved to be quite a handful. For the other residents, getting work done was a challenge with the animated poet dancing around the house nude and taking turns with openly homosexual artist Simeon Solomon sliding down the handrail naked. Although unpredictable, Swinburne did manage to write as well, and in 1865 he composed a poem 'Before the Mirror' inspired by Whistler's new *Symphony in White, No. 2: The Little White Girl*, a follow-up to the previous painting featuring Jo once again in her white dress.

Unlike its predecessor, *The Little White Girl* was accepted at the Royal Academy where an extract of Swinburne's poem appeared in the catalogue and a few lines were printed on the picture frame. The poem was, wrote Whistler, 'a rare and graceful tribute from the poet to the painter – a noble recognition of work by the production of a nobler one'.[11] Swinburne's greatest work was just on the horizon. The year after Whistler's *White Girl* was shown, Swinburne published the same poem in his canonical volume, *Poems and Ballads*, which was met with deeply divided reviews, mostly negative. The poems were a revelation and a shock to Victorian sensibilities dealing as they did with erotic lesbian love and with a fixation on flagellation and 'filth'. One critic dismissed them as 'unclean for the sake of uncleanness'.[12]

In this milieu, Whistler ripened as an artist. He shared a temporary residence nearby on Queen's Road with his 'White Girl' until they could settle into their own home just a few minutes away from Rossetti's at Lindsey House. Although smaller, it soon rivalled Rossetti's house in Cheyne Walk as a buzzing hive of artists, writers and intellectuals; his collection of porcelain also grew to rival that of his neighbour, and he instigated a new ritual that would become a staple of social life amongst the bohemian clique. Perhaps in an attempt to make Chelsea slightly more Parisian, Whistler flung open his doors on Sundays to his friends and neighbours. His raucous Sunday brunches soon became a Chelsea institution. To Whistler's dining room flocked the greatest figures of the day, invited to a home-cooked meal and an afternoon of conversation and painting in the studio.

With Rossetti's *Bocca Baciata*, Swinburne's *Poems and Ballads* and Whistler's *White Girl* 'symphonies', the Chelsea set were well on the way to establishing a new aesthetic school – the 'fleshly school' as they were called – prized for their use of colour and 'harmonious sensuality' over narrative functionality. They presented some of the earliest examples in England of a new breed of art that, first conceived in Paris, was finally being given credence in London. This 'fleshly' art and poetry would soon dominate the studios and salons of Chelsea as a variant of a broader aesthetic movement in British art. As the chief proponents of this new school of thought lived in Chelsea, this tiny village along the Thames became its default headquarters. Down by the river, artists lived in rented accommodation, in dilapidated old houses, with models and mistresses out of wedlock. None of them had enough money or esteem to build exotic palaces as celebrity artists Val Princeps, Marcus Stone, Lord Leighton and Luke Fildes were doing further north in Kensington.

This decadent charm led Chelsea to become one of the first quarters of London to be referred to as 'bohemian'. At Cheyne Walk, visitors found dark rooms full of dusty old books and paintings, sketches and prints alongside shelves full of the best porcelain and Japanese pottery. At nearby Lindsey House, Whistler's love of Japanese art and design, developed while in Paris, had flowered into an obsession whose flames were fanned by competition with Rossetti, also an avid collector. At Cheyne Walk there was a noisy dining room peopled by Swinburne, Solomon, Meredith, Whistler, William Morris and Edward Burne-Jones.

Venturing into the rear garden they would find a menagerie of exotic plants and animals – kangaroos, raccoons, peacocks, wallabies, chameleons, gazelles, woodcocks, monkeys and parakeets, a raven, an armadillo and (until it died after eating Rossetti's cigars) a wombat.

The etcher Alphonse Legros, a friend of Whistler's in Paris, had come to London and was living with the artist to escape his father's creditors. They shared Lindsey House for a short time, establishing an English outpost of French artistic life. Their bohemian bubble was soon to burst when Whistler learned that his beloved mother intended to come over from America and stay with him as a live-in guest. In 1864 Anna McNeill Whistler departed from the United States to join her son and his half-sister Deborah Seymour Haden who were both living in Chelsea. A pious and religious woman, Anna's role was to regulate 'the everyday realities' of her son's existence. Despite his 'bright hopes . . . his income is very precarious'.[13] It was true. Respectable society dared not go near Whistler's 'amoral' clique for fear of being mixed up in some scandal.[14] The imminent arrival of his mother necessitated the eviction of Legros and the removal of his mistress Jo to lodgings further afield.

Anna Whistler tidied up Lindsey House in her own maternal way. Mistresses were kept at bay, brunches were tamed, and the household garnered an element of conservative stability needed to attract respectable patrons and much-needed income. As far as possible, the conservative New Englander coolly tolerated her son's friends, but their 'aesthetic' values and seeming lack of morals did not entirely escape her attention. To her, and indeed to many others, they were dismissed as 'visionary and unreal'[15] – tortured romantics and desperate lovers.

The arrival of his mother did change Whistler's life and career. First, the widow, in her austere black dress, provided the inspiration for a portrait. *Arrangement in Grey and Black, No. 1* earned the artist considerable fame and had the effect of attracting lucrative portrait commissions such as the great 'Sage of Chelsea' Thomas Carlyle and the famous jump-rope dancer Cicely Alexander. In the meantime, Whistler had also found a powerful ally and patron in the wealthy industrialist Frederick Leyland. Leyland belonged to the newly wealthy industrial class, rising from a meagre apprentice in a shipbuilding firm he took the reins of the Liverpool based company and made a fortune from a shipping line. He had also become a generous patron of artists like Whistler, gaining the nickname the 'Liverpool Medici'. In 1871 Leyland commissioned Whistler to paint portraits of his entire family.

As the commissions began to stream in, Whistler was finally beginning to reap the financial rewards of being a professional artist. Nonetheless, he did manage to make a number of significant enemies. Sometimes his temper turned violent. He had pushed his brother-in-law Francis Seymour-Haden through a shop window and had a punch-up with Alphonse Legros. Other times he was more subtle. When the Royal Academy showed reluctance to exhibit his mother's portrait, *Arrangement in Grey and Black, No. 1*, in the 1872 exhibition, Whistler decided it would be his last work submitted for exhibition there.

Arrangement in Grey and Black, No. 1: Portrait of the Artist's Mother by James Abbott McNeill Whistler, 1871

While friends and enemies were being made and lost, the legend of Whistler was being created – a legend closely tied to the streets of Chelsea. By the mid-1870s the once close circle of artists and writers, the tapestry of those 'visionary and unreal' eccentrics along the Chelsea riverfront had already begun to unravel. Meredith had settled in Surrey, Swinburne, the 'libidinous laureate', was relocated across the river in Putney, and increasingly the walls of Cheyne Walk had become a prison for an ageing and anti-social Rossetti. The jovial scenes of brawls and brunches were coming to a close. Whistler's career, on the other hand, was on a steady progression upwards. He temporarily left Chelsea and for a moment it seemed as if artistic life had receded altogether from its shores, but there were bigger changes on the horizon that the artists of Cheyne Walk and Lindsey House could not anticipate.

2.

PARADISE LOST

If here is Paradise, we will travel in some other direction.
– Charles Dickens Jr.

For centuries Chelsea had been a small village of artists, artisans and aristocrats living peacefully on the outskirts of London. But it was in 1834 that Chelsea's artistic and intellectual epoch officially began, when Jane and Thomas Carlyle arrived and settled into their new house in Cheyne Row. Here the 'Sage of Chelsea' would write his influential *History of the French Revolution*, and the house itself would become a pilgrimage site for almost every intellectual, artistic and literary person of the age from Charles Dickens and the Brownings to Virginia Woolf.

Meanwhile, in 1846, at the far end of Chelsea Reach, past Lindsey House, in a small cottage a homely landlady called Mrs Booth bought a twenty-one-year lease. A mysterious gentleman lodger accompanied her, but wished to remain known simply as 'Mr Booth'. This seventy-one-year-old man with short thick legs, a red, weather-beaten face, and piercing grey eyes was none other than J.M.W. Turner. The ageing artist had come to Chelsea in search of peace and anonymity in his fading years. Turner spent much of his time here simply watching the misty river from his upper-floor window. So secretive was the artist about his Chelsea residence that when leaving a party in the West End his host, after helping him into a cab, asked which address to give the driver. 'Tell the fellow to drive to Oxford Street,' said Turner, 'and then I will direct him from there.'[1] Thus Turner spent the remaining days of his life in his dingy Chelsea lodgings where he continued to paint until his death.

A generation after Turner's death, along the Thames shores, a new, distinctive Chelsea set were making themselves known. By 1875, a new London had emerged from the fissures of industrialism and empire, and had all but engulfed the little village on its fringe. Alongside the many marvels of Imperial London stood the new Chelsea Embankment and a narrow lane branching off to the north – a seemingly insignificant little thoroughfare that would eventually blossom into a thriving artistic quarter as the newly paved Tite Street.

Tite Street owes its existence to the hot, dry summer of 1855. The Industrial Revolution of the previous century sent the rural poor flooding into urban centres in search of work. In spite of this influx of newcomers, London had failed to keep up with the pace of progress and modernisation. The capital was impossibly crowded and incredibly dangerous. At the beginning of the nineteenth century, London housed a mere one million people, but by the 1850s this number had more than tripled.[2] Parliament hastily established one of the greatest bureaucratic marvels of the Victorian age, the Metropolitan Board of Works. Comprised of civil engineers and urban planners (including Sir William Tite) the Board of Works would oversee the development of London as a modern, functioning city.

Perched on the edge of the expanding city, between the age-old King's Road and the Thames, sat Chelsea. When Whistler arrived it was a quaint village with a few modest inns, brothels, churches, a pottery and a brewery punctuated by a handful of stately homes. Like Turner, Whistler found himself drawn to the murky, misty, mysterious Thames. There was nowhere better to settle than in Chelsea, nestled along the river, away from the bustle of the crowded metropolis and yet still within easy reach of the West End theatres and galleries.

By 1865 construction on the Embankment scheme was already in progress, and with it much of the old riverfront was swept away. Artists, writers and intellectuals were not oblivious to the changes taking place in their capital. To escape this rugged industrialisation, critic John Ruskin sought solace in the stones of old Venice, while the early Pre-Raphaelites had already turned to the mosaics of Renaissance Italy. Whistler would revert to the pure, unpolluted art of Japan. By the late 1860s, Whistler had begun to restrict his palette to subdued colours, reduced detail, and concentrated on the careful arrangement of large, simple forms and areas of harmonious colour. But when he applied this to the chaotic, dirty urban scene of Victorian London, the visual experience in turn created an awkward, somewhat unpleasant conflict between style and subject matter. Throughout the late 1860s and early 1870s, Whistler struggled to successfully combine the ethereal Japanese style with the grim reality of London.

One night on his way home from Westminster with his mother, Whistler found 'the river in a glow of rare transparency an hour before sunset', and was 'inspired to begin a picture and rushed upstairs to his Studio, carrying an easel and brushes'.[3] That night, Whistler developed a new style of painting, which would become his famous 'nocturnes'. *Nocturne: Blue and Silver – Chelsea* was a glimpse of Japanese-inspired colour harmony begun in *The White Girl* and now perfected. The river itself and the shoreline could barely be detected, but the cool colours were a sensual treat and evocative of a particular ethereality evoked in Japanese watercolour.

Ever since he had moved to London, Whistler had been having a love affair with the Thames. Over the next ten years it would develop into an obsession. 'The river,' writes Margaret MacDonald and Patricia De Montfort, 'as a late nineteenth-century social, economic and geographic phenomenon, is the essential backdrop to [Whistler's] art and

Construction of the Chelsea Embankment, 1873

was crucial to the development of a Whistlerian aesthetic.'[4] At night he would row out onto the river with local Chelsea artist Walter Greaves as his oarsman. They would start out at twilight and sometimes remain on the river well past midnight. All along the Chelsea riverfront Whistler, encumbered with easel and brushes, would paint the dusky, misty Thames from Battersea Bridge to Cremorne.

At the far end of Chelsea, Cremorne Gardens had been created in 1845 as an enormous pleasure garden that stretched from the King's Road down to the River Thames, just slightly upriver from Lindsey House where Whistler and his mother were living. Cremorne was a feast for the senses, a noisy and colourful pleasure garden complete with restaurants, entertainments, dancing, hot air balloon rides and topped off with incredible fireworks and rocket displays. Living nearby, Whistler had taken an interest in Cremorne from his earliest days in Chelsea and in 1875 he completed a series of nocturnes of Cremorne which feature one of these rockets falling from a dark sky. *Nocturne in Black and Gold: The Falling Rocket* would change Whistler's life and would become one of the most infamous paintings of the nineteenth century.

Painted at dusk, Whistler's eerie, serene nocturnes document the demise of an old, tranquil village. The Chelsea of the 1860s and 1870s had not yet been swallowed up by the expanding metropolis and was still a world described by Thomas Carlyle as a 'singularly heterogeneous kind of spot, very dirty and confused in some places, quite beautiful in others'.[5] There were still old-fashioned inns and taverns and coffee shops dotted along the riverfront, punctuated with pockets of extreme poverty.

The Duke and Duchess of Edinburgh opening the new Chelsea Embankment, 1874

A small dockland with three wharves – Paradise Wharf, Bull Wharf and Swan Wharf – supplied Chelsea with goods brought from nearby London. On the edge of Swan Wharf was Stansfeld & Co's Swan Brewery and Old Swan Inn where Pepys stayed on his journey to Chelsea in 1666. Just opposite on Swan Walk, the botanist Joseph Banks was raised inhaling the scents of the Chelsea Physic Garden across the street. The odours of the Physic Garden, however, did little to mask the putrid poverty that arose just a few steps in the opposite direction. Up from Paradise Wharf ran a notorious little stretch ironically named Paradise Walk, which took its name from the Paradise Chapel on its eastern side. The lane of tiny workers' cottages itself was anything but paradise. Here lived some of Chelsea's poorest residents. Over time the narrow thoroughfare and adjoining timber yard had gained a reputation for vagrants and prostitutes plying their trade for local dockworkers and shipmen.[6]

When Charles Dickens Jr. visited the area in 1888, he described his walk through this part of Chelsea: 'Away from the river leads the Queen's Road[7] . . . The policeman standing there, and the costermonger with his barrow farther on, have never heard of Paradise Row, or receive the suggestion that perhaps it is this very street, with anything but credulity and with a slight doubt as to the good faith of the questioner. But there is Paradise Walk. Always there is Paradise Walk . . . But what a glimpse of Paradise we gain looking down this walk; the houses small and ancient, with a ferocious kind of gloom about them! If here is Paradise, we will travel in some other direction.'[8]

Pleasure gardens and Paradise Walk however were soon lost. The Chelsea of Cremorne Gardens, Turner and Carlyle would not survive the greedy clutches of the encroaching city. The new Embankment scheme was one of the most enduring engineering marvels of the Victorian age, creating a lasting infrastructure 'worthy of an Imperial capital'. With one sewer housed under the Chelsea Embankment, the 'unpleasant mud banks' of the Thames would be replaced by 'pleasant drives and ornamental gardens.'[9] Despite an urgent public outcry against Lord Cadogan's policy of demolishing poor housing for property development, by the late 1860s, the Board of Works had forced compulsory purchase of the land along the riverfront from the Cadogan Estate. With the Board now in firm control of the land around the Embankment, the maze of twisting lanes along the river were mostly flattened and replaced with paved streets whose plots were leased out to prospective builders for development at affordable rates. Modern London had finally arrived at Chelsea's door, and she was hungry.

Lord Carbery's old, disused Gough House had been converted into a hospital for children in 1866 (the second of its kind in London, the other being Great Ormond Street Hospital). With the building boom, a host of new streets were created on top of the old side-lanes. The task of naming the streets fell to the local Chelsea Vestry, who would propose names to be submitted to the Board of Works for approval. When it came to the street alongside the Victoria Hospital, the Vestry debated a suitable name.

Sir William Tite was a London-born architect famous for the rebuilding of the Royal Exchange in 1844. The Vestry had been in his debt since 1846 when a lack of funding threatened the cancellation of the 'embankment and roadway between Vauxhall and Battersea bridges' and 'the construction of suspension bridge at Chelsea'.[10] Tite came to the rescue. A well-respected, prominent Victorian, former President of the Board of Works and an MP, Tite had plenty of clout. As an activist for sensible urban planning and development, he was approached by the Vestry to help. Tite appealed to the Board of Works to undertake the work independently of Government assistance. As a result the roadway and suspension bridges were built ahead of schedule and on budget.

Ever since Tite's death in 1873, the Vestry had been in search of an appropriate means of preserving his memory to posterity. A list of ideas was formulated: a statue of him in Sloane Square? A fountain? Or a park? On 10 December 1875 a motion was put forward to the Board of Works from the Vestry that the lane 'from Queen's Road West to the Chelsea Embankment be named "Tite-street"' in commemoration of Sir William's services to the borough.[11] The motion was passed by twelve votes to four. The newly created Tite Street would serve to connect the age-old Royal Hospital Road to the new Chelsea Embankment. Over time, it would live up to its role in connecting the old with the new both in geography and art. Thus through Victorian progress and expansion a street was created that would eventually challenge the values of the age and embody the new aesthetic in art and architecture well into the twentieth century. Tite Street was born.

Nocturne: Blue and Silver – Chelsea by James Abbott McNeill Whistler, 1871

Entrance of the Grosvenor Gallery, New Bond Street, London from *The Graphic*, 19 May 1877

3.

The WICKED EARL
& the BUTTERFLY

The opening of the Grosvenor Gallery was to be an epoch-making
event, said rumour, and for once rumour spoke the truth.
– W. Graham Robertson

New Bond Street, London, 1 May 1877. Three miles north-east of the newly created Tite Street, crowds gather as horse-drawn carriages line the streets of Mayfair. Bejewelled royalty mix with Victorian celebrity and a host of artists, writers and journalists all sweep along a red carpet, disappearing through the quasi-Greek facade of Sir Coutts Lindsay's new Grosvenor Gallery. Dubbed by Walter Crane as the 'modern day Lorenzo [Medici]', Lindsay was a collector and patron of the arts who, along with his wife Blanche, had pioneered a 'temple of art' in the heart of Mayfair. The Grosvenor Gallery would revolutionise the London art world. Upon its walls hung works by contemporary artists – young, unrecognised talent or more avant-garde artists like Whistler and Crane – rejected or ignored by the Royal Academy.

Of course, contemporary art galleries had existed in London alongside the Royal Academy for years. The Dudley Gallery, the Pall Mall Gallery, Berners Gallery and the Grafton Street Gallery had all thrived on the periphery, but the Grosvenor posed a new and very real threat for several reasons. First, it contained five cavernous galleries with more than enough space to stage blockbuster exhibitions. Secondly, it dared to host these shows at the same time as the Royal Academy's summer exhibition. More importantly, it had a somewhat controversial remit: to exhibit avant-garde works by new, up-and-coming and often non-traditional artists, thus undermining the Academy's authority as the final word on British art and aesthetic tastes. The Grosvenor warmly opened its arms to Academy outcasts like Whistler, who were refusing to play by the rules.

Years later Lord Henry Wotton in *The Picture of Dorian Gray* complained that the Royal Academy was 'too large and too vulgar. Whenever I have gone there, there have been either so many people that I have not been able to see the pictures, which was dreadful, or so many pictures that I have not been able to see the people, which was worse. The Grosvenor is really the only place.'[1] On its opening night the Grosvenor Gallery was indeed the only place to be. The event drew the biggest names of London society. The Prince and Princess of Wales were there along with the young Oscar Wilde[2] and the veteran Pre-Raphaelite painter John Everett Millais. The Gallery hosted an eclectic mixture of new talent like Edward Burne-Jones, who had a total of eight paintings hanging in the gallery, including the legendary *The Beguiling of Merlin*, alongside works by some well-known and respected artists such as George Frederic Watts and Lawrence Alma-Tadema. Whistler had an entire gallery dedicated to his nocturnes and appropriately decorated the room with a frieze of peacocks and butterflies.

Circulating among the crowd that night was London's most daring architect and designer, Edward William Godwin. Throughout his life Godwin would assume many roles – architect, interior designer, theatre director, and he would assume just as many nicknames. Max Beerbohm thought he was the 'greatest aesthete of them all',[3] while Oscar Wilde called him 'one of the most artistic spirits of [the nineteenth century] in England'.[4] The artist Louise Jopling curiously referred to him as 'the Wicked Earl'. Born the son of a builder-decorator and antiquary, Godwin spent his childhood surrounded by the past, with 'fragments and crumbling bits from old churches' that his father had meticulously collected and preserved in their garden. He was born into a turbulent period of British history. With the industrial revolution in full swing, urban centres were transformed by mass migration from rural farmsteads. Critics such as John Ruskin sought peace of mind in a return to the simplicity of the middle ages. Their ideas were indicative of a cultural nostalgia gripping Victorian Britain, manifest in architecture as Gothic Revival. Nowhere was this style more apparent than at the very heart of Britain's government with the new Palaces of Westminster.

For the first twenty years of his career Godwin worked in the Gothic Revival style mainly on civic ventures, designing schools, town halls and warehouses. In 1861 his career launched when he won a competition to design the new town hall in Northampton using a fashionable Italian Gothic design.[5] By the late 1860s, however, Godwin had begun to break from popular trends. The influence of Japanese art and design increasingly played a part in his works as designs for the interior of Dromore Castle, County Kerry, in Ireland indicate – for the first time a motif of oriental flowers and butterflies, with clean and simple lines formed the basis of Godwin's design.

The integration of Japanese art and design had increased in Britain since the mid-nineteenth century as Japanese trade slowly resumed after a prolonged period of isolation from the West. One of the first significant steps towards this new acquaintance came with the landmark International Japanese Court exhibition held in London in 1862, displaying a mouth-watering assortment of more than one thousand crafted objects, textiles, ceramics and wood-block prints from the Far East.

The attraction of Japanese design for aesthetes like Godwin was its innate quality and simple naturalism. Godwin held Japanese artists in high esteem. Unlike the modernised and industrialised Western Europe, Japanese artists were, he believed, 'under the influence of a free and informal naturalism'. There still existed in Japan 'a living art, an art of the people, in which traditions and craftsmanship were unbroken, and the results full of attractive variety, quickness and naturalistic force.'[6]

When the Grosvenor Gallery opened, London was still recuperating from the massive reconstructive surgery of the 1860s. The social geography of the city had changed. Public transport had been implanted and the middle-classes now stretched their legs in the new roomier, leafier suburbs of Kensington and St John's Wood to the north. The popular taste for domestic architecture in London, however, did not adopt these influences easily. Victorian eclecticism gave way to a growing trend of Dutch-inspired designs which has vaguely become known as 'Queen Anne'. The red-brick, yellow-trimmed Queen Anne houses soon dominated the urban landscape of London's suburbs.

In the beginning, Godwin supported this trend, but as areas like Holland Park and Chelsea blossomed with fresh artistic life, he soon began calling for a more relevant architecture that would express a contemporary (although not particularly 'British') identity, something original, something more than a safe resurrection of a past vernacular as the Victorian Gothic Revival had done. Godwin called for 'a living style' of architecture that would be 'big enough to embrace town halls and law courts, chapels and cathedrals, as well as suburban villas', and yet strong enough 'to influence the whole character of modern manufacture'. This new architecture would have to be a creative and original endeavour, embracing the realities of the modern world, and it would have to be 'the builder's work, naked of ornament, void of style and answering to only one name – Utility.'[7]

While Godwin's professional life had begun to show signs of progression and clarity, his personal life was becoming increasingly complicated. After the death of his first wife, Godwin began a love affair with an actress, Ellen Terry, the young wife of artist George Frederic Watts. Watts had refused to divorce his child bride, so when they fell out of love she and Godwin lived out of wedlock and together they had two children, Edith Craig and Edward Gordon Craig. As the years passed, however, Terry was replaced by an aspiring young artist named Beatrice Philip, the daughter of artist John Bernie Philip. Godwin eloped with Beatrice and the couple were married in 1875. Nearly a quarter of a century younger than her husband, the handsome brunette complemented her husband's creative fires. She proved to be much more than a simple Victorian housewife; she was a pupil, secretary, collaborator and an aspiring bohemian who provided a feminine touch to an otherwise male-dominated clique, and she was particularly fond of her husband's friend, Whistler.[8]

Godwin and Whistler were already good friends by the time the Grosvenor Gallery opened. The Wicked Earl had become an established visitor in Chelsea, and his love of everything Japanese endeared him to Dante Gabriel Rossetti. Whistler had been collecting Japanese prints and pottery since his days in Paris, and people flocked to Lindsey House to admire his 'very rare collection of Japanese and Chinese' porcelain. George Price Boyce, artist, devoted collector and frequent visitor to Chelsea declared Whistler's collection to be 'the most interesting collection of old blue china porcelain' he had ever seen.[9]

Meanwhile Whistler was in the process of transformation. In the cocoon of Chelsea, he was maturing, and he even began to sign his letters and paintings with an intricate butterfly signature. The climax of Whistler's 'chinamania'[10] came when his patron Frederick Leyland bought 49 Prince's Gate and commissioned Thomas Jeckyll to decorate the interior. Leyland had initially asked Whistler to decorate some panels in the hallway, but when Jeckyll suffered a mental collapse he was asked to complete the room according to Jeckyll's design. But it was not long before Whistler had overstepped his assignment and plunged in headfirst developing an elaborate 'Peacock' scheme for the room. The walls and ceilings were painted in blue and gold with peacock feather designs and the closed shutters with peacocks. He soon lost himself in the room. 'I just painted it as I went on,' he wrote, 'without design or sketch.'[11]

Whistler wrote to Leyland, who was away in Liverpool, that his dining room was 'something quite wonderful' and 'thoroughly new and most gorgeous though refined'.[12] The work dragged on, and Whistler, unable to control himself, added more and more embellishments. Immersed in perfecting every detail, the artist soon 'forgot everything' in his 'joy' of creating what would later become known as the Peacock Room. Yet not everyone was quite so joyous, least of all the owner, who considered his 'dining room ruined and Whistler's time wasted.'[13] In spite of this sting of disapproval, Whistler held a press view of the room without Leyland's consent, and invited many notables including Princess Louise and the Marquis of Westminster. Leyland was furious. To add insult to injury, Whistler asked for a staggering £2,000 for the project but his patron flatly refused to pay more than £1,000. Leyland returned the insult by deliberately paying Whistler in pounds, like a tradesman, as opposed to guineas, like a gentleman. Whistler had made yet another enemy, and it would not be his last.

The Peacock Room created a sensation. 'Peacocks have been painted before,' wrote Joseph Comyns Carr, but 'in Mr Whistler's hands these familiar materials take an entirely new form and become a thing of original and independent invention.'[14] The melding of Japanese art and architecture embodied in the Peacock Room only fuelled Whistler's chinamania. Together with Godwin, the 'Butterfly' set upon his next collaboration with heightened enthusiasm.

Whistler and Godwin were not alone. From 1877 onwards there was a new voice in the British art world, giving authority and recognition to aesthetes like the Wicked Earl and the Butterfly. The opening of the Grosvenor Gallery temporarily ushered a new spring of youth and optimism in art and architecture which would coincide with another landmark in

James Abbott McNeill Whistler, his butterfly signature in the right corner, 1885

Harmony in Blue and Gold: the Peacock Room, designed by James Abbott
McNeill Whistler, 1876–7

British art. The Peacock Room was merely a starter. The main course would be a much larger collaboration between the two aesthetes – a work of art in bricks and mortar that would redefine Godwin's architectural career, bankrupt Whistler, and ensure Tite Street's place at the heart of the artistic map of London for over a century to come.

4.

The WHITE HOUSE

The leader of the reaction against this method of Millais was undoubtedly
Whistler – a man of great originality, whose influence on modern art can
hardly be exaggerated. The chief characteristics of his portrait, as of his other
work are a great subtlety of tone, harmonious colouring, pitched in a very
subdued key, and a simplicity of arrangement that is carried so far at times as
to seem to the natural man mere wilful eccentricity.
– John Collier, *The Art of Portrait Painting*, 1905

When the Grosvenor Gallery opened, Tite Street was almost completely unknown and
stark naked. Sewers had been laid and lampposts installed, but the lots were mostly vacant.
The old Gough House stood in its austere brick form now converted to a children's hospital, and opposite, a pair of architects-cum-property developers, Frederick Beeston and
Francis Butler, had bought seven empty plots on the north-west side of Tite Street where
construction had already begun on a row of red-brick, Queen Anne-style houses. The two
architects jointly bankrolled the investment in a speculative gamble that paid off. One by
one the houses were built, and less than a year later they all were inhabited.

The riverfront of Chelsea had already changed dramatically. The mud banks had been
replaced with a new tree-lined embankment. Along the new embankment from the Royal
Hospital to the Chelsea Physic Garden, a row of elegant houses had been built. Numbers
4, 5 and 6 Chelsea Embankment, near the corner of Tite Street, were the work of E.W.
Godwin. Sir Percy Shelley, son of the Romantic poet, commissioned Joseph Peacock to
build him a house on the Embankment, and so the great and good of London migrated to
the fashionable Chelsea riverfront.

Ever the self-promoting artist, Whistler needed an abode to match his Holland Park
contemporaries, to attract patrons, but more importantly, to stake his flag and claim his
own turf. Lindsey House seemed increasingly dull and traditional. Whistler found his
studio was poorly lit, and he complained about the 'cramped space in which [he was]
obliged to carry on [his] work'.[1] With the Peacock Room and other commissions he was

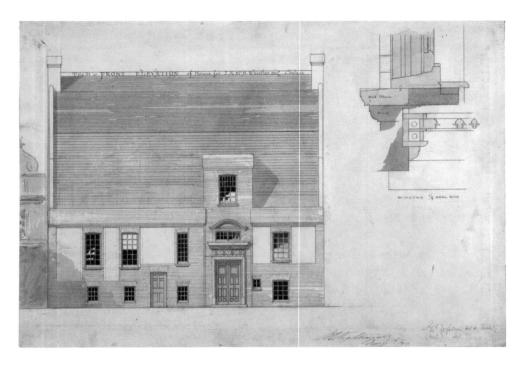

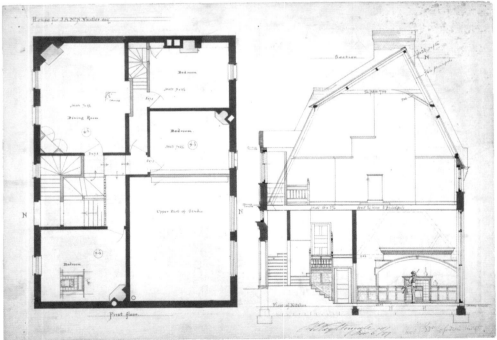

E. W. Godwin's designs for the White House, 1877, rejected by the Metropolitan Board of Works

now earning a very suitable income, enough to consider erecting his own aesthetic temple, a self-publicity campaign in stone.

So Whistler had begun looking for a studio-house. Years earlier, his mother wrote to a friend that 'all the Studios now being built are totally wrong,' and that, 'he must therefore have one and as soon as possible, built according to his own views.'[2] The general idea was to design a unique house with a large studio on the top floor. This would be used as a Parisian-style atelier anticipating, correctly, that hordes of bright-eyed young students and admirers would come knocking on his door. He set about scouting several locations around his beloved Chelsea and nearby Fulham.

The architect and designer of choice would be none other than his good friend E.W. Godwin. An architect unafraid of experimenting in the new modernist style, Godwin was the only man who could have built a house to Whistler's satisfaction. Godwin, who was already engaged on the Chelsea Embankment houses, suggested the new, unknown Tite Street to his friend as a prime location. Just a few months after the momentous Grosvenor Gallery opening, on 23 October 1877, Whistler signed an agreement to build a studio-house on a double plot on the south-east side of Tite Street for a rent of just £29 a year.

Tite Street was the perfect location for Whistler. To begin with, it was cheap. With the Embankment schemes the Metropolitan Board of Works now had vast acreage of land that needed to be developed, and they leased the plots relatively cheaply. The proximity to the river was another huge bonus, and the bohemian environment of Chelsea was one that Whistler did not wish to abandon. Furthermore, Cheyne Walk and Melbury Road already had their own artistic overlords (Rossetti and Leighton, respectively), and Whistler was not in the habit of playing second-fiddle to anyone. The new Tite Street needed a master of ceremonies and Whistler would gladly fill that role. With plenty of other plots still available to be snatched up by his young admirers, he was ready to claim Tite Street as his own. And so the Butterfly set to work with Godwin to build a house that would be as unorthodox, novel and whimsical as himself. There was only one obstacle standing in their way – the Metropolitan Board of Works.

The Board of Works was not receptive to the aesthetic aims of Whistler and Godwin. Although Whistler had obtained a bargain in his lease, his contract clearly stipulated that he must 'submit plans and elevations of the buildings proposed to be built for the approval of the Architect of the Board and that the buildings shall be built in strict conformity to the elevations when approved.'[3] Even before the opening of the Grosvenor Gallery, Godwin, his new bride Beatrice, and Whistler had been in collaboration to design his new studio-house. The project advanced quickly. Almost immediately Godwin submitted the plans to the Board while Whistler, eager to get started (with or without their approval) contracted the builder, Benjamin Nightingale, to undertake the construction of what would become known as the White House. Nightingale began work immediately on Whistler's orders, and without the Board's consent. When the Board's chief adviser, George Vulliamy, inspected the site before the plans had been approved, he was surprised to find the walls had already 'gone up ten to twelve feet'.[4]

Vulliamy was himself an architect and had designed the sturgeon lampposts adorning the Embankment. He had the unlucky position of being the middleman between a traditional, bureaucratic Board of Works and the rebellious individualism of the two aesthetes. In his report to the Board, Vulliamy was diplomatic, describing the design as presenting 'some novel features', and concluded 'the appearance of the building is unusual but [he did] not think that the Board can withhold its approval upon that account. The building is intended for a particular purpose and the peculiarity of the design is due to its being constructed in a manner adapted to that purpose.'[5] With fancy curlicues, cupids, gothic spires and frilly embellishments decorating the houses of London, the stark, clean-lines of the White House were nothing less than architectural sacrilege. There was no movement or fluidity in its stark, efficient design. The committee disagreed with Vulliamy's diplomatic suggestions and rejected Godwin's elevations outright, condemning the 'dead house' as 'all roof'.[6]

After a furious exchange of sharply worded missives and legal threats, Godwin was eventually forced to submit slightly amended plans which were likewise rejected. Whistler, the rogue American, had refused to pay any attention to the Board's admonitions and defiantly ordered his builders to carry on without interruption. Construction was swift and relatively unhindered. He visited the construction site in Tite Street almost on a daily basis, carefully monitoring its progress. By February, Vulliamy reported back to the Board that despite his repeated notifications to Whistler, the house was all but complete.

The Board was furious. Its solicitor informed the committee that it now had the right to take back the site and keep the deposit, but as 'the only objection which the Board had is that the elevation is of an ugly and unsightly character,'[7] he suggested the committee content itself with threatening to take up its rights unless Whistler agreed to make whatever alterations it required. At Vulliamy's suggestion, Godwin made a number of alterations consisting of stone surrounds to the door and windows and inserted two panels filled with sculpture (Whistler had preferred mosaics), one in the parapet and one between two windows. The amended designs were subsequently approved and a few months later, in July 1878, Whistler was finally able to move into the White House along with his mistress and model Maud Franklin.

There it stood. The first studio-house in Tite Street – a white block facade with a slanted, green-tiled roof. The paint barely had time to dry before Whistler's door was open to an eager and curious public beyond. Yet for many of his friends and visitors, the White House remained an enigma, unlike anything they had seen before. To the actress Lillie Langtry, the entire house had 'an effect of studied eccentricity quite in keeping with its

The White House, *c*.1880

owner's whimsical personality', but it was 'nothing more than a jumble of narrow stairs and passages, quaintly-shaped rooms, low ceilings, mustard-yellow walls, matted floors and blue and white china.'[8]

The revolutionary White House, as it became known for its austere white facade, welcomed curious friends, admirers and critics who came to see it for themselves. Visitors entered directly from the street onto a flight of stairs that led down to a large low-ceilinged, terracotta-coloured room with white trimmings. This lower room had two long windows about sixteen feet high looking over a little bit of garden behind and on the adjacent wall a shallow alcove with a fireplace. The solitary fireplace was completed in yellow brick with a sideboard with triangular shelves ornamented with red-and-yellow Kaga porcelain. The floor of the room was covered in matting and furnished with a few sparse chairs. At one end of the room stood a Godwin-designed table with Whistler's portrait of Henry Irving as Philip II above a piano at the other end of the room.[9] Going up the stairs led to the dining room and at the very top of the house was a vast studio whose walls were coloured a sort of grey flesh tint – 'a singularly cold and unsympathetic hue.'[10]

For aesthetes like Godwin and Whistler, architecture did not stop with the construction of the physical building. Harmony was the key to its success and to that end the entire house, its contents and its inhabitants, would be a cohesive, artistic package. Godwin wrote in the *British Architect* that 'the architect's work should not be confined to the mere bricks and mortar of a house. The decorator, the upholsterer, and the cabinet maker should be as much subject to the architect as the joiner, the plumber or the glazier.'[11] The interior that Godwin created in the White House was a work of art in itself. Tables had legs of brass and furniture rested on a yellow-brown velvet rug. The armchairs and couches were upholstered in pure yellow velvet, darker than that of the walls, and fringed with yellow.

Some visitors complained that style was given priority over comfort. Indeed one visitor remarked that the rooms 'were meant for the photographer and not for human habitation.'[12] Godwin did not hide the fact that he despised anything suggesting laziness, an attitude shared by Whistler who, when asked for a padded seat, simply answered, 'if you want to be comfortable go to bed.'[13] Harper Pennington commented somewhat humorously on the scarcity of furnishings, noting that Whistler's 'furniture was limited to the barest necessities and frequently, too few of those. The studio could boast only four or five small cane-seated chairs (always requisitioned for the dining room on Sunday) and the most uncomfortable bamboo sofa ever made. Nobody, except some luckless model, sat upon it twice.'[14]

But Whistler loved his new house. The taste of victory was sweet. 'We have beaten them,' he boasted. 'A triumph of Art and ingenuity.'[15] Certainly, he had won the battle against the Board of Works and the house was built to his tastes. The trick for Whistler was to keep the house clean whilst a flurry of construction was taking place, as scaffolding was erected on all sides and Tite Street began to flourish with new artistic life.

5.

ARCHIE & APE

Whistler was convinced that he was the chosen painter of Chelsea,
with those aubergine-coloured brick houses and their blackened
ironwork, the chequer-patterned squares, the wooden piles of
Battersea Bridge, so reminiscent of Hokusai's drawings, with a
pinnace[1] on the river; of all things ugly, which fog turns into the poems
of the night, mirage edifices that vanish while the beholder watchers.
– Jacques-Emile Blanche, *Portraits of a Lifetime*, 1937

With a maverick new house and a raffish reputation, the final ingredient necessary in
Whistler's recipe for a Tite Street artists' colony was a devoted following of artists. Just as
the scaffolding for the White House was going up, Godwin had a new project land on his
drawing table. The commission came from a handsome, golden-haired young aristocrat,
Archibald Stuart-Wortley, and his flamboyant Italian friend, Carlo Pellegrini, better known
as the outlandish *Vanity Fair* caricaturist 'Ape'. Together Archie and Ape were an odd couple
of gentlemen bohemians, of a variety that would come to typify the Tite Street personality.

The reserved, respectable Archie descended from a distinguished line of political power
including former Prime Minister, John Stuart, 3rd Earl of Bute and the eighteenth-century
poet and diarist Lady Mary Wortley-Montagu. He had led the wholly conventional life
of a budding English aristocrat. From early days of boating at Eton he developed into a
keen sportsman, and he demonstrated a considerable penchant for shooting grouse on his
family's vast Yorkshire estates. But he surprised his friends and family when he showed an
even more remarkable skill with the brush. In due course, he announced his intention to
study at the Slade School of Art in London.

Of course, there was no shame in a career as an artist. By the 1860s the social status of
the artist in England had never been better. Indeed, it had almost become a necessity for any
respectable society hostess to have a Leighton, a Watts or a Burne-Jones ornamenting her
drawing-room. 'The ideal dinner party,' wrote Lady Tweedsmuir, consisted of 'one or two
Cabinet Ministers, a diplomat or viceroy, a sprinkling of women famous for their beauty,

a musician who might be induced to perform, and a painter.'[2] The biggest names in the art world mixed in the highest circles of society, and some earned annual incomes that would be the envy of even the wealthiest banker or landed baronet.[3] Archie had an added advantage in that he was endowed with enviable social connections, which certainly paid off when his father convinced John Everett Millais to take on young Archie as a pupil.

In 1874 the carefree twenty-five-year-old, in a 'happy state of irresponsible bachelor-hood … with no particular profession to hamper his movements nor any settled views as to his future,'[4] arrived at Millais's studio. One of the founding members of the Pre-Raphaelite Brotherhood, Millais was a well-seasoned and respected artist in spite of the tarnish of scandal in his early life when he had fallen in love with John Ruskin's wife Effie, and eventually married her after the marriage to Ruskin was annulled for non-consummation. Millais recognised talent in Archie and set to teaching the young man everything he knew about artistic technique. The master and pupil only spent a few days together; the former painted while the latter diligently watched. Finally, the young artist was handed a brush and palette and alongside the great master, with 'his frequent hints, scoldings or encouragement,' began to paint.[5]

LEFT Carlo 'Ape' Pellegrini by Arthur Marks in *Vanity Fair*, April 1889
RIGHT Archibald Stuart-Wortley by Leslie 'Spy' Ward in *Vanity Fair*, January 1890

Inexperienced as he was, Archie's work quickly made its way into the Royal Academy with a winter scene of his family's Yorkshire estate, Wharncliffe Chase. While he was content to paint what he loved – blood sport and rugged landscapes – it was Millais who encouraged him to focus on portraiture as a means of improving his art and earning a viable income. Archie listened. Wasting no time, he collected his family and friends and anyone he could find to sit for him and rigorously and steadfastly began to master the art of portraiture. He worked quickly.[6] In 1875, he submitted three portraits to the Royal Academy including a striking portrait of his younger sister, *Miss Margaret Stuart Wortley*, which Ruskin hailed as 'the rightest and most dignified female portrait' at the exhibition.[7]

The up-and-coming painter gained membership to several prominent societies that had sprung up around London since the early part of the century. The most famous of these was the Arts Club opened in 1863 in Hanover Square with a members' list that included Dickens, Millais, Whistler and Degas. The Beefsteak Club was another, and it was here that Archie most likely met Whistler. Archie quickly found his feet in London's bohemian art world and was soon comfortably nestled in Whistler's circle. This was helped no doubt by the fact that Whistler was friends with Archie's cousin Edward, who owned Wortley Hall in Yorkshire.

One of the many artists Archie met at the Beefsteak was the colourful Italian cartoonist, Carlo Pellegrini. In contrast to the athletic, aristocratic Stuart-Wortley, Pellegrini was an absurdly vibrant character, short and portly, standing at five-feet with a large head and tiny feet. Born in Naples, Pellegrini claimed to be descended from the Medici dynasty. He had spent his younger days flirting with Neapolitan society and making caricatures in private. When the Prince of Wales made his Grand Tour through Italy, Pellegrini had taken his arm and introduced him to the greatest court beauties Naples could offer. But after a disastrous love affair, and the death of his sister, Pellegrini decided to leave Italy. Two years later he arrived in London a friendless, penniless bohemian forced to sleep on empty doorsteps in Piccadilly and St James.[8]

Less than five years later, Pellegrini had sketched his way out of poverty and into the best houses of London. He was now dining at the tables of the Prince of Wales in nearby Marlborough House and Buckingham Palace. In 1868, Thomas Gibson Bowles started a new weekly magazine, *Vanity Fair,* which aimed to 'expose contemporary vanities of Victorian society', which was as its subtitle suggests, 'A Weekly Show of Political, Social and Literary Wares'. Bowles saw potential in Pellegrini's caricatures and hired him to sketch the most famous and notable people of the day. Adopting the sobriquet 'Ape', Pellegrini became *Vanity Fair*'s first caricaturist. In an age when photography was in its infancy, the art of caricature was vital to the publishing industry, a precursor to the paparazzi.

Political cartoons and caricatures had developed in Britain through periodicals, journals and posters, gaining incredible popularity in the eighteenth century with the work of James Gillray, Thomas Rowlandson and George Cruikshank. These cartoons and caricatures tended towards strongly exaggerated, heavily politicised renderings, tied to the witty commentary that accompanied them. Ape's forms, however, took centre stage. They were striking and easily recognisable likenesses with only very slight exaggerations of the subject's features.

The art of caricature was tricky. Subjects rarely ever sat in person. Ape would take notes and then the sketches were later made from memory. 'He did not give his sitters much trouble in the way of posing,' wrote Chelsea-based artist Louise Jopling, 'he would make a note of any personage on his thumb nail, or on his shirt cuff, but generally it was sufficient for him to follow his intended victim about, for two or three days, and he would thus learn him by heart, and, in his Studio, with only the mental image of the man before his mind's eye, he would produce the salient points.'[9]

Most had no idea they were the subject of a caricature until they opened the pages of *Vanity Fair*. His sketches became an instant success and the Prince of Wales commissioned him to draw up caricatures of his friends known as the Marlborough House set. He began to caricature all the famous names in society, the art world and politics. His first major hit was a caricature of the Prime Minister, Benjamin Disraeli (also a member of the Beefsteak), for the first issue of *Vanity Fair*. 'He educated the Tories and dished the Whigs to pass Reform,' reads the subscript beneath the picture, 'but to have become what he is from what he was is the greatest Reform of all.' He followed this with a caricature of Gladstone – leader of the opposition and Disraeli's greatest rival.

Ape quickly became one of the most well-connected men in London – the Cecil Beaton or Mario Testino of the 1870s – and at the centre of the city's bohemian set. He dined late at Paganini's in Great Portland Street and went to see the Bancrofts' theatre with the Prince of Wales and Lord Leighton. He went to and from Paris regularly, where Degas painted his portrait, and he spent many evenings at the Beefsteak Club where he inevitably met Whistler and Archie Stuart-Wortley. Archie was living in a small studio flat in William Street where a number of other artists, including his future Tite Street neighbour, John Collier, lived. The rooms, however, were small and crowded, quite unsuitable for an aspiring society artist.

The prestige and respect that artists enjoyed in the nineteenth century necessitated suitable environments to match their elevated social status. By this time it had become a reality, a new phenomenon in fact, that the success of an artist was correlative to their physical location. To attract wealthy, fashionable sitters and patrons, and publicity, a portrait artist needed to have a studio-home worth visiting.[10] Leighton, Fildes, Alma-Tadema, and now Whistler had all launched a trend of the studio-house no longer being merely a service point like a tailor or a barber, but a destination in itself, a place of entertainment where patrons, artists and guests engaged in debates, dinners and occasional debauchery. For an artist to be taken seriously and to keep abreast of competition it was vital to have his or her own studio. Archie knew this. There were practical concerns too; lighting, space and comfort were all taken into consideration. For Archie, however, there was just one problem; though his family was wealthy, he was not. He was dependent upon his father to supplement the income from his portraiture and simply could not afford to design and build a new house on his own.

"He educated the Tories and dished the Whigs to pass Reform, but to have
become what he is from what he was is the greatest Reform of all."

Benjamin Disraeli by Carlo 'Ape' Pellegrini in *Vanity Fair*, January 1869

A view of Tite Street with Chelsea Lodge (left) and the White House (right), *c.*1880s

Meanwhile, Ape was attempting to take his career in a new direction and set about learning the art of serious portraiture. He too thought it was time for a change of scenery. Neither Archie nor Ape could afford the luxury of a new house on their own, so they joined forces and set about commissioning Godwin to design his second studio-house in Tite Street, directly opposite the one he had just completed for Whistler. Godwin accepted. The space they chose was somewhat awkwardly perched on the corner of Dilke Street and Tite Street, but when the Board of Works merged their corner plot with another smaller plot directly to the north, Godwin had enough space to play with, and the plans proceeded without delay.

'I wish to have nothing but light,' demanded Ape, 'walls and roof and everything.'[11] Having a corner house, light was not going to be a problem as windows could be placed on three sides. Plans were drawn up. The interior was divided into two living units with separate entrances: Archie's on the Dilke Street corner with Ape's in the rear garden near Paradise Walk. The ground floor was a general living quarter while the top floor held two enormous studios. It was soon apparent that this house was more conventional than the White House, with a cottagey Arts and Crafts façade which the Board of Works approved. Godwin's newest creation had 'nothing in it in common with Mr Whistler's house' as the *Building News* was quick to point out, 'It is a plain Old English type of house, with mullioned casements, and seventeenth-century details.'[12] As soon as he had finished Whistler's house, the builder, Nightingale, simply moved his team across the street and started building again in June 1878. In the space of just two years, Godwin had created just as many houses, only a few yards apart. The golden age of Tite Street was now firmly under way.

6.

AESTHETES & DANDIES

There's a Portuguese person named Howell,
Who lays on his lies with a trowel:
When he gives-over lying
It will be when he's dying
For living is lying with Howell.[1]
– Dante Gabriel Rossetti

While most streets and squares in London consisted of rows of symmetric Georgian houses or Victorian terraces, Tite Street was a new complex comprised of independent studio-houses. This unique visual asymmetry was a reflection not only of each artist's personality and beliefs, but was also a commentary on the non-conformist ideology that pervaded the street as a whole. This collective identity, however superficial, was taken very seriously. On numerous occasions Whistler made puns about living in 'Tight Street', but these artists would still do what they could to shape their environment and make it more suitable to their collective image. In 1879 the *British Architect* published a letter from the artists of Tite Street to the Metropolitan Board of Works:

> We trust the Metropolitan Board of Works will not refuse to grant this simple request of the artists and others who own property in Tite-street, Chelsea, that the name of the street be altered to Holbein Walk or Turner's Walk or Prince of Wales Road. A memorial to this effect has been signed by Mr James. A. Whistler, Mr Stuart-Wortley, Mr Frank Miles and Messrs. Gillow, whose houses (all designed by Mr E.W. Godwin, F.S.A.) face this street.[2]

The Board, unsurprisingly, dismissed the request without acknowledgement. Regardless of the name, the street was soon a fashionable outpost for London society. The Prince of Wales and his new mistress Lillie Langtry passed within close range of Tite Street's artists, flower-girls-cum-models, art swindlers and the occasional prostitute, both female and

Miss Maud Franklin by James Abbott McNeill Whistler, *c*.1872–3

male, in these newly designed studio-houses which became salons for London's celebrity and literati.

The centre of this fashionable colony was the White House, where Whistler was living at a 'rate that would have killed most men'.[3] During the week he would rise early and set to work in the studio then perhaps head off to the West End for lunch and not return to Tite Street until after he had been to the theatre. If weekday evenings were spent on the town, Sundays were a Tite Street affair. Whistler's social calendar had revolved around his Sunday breakfasts for many years. They were legendary, as fellow artist George Boughton wrote, '[N]othing exactly like them have ever been seen in the world. They were as original as himself and his work, and equally memorable.'[4] Whistler took great pains to ensure that every detail was perfect. He designed the invitations himself, arranged the table with 'blue and white plates, coffee-cups, and other accessories being of Oriental design', polished silver, starched linen, Japanese bowls with goldfish, and a jar of flowers in the centre.

Whistler also prepared the menu and cooked the food himself. Fruits and fish were hand selected from shops around Chelsea and nearby Pimlico on Saturday afternoon. The dishes were part American, part French concoctions complete with buckwheat cakes, and cream corn, which bewildered his English guests. His menus were as creative as his paintings and consisted of oyster soup, fried sole, mutton cutlets, Parisian beefsteaks, little pastries, cheese omelette and coffee, while 'scattered over the table were queer little dishes containing mysterious relishes and compounds'.[5]

Sunday mornings were spent slaving over a hot stove. When guests started to arrive they were often asked to talk among themselves while, in the room adjacent, they could hear Whistler splashing around in the bath. They would also meet Whistler's newest mistress, Maud Franklin, who had been living with him at Lindsey House and was now installed in the White House as his model and mistress. Maud was one of many aspiring artists who fell under his spell. She had lived with Whistler on and off since the early 1870s and modelled for several portraits.[6] No doubt Whistler promised to teach her his techniques and she soon became hopelessly devoted to the artist.

Although not classically beautiful, she was a typical Whistler girl – demure, Celtic-looking, pale skinned and red-headed – but a mutual friend bruisingly described her as 'not pretty, with prominent teeth, a real British type'.[7] Maud had already given birth to at least one illegitimate child fathered by Whistler with a second one on the way. As an unmarried mother, mistress and model, Maud would never find acceptance into polite society. While it was perfectly acceptable for gentlemen and ladies to be received in her company at the White House, invitations including Maud were not reciprocated. Whistler, on the other hand, was free to do as he pleased.

One of the very first socialites to grace Tite Street was Lillie Langtry. She became a confidante and regular visitor to the studio and a staple feature at Whistler's Sunday breakfasts. Whistler had also been plotting a portrait of the actress as *Arrangement in Yellow: Portrait of Lillie Langtry*. She modelled for Whistler several times after their brunches, but the portrait never came to fruition. The artist doted on Langtry, saying 'she is perfect. Her beauty is simply exquisite, but her manner is more exquisite still.'[8]

For all its idealistic artists and genteel aristocrats, available models and haughty mistresses, the bohemian hen-coop of Tite Street was not without the occasional fox on its borders. Charles Augustus Howell was an agent, dealer, and notorious rogue who wove in and out of the London art world throughout the 1860s until his death in 1890. After being fired as Ruskin's secretary he became an unavoidable member of Chelsea's bohemian set, famously helping to exhume a volume of Dante Gabriel Rossetti's poems from the grave of the poet's dead wife Lizzie Siddal at Highgate Cemetery. 'It was easier to get involved with Howell than to get rid of him,' said Whistler, who described him as 'the Robinson Crusoe hero out of his proper time, the creature of top-boots and plumes, splendidly flamboyant, the real hero of the Picaresque novel, forced by modern conditions into other adventures, and along other roads.'[9]

On several occasions, Howell had come to Whistler's rescue. On one particular occasion, shortly after Whistler had drawn the newly rebuilt Brompton Rectory and was in financial straits, Howell came to his studio, took the drawing and rushed off to a pawnbroker, returning with an astonishingly large amount of money. A few weeks later Whistler passed the same pawnshop and saw his sketch in the window, labelled 'Michelangelo's first Drawing for St Peter's.' 'He was really wonderful,' said Whistler. 'You couldn't keep anything from him and you always did exactly as he told you.'[10]

In September of 1878 Whistler was paid a hundred guineas by Howell to paint a portrait of his lover Rosa Corder. Ellen Terry described Corder as 'one of those plain-beautiful women who are far more attractive than some of the pretty ones. She had wonderful hair – like a fair pale veil, a white waxen face and a very good figure; and she wore very odd clothes.'[11] Others believed she 'exuded sexual appeal and knew it'.[12] The sexy and eccentrically dressed Corder had initially studied music but later took up painting racehorses until she was eventually ensnared by the man she confessed was 'half mad, and half a devil but always a man and a gentleman'.[13] Howell was in the business of producing and selling forgeries of Reynolds and Gainsborough, and before long he had perverted her talents to the same end. Together they produced forged paintings and etchings by Fuseli, Millais and even Rossetti's *St George Slaying the Dragon*, as depicted in Max Beerbohm's *Mr__ and Miss__ Nervously Perpetuating the Touch of the Vanished Hand*. Howell is pictured eavesdropping while Corder forges art, with a copy of Rossetti's *Bocca Baciata* in the background.

Corder was no stranger to Whistler or the Chelsea set. As early as 1874 she worked as an assistant to Rossetti just around the corner from where Whistler was living at Lindsey Row, and she was now a regular face at the White House brunch table. She soon inspired a portrait from Whistler. According to W. Graham Robertson, the idea for *Arrangement in Brown and Black* came to Whistler during one such brunch when he saw Corder in a brown

Lillie Langtry by Frank Miles, 1884

Arrangement in Brown and Black: Portrait of Miss Rosa Corder by James Abbott McNeill Whistler, 1876–8

Mr__ and Miss__ Nervously Perpetuating the Touch of the Vanished Hand by Max Beerbohm, 1918

dress pass a black door. At his studio she posed over at least forty gruelling sittings, 'standing in a doorway with the darkness of a shuttered room beyond her'.[14] Posing for Whistler was no easy affair and involved 'long sittings, lasting on occasions until she fainted, and at last she refused to go on with them.'[15] Unlike many other sitters, Whistler was sympathetic towards Corder and wrote a uniquely compassionate note, 'I want to thank you for your kind endurance. The work is complete and an hour or two longer or less will entirely end the matter – I am charmed myself and one of these days you will forgive me.'[16]

Arrangement in Brown and Black: Portrait of Miss Rosa Corder was Whistler's first successfully completed portrait in Tite Street. Corder's strong contrapposto stance, the angle of her up-tilted head, and the dynamic lines of her attire convey vitality and self-possession, while the gesture of her left arm, bent at the elbow with her hand resting on her hip contributes a note of assertiveness. Soft light focuses attention on her pale face turned in pure profile to reveal her straight nose, full lips and strong chin. The painting was exhibited

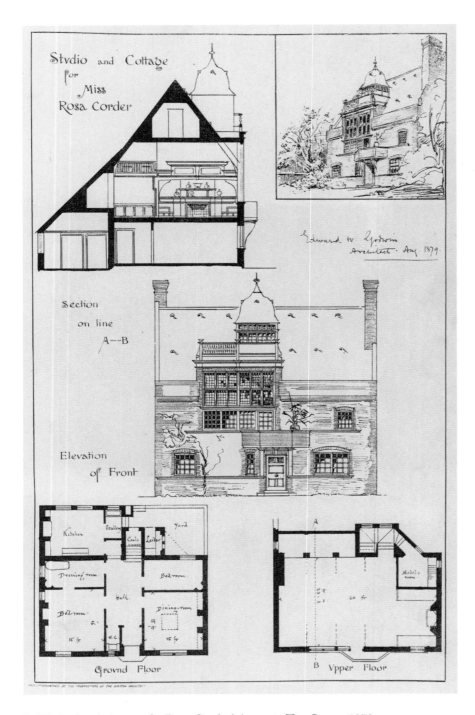

Studio and Cottage
for Miss
Rosa Corder

Section
on line
A—B

Elevation
of Front

Edward W. Godwin
Architect. Aug. 1879.

Kitchen
Scullery
Coals
Cinder
Larder
Yard
Dressing room
Bed-room
Hall
Bed-room
Dining-room
15 ft
W.C
15 ft

Ground Floor

A
Models
room
40 ft

B Upper Floor

E. W. Godwin's designs for Rosa Corder's house in Tite Street, 1879

for the first time at the Grosvenor Gallery in the spring of 1879. William Rothenstein later praised it as 'a triumph of unaffected ease,' while the *Echo de la Semaine* in Paris hailed it as 'one of the most noble feminine figures that one could encounter . . . the model, serious, almost grave displays a quiet authority, a mild serenity.'[17] Even *The World* was discussing its '[B]road, grand passages of execution worthy of Velazquez.'[18]

Corder's place among Whistler's Tite Street circle had all but been cemented with *Arrangement in Brown and Black*, but she was determined to go one step further. There still stood a gaping space between the White House and the Victoria Hospital. Howell and Corder entertained the idea of having their own house in Tite Street and Godwin managed to tentatively secure a small plot with the intention of designing a house for them. While Whistler was painting Corder's portrait, Godwin was busy designing her Tite Street house Corder's house smaller than the White House, with a softer, more feminine touch. It had a steep pitched roof and a single cupola centred almost directly above the door with a good deal of quaint, even dainty, detailing around the studio window.

Everything seemed to be going well with the project until the time came to discuss money. Suddenly both Corder and Howell were conspicuously difficult to contact. In reality neither of them could afford the project. Godwin did not have the funds to bankroll a speculative venture as individually tailored as the Corder designs and was instead forced to relinquish the leasehold. Howell and Corder apologised profusely but the designs were shelved. Perhaps it was all for the best as a storm was brewing over Tite Street.

Nocturne in Black and Gold: The Falling Rocket by James Abbott McNeill Whistler, 1875

7.

BETWEEN *the* BRUSH *&* *the* PEN

There's a combative artist named Whistler
Who is, like his own hog-hairs, a bristler:
A tube of white lead
And a punch on the head
Offer varied attractions to Whistler.
– Dante Gabriel Rossetti

Every silver lining has its cloud. Almost from the very beginning dark clouds gathered over Tite Street. The fate of the White House would be directly affected by the events that led from a warm July evening in 1877. Just a month after the opening of the Grosvenor Gallery, seated at the Arts Club in Hanover Square, Whistler came across an article in *Fors Clavigera*. The art critic John Ruskin had written a sharp piece lambasting his *Nocturne in Black and Gold: The Falling Rocket*:

> For Mr Whistler's own sake, no less than for the protection of the purchaser, Sir Coutts Lindsay ought not to have admitted works into the gallery in which the ill-educated conceit of the artist so nearly approached the aspect of wilful imposture. I have seen, and heard, much of Cockney impudence before now; but never expected to hear a coxcomb ask two hundred guineas for flinging a pot of paint in the public's face.[1]

The ruffled artist slapped the paper on the coffee table. 'It is the most debased style of criticism I have had thrown at me yet,'[2] he declared. A few weeks later Ruskin was served with a writ for libel. Ruskin had been a prominent art critic and historian for nearly half a century. His taste for Italian – especially Venetian – art had influenced a generation of artists and architects including, for a time, Godwin. With his study, *Modern Painters,* Ruskin had championed the work of J.M.W. Turner and later defended the avant-garde Pre-Raphaelite Brotherhood. He believed that art should serve a moral as well as an aesthetic purpose in cultivating and elevating society and should not exist merely for itself alone. To the Whistler-Godwin camp, Ruskin's ideas had become redundant and highly populist.[3] But when his Grosvenor Gallery review appeared, Whistler was outraged. In an attempt to defuse the situation somewhat, William Rossetti suggested that the ageing critic had suffered from a mental collapse. Perhaps Whistler would have let the insult pass unanswered had it not been for the direct consequence that commissions immediately dried up, or at least that is what he claimed.

Ruskin had thrown down his glove and Whistler prepared for battle. He had endured, indeed enjoyed, reams of criticism in the past, but Ruskin's words struck a blow not only at the artist's principles, but at his livelihood. He wanted revenge, and if it also provided a public forum to espouse his artistic beliefs, so be it. The taste of blood was on his lips after his victory with the White House, and now he had a new enemy. Ruskin was an amateur watercolourist and draughtsman, but Whistler still felt he had no place criticising art. To Whistler the fight against Ruskin was the fight 'between the brush and the pen,'[4] the artist versus the critic, to determine whether the artist should rule or be ruled when it came to art.

Less than a month after moving into his new Tite Street abode the showdown began. On 25 November 1878 he took the stand in a pantomime trial starring Whistler as the wounded artist and Ruskin as the prescribed villain. A host of witnesses were called for both sides. Edward Burne-Jones, a friend to both parties, reluctantly took the stand but later described the trial as a 'hateful affair'. When asked by the Attorney General how long it had taken to 'knock out' the painting in question, Whistler answered that it had taken approximately 'two days'. 'The labour of two days,' argued the Defence, 'is that for which you ask two hundred guineas?' 'No,' replied Whistler defiantly, 'I ask it for the knowledge of a lifetime.' He then went on to hit at the core issue of the entire trial. 'It is not only when criticism is inimical that I object to it,' he argued, 'but also when it is incompetent. I hold that none but the artist can be a competent critic.'[5]

Witnesses were called and the jury were shown the painting in question, *Nocturne in Black and Gold*, alongside a Titian for comparison. Overall the show trial was 'a complete fiasco on both sides . . . unworthy of either as men of genius with any pretensions to common sense,'[6] wrote Francis Mewburn, a solicitor and friend of E.W. Godwin. The jury agreed. After only an hour's deliberation they delivered their verdict in favour of Whistler – damages of one farthing.

For Whistler the three-day trial had been a defence of strongly held principles, and the verdict was a justification of his beliefs. The artist did not accept his victory with quiet humility. Instead he held a celebration party in Tite Street and had the famous farthing put on a chain which he wore boastfully around his neck. He did not stop with trivial gimmicks either. Less than a month after the trial Whistler had efficiently collated a transcript of the entire trial along with relevant newspaper clippings and letters. He took on the job of printing the pamphlets from an old printing press he kept in the attic of the White House.

AN APPEAL TO THE LAW.
NAUGHTY CRITIC, TO USE BAD LANGUAGE! SILLY PAINTER, TO GO TO LAW ABOUT IT!

'Naughty critic, to use such bad language! Silly painter, to go to law about it!'
Whistler versus Ruskin in *Punch*, December 1878

The self-congratulatory publication, *Whistler v. Ruskin – Art and Art Critics*, was available almost immediately.

The trial had become ripe ammunition for the press. Across the country articles and cartoons depicted Ruskin as a senile old critic or Whistler as the fey aesthete. *Punch* was most prominent. Whistler wrote to the cartoonist Linley Sambourne after a cartoon of him was published in *Punch*: 'To have brought about an "Arrangement in Frith, Jones, Punch and Ruskin, with a touch of Titian" is a joy! And in itself sufficient to satisfy even my craving for curious "combinations".'[7] Whatever their individual preferences, everyone called the trial what it really was – a farce.

The Gold Scab: Eruption in Frilthy Lucre (The Creditor) by James Abbott McNeill Whistler, 1879

The publicity from the trial placed Tite Street in the public spotlight. The victory celebration could only last for so long, however, as soon afterwards Whistler's life and the grand aesthetic dream of the White House began to crumble. Whistler may have won the farcical farthing, but he was not awarded legal costs which had swiftly accumulated. When the dust finally settled and everything was added up, the costs of the trial, combined with the outstanding building costs of the White House, totalled more than triple his annual income.

Meanwhile, throughout the trial and the months that followed, poor Maud Franklin, who was now eight months pregnant with their second child, had been stashed away in a London hotel while Whistler had tricked her into thinking he was away in Paris. In February 1879 Maud gave birth to a little girl, and by May she had moved back to Tite Street. By then creditors were circling like vultures over the White House, and she found the house was full of bailiff's men. Throughout the spring and summer of 1879 Whistler slipped further and further into debt but continued with his busy social life as if nothing had happened. In an effort to make some money, and escape the dogged bailiffs, he busied himself with a series of etchings of the area around Tite Street and the Embankment, including *Nocturne: Grey and Silver – Chelsea Embankment, Winter*. He used his old printing press to begin churning out his etchings for sale.

Less than fourteen months after moving in to the White House, on 9 May 1879 Whistler was officially declared bankrupt with debts of over £4,500. He tried to stem the disaster by meeting with his creditors. His old patron Frederick Leyland was present at the meeting. Whistler proceeded to cut into Leyland, calling him the archetypal capitalist, and blaming him for his financial fall. As if this were not enough, Whistler went a step further to caricature Leyland in a series of paintings, the first of which was *The Love of Lobsters: Arrangement in Rats* depicting a lobster wearing a frilled shirt similar to the ones that Leyland wore. Another was called *The Gold Scab* showing a hunched figure representing Leyland covered in scales the shape of gold pieces, playing the piano while seated on top of the White House.

By the end of the summer Whistler was no longer opening his post but forwarding all letters to his solicitor. Bailiffs were now in possession of the White House, but they would not get an easy ride. Whistler immediately put them to work around the house. The famous Sunday brunches continued uninterrupted. When a guest arrived one Sunday for brunch she was met by two or three men waiting on the table. 'Why Jimmie, I am glad to see you've grown so wealthy,' she said. 'Bailiffs!' Whistler snorted. 'You know I had to put them to some use!' William Rossetti and his wife also found the same 'liveried attendants' and commented that Whistler's servants were 'extremely attentive and anxious to please.' 'Oh yes,' Whistler replied, 'I assure you they wouldn't leave me.' [8] And he was right. When things got desperate, bills covered the front of the house, announcing the approaching sale.

Along with the bailiffs Whistler's friend Howell descended upon Tite Street at the smell of blood to help smuggle works of art out of the house without detection. The painting of Corder was the first to go. It was not until a decade later, when Howell died, that the true extent of his business cunning would be thoroughly revealed. The day after Howell's death W. Graham Robertson received a telegram from Ellen Terry: 'Howell is *really* dead this time, do go to Christie's and see what turns up.' Both Robertson and Whistler met in the auction room. As lot by lot of Howell's loot went under the hammer, Whistler sat placidly identifying many of the pictures. '[T]hat was Rossetti's – that's mine – that's Swinburne's!'[9] One of the paintings to appear was the portrait of Rosa Corder along with numerous other pictures he had 'kept for safekeeping' during Whistler's bankruptcy.

The party was clearly over. All that the artist had accumulated – his beloved White House, his blue and white porcelain, his pictures – had to be sold off to pay his debts. Undeterred by his impending homelessness, Whistler made arrangements to go to Venice[10] to complete a series of etchings there. The Fine Art Society had given Whistler a commission for twelve plates. One hundred proofs of each were to be printed, and he was to receive a handsome twelve hundred pounds in return.

Despite all the turmoil in Tite Street, Whistler was 'apparently in great spirits', busily 'arranging his route to Venice'.[11] The bailiff's receiver had given him permission to destroy any unfinished works, in order that they not be sold and displayed to the public. Copper plates from his etchings were scratched over with gum. Most of his precious items had long been smuggled out of the house and were now lodged with Howell or with friends around Chelsea.[12] When next to nothing was left, he packed his trunks and wrote – slightly misquoted – over his front door, 'Except the Lord build the house, their labour is but lost that build it – E. W. Godwin, F.S.A., built this one,' and he set off along Tite Street bound for Venice.

8.

FRANK MILES, OSCAR WILDE & KEATS HOUSE

Laughter is not at all a bad beginning for a friendship,
and it is by far the best ending for one.
– Oscar Wilde

'I am trying to settle a new house, where Mr Miles and I are going to live,' wrote Oscar Wilde to Margaret Hunt in the summer of 1880. 'The address is horrid but the house very pretty.'[1] Within a year of the White House being finished, Tite Street, despite its 'horrid' name, was becoming synonymous with art. Empty plots of land were being purchased quickly, so it was necessary to act fast. He had barely signed off Archie and Ape's designs when Godwin found yet another handsome young man standing by his drawing table, requesting a new studio-house in Tite Street. This time it was Mr Frank Miles.

Miles found a plot of land on the river side of the red-brick terraces that had just been completed. Like Whistler he took a lease from the Board of Works and gave Godwin free rein in design. Godwin took his time, and spent several months letting his imagination run wild. Whistler had given his input and Godwin's wife Beatrice whispered subtle suggestions over his shoulder. Eventually the plans took shape, but getting them approved was not going to be easy. Miles's lease, like Whistler's, stipulated that designs had to be approved before they were built. Once again the appearance of Tite Street would be dictated at the bureaucratic level.

The elevations that Godwin submitted to the Board were somewhat unusual. Externally the house appeared less stark than Whistler's and therefore perhaps more characterful. The facade consisted of an irregular arrangement of rectangles of alternating red and yellow brickwork topped with a green slate roof, and vertical windows placed off-centre. Godwin had certainly taken Miles's character and interests into consideration when he designed the

Design for Frank Miles by E. W. Godwin, 1879, rejected by the Metropolitan Board of Works

house. Miles was a passionate botanist, with a love of flowers and horticulture, and the most unusual feature of the house was a balcony in the shape of a lily projecting onto Tite Street. For the interior Godwin suggested a similar colour scheme to the one he implemented in Whistler's house, a delicate Japanese-inspired harmony of lemon yellow, blue, light brown, dark green and light pink.

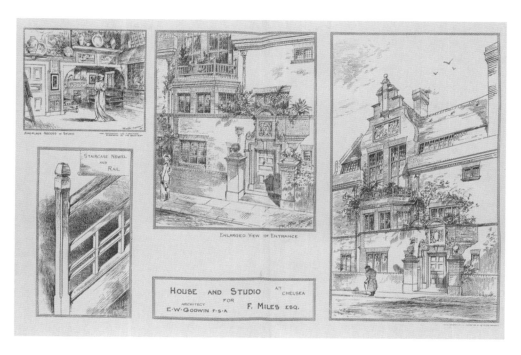

House and studio for Frank Miles by E. W. Godwin, 1879

The designs were inspected by the Board of Works, and Vulliamy, still sour over the White House debacle, dismissed them as 'worse than Whistler's'.[2] The Board's decision went to a vote – seven 'yes' and seven 'nay' – with the chairman breaking the tie by voting against the designs. Godwin flew into a rage. '[W]hat right have retired farmers and cheese mongers, who never drew a line nor saw a drawing till yesterday!'[3] he fumed. '[W]ho are they to sit and judge on my work?'[4] Once calmed, Godwin returned to his drawing table and produced a revised drawing, removing the floral balcony and embellishing the facade with a more Queen Anne style of ornamentation to placate the Board. The plan worked and the Board reluctantly approved the amended designs. Miles hired a builder to start the work. But this was Godwin's baby, and he did not leave anything to chance. Building commenced in May 1879, and the architect spent nearly every day that summer supervising the construction and interiors, spending hours 'mixing colours'[5] until every detail was perfected.

The house was not ready for occupancy until the following summer. Despite the decorative changes he was forced to make, Godwin still boasted it was the 'best work' he had ever done. The house, both interior and exterior, rivalled Whistler's in its aesthetic properties. 'It is for a bachelor, is unpretentious, containing about nine rooms besides a studio,' said Godwin. 'The latter is at the top of the house. The whole house was designed with balconies and other accessories to meet the taste of a lover of flowers.'[6] Inside the walls were all pale and distempered with bare wood floors and sparse furnishings. The spacious drawing room was decorated in a warm, inviting yellow colour scheme with 'walls and ceilings toned golden yellow and wood cinnamon.'[7] The hallway and staircase were painted ivory with a ceiling in light brown, and black mahogany railing complete with Japanese latticework design and elegant brass-capped finials.

The narrow stairs that led up to the studio were covered with soft felt. For the studio Godwin installed Japanese-inspired inglenooks with rounded lintels but in a more austere scheme of ivory-coloured woodwork, white walls, and a slightly darker ivory-coloured ceiling. The floor was covered in durable Chinese woven matting. The bedrooms meanwhile, just below the studio, were in a blue and grey scheme of a Whistlerian nocturne with 'wood blue, walls grey, blue-green ceiling,' and blue cretonne curtains in a Japanese bird pattern with a thin blue lining over the windows set above bare, dark, stained floors.

Miles was a bachelor. However he would not be enjoying his new studio-house alone. Although he had commissioned Godwin and had paid for the house, he would soon be overshadowed by his young friend Oscar Wilde, who accompanied him into Tite Street. Miles and Wilde had already been sharing rooms in a dark, rustic block of studio-flats in Salisbury Street off the Strand. While Miles had an impressive array of friends and visitors, the young Irishman, fresh from Oxford, was all but unknown to London's society. But what he lacked in social connections he made up for in witty repartee and aesthetic idealism.

As a child Miles had been raised in the idyllic countryside of Nottinghamshire where he developed a love of nature and a passion for plants. As a young man he had moved to London and taken art classes at the Royal Academy schools. Wilde's background, however, was decidedly more cosmopolitan. He had been raised in a grand Georgian house in Merrion Square in the fashionable end of Dublin. After a successful time at Trinity College Dublin, he was awarded a scholarship to Magdalen College, Oxford, and after graduating with a double first, he moved to London.

The Salisbury Street studio had been visited by the high and low of Victorian society. In 1879 Wilde met the society belle Lillie Langtry. Born in Jersey in the Channel Islands, Lillie married a wealthy Irish landowner Edward Langtry in 1874, and when she came to London became good friends with Frank Miles. Miles completed a sketch of Langtry which brought her to the attention of Millais, who, in 1878, painted the famous portrait of the 'Jersey Lily'. Wilde and Miles both adored Langtry. They were not alone. Prince Leopold, the artistic, haemophiliac fourth son of Queen Victoria, was at Miles's studio when he sketched Langtry. When the portrait was finished he quickly purchased it and found a home for it over his bed in Buckingham Palace. According to Langtry, the Queen visited the Prince's bedroom one day when he was ill and spotted the drawing on the wall. She was not amused by what she saw, and took the portrait down.[8]

Miles continued to achieve recognition as a painter of portraits and landscapes. Between 1874 and 1878 he had exhibited several works at the Royal Academy before being awarded the Turner Gold Medal for his landscape *An Ocean Coast, Llangranog*. With a series of successful Academy exhibits including *Mrs Cornwallis-West*, Miles's soft, angelic ladies were soon distributed to the mass market by the thousands, reproduced and tinted to such a superb quality that people often thought they had bought originals. It was not long before these reproductions quickly 'filled the windows of every stationer's shop in the kingdom'.[9]

Tite Street's two newest young aesthetes, Miles and Wilde, revelled in their notoriety which spread to the upper echelons of society. The seeming lack of morality in Tite Street did not deter royalty from visiting. The Prince, who had been asked to meet Oscar Wilde, declared, 'I do not know Mr Wilde, and not to know Mr Wilde is not to be known.'[10] In June 1881 the wait to meet Wilde was over when he came to a thought-reading séance in Tite Street.

In the same year that Miles's house was being built, Langtry herself, with the approval of the Prince, had considered building an inexpensive house in the street on a vacant plot opposite No. 44. For weeks she spent evenings with her 'triumvirate of counsellors' – Wilde, Miles and Whistler – all plotting and planning the newest house. In 1879, Langtry was at the height of London fashion. Her presence in Tite Street would complete the circle, bringing a splash of celebrity into their already blooming community. Ideas and suggestions were tossed around in the air, but when Godwin inspected their rough designs he pointed out a small oversight. In their overzealous plans the bumbling aesthetes had neglected the practicality of a staircase to connect the upper floors with the rest of the house.[11]

The idealistic project would never materialise. Things were not going well for the 'Jersey Lily'. Her husband had gone bankrupt, and the Prince of Wales could only nominally support her. So it fell to her to pull up her stockings and earn a living. Miles suggested she become a farmer, but Wilde protested, '[W]ould you have our Lillie tramping around in the mud?' No. Wilde had a better idea. With her good looks, charisma and popularity there was only one profession – she should become an actress. Lillie agreed. By 1882 her acting career was in full swing and she was embraced by the United States, and the flimsy fancy of having a Tite Street house was stamped out.

If nothing else, Miles became a specialist in portraying royal mistresses. He found a particularly devoted patron in his new friend the Prince of Wales. If a beautiful lady found her way into Bertie's bedroom, it was highly likely that she would eventually find her way into Miles's studio as well. At the height of his popularity Miles was appointed artist-in-chief to *Life* magazine, where he had already submitted a number of works.[12] The magazine's owner Heinrich Felbermann records that 'no one could bring out better than Miles the points of a face, idealising where there was charm, concealing where there was harshness in expression. And yet his drawings retained a perfect likeness. It soon became the rage among society beauties to be "done" by Frank Miles and be published in *Life*.'[13]

In November 1880, the magazine quoted the Prince as saying that Miles's pictures were 'the most charming I have seen of ladies … they are the only pictures that do them justice.'[14]

The following year the Prince purchased Miles's oil, *For Pity and Love are Akin*, which was subsequently displayed in Marlborough House and later transferred to Buckingham Palace. The Prince purchased another of Miles's Academy works, *The Flower Girl*, and commissioned him to do portraits of his wife, the future Queen Alexandra, and a pencil drawing of a group made up of Princess Victoria, Princess Maud and Princess Louise of Wales in 1881.

When he arrived with Miles in Tite Street, Wilde did his best to make the street more befitting of his image as a literary prophet. The young aesthete who, several years prior, had 'prostrated himself on the grass' in front of Keats's grave declaring it the 'holiest place in Rome,' christened his new residence Keats House. He would also have been aware of his neighbour, Sir Percy Shelley, son of the Romantic poet. Wilde and Miles immediately settled into Keats House, not as lovers – they slept in separate rooms – but as friends with mutual perks; Miles had respect as an artist and enviable society connections, and Wilde provided entertainment with bravura wit.

While the rest of Tite Street was a veritable construction zone, Keats House was constantly astir with visitors and guests flocking to see two young aesthetes in London's newest aesthetic house. Miles painted while Wilde talked. When Laura Troubridge, a future neighbour, visited, she wrote in her diary, 'To tea with Oscar Wilde, the poet. Fell awfully in love with him, thought him quite delightful.'[15] In July she returned to be greeted by 'lots of vague "intense" men, such duffers, who amused us awfully.'[16] Not everyone found Wilde 'delightful' however. Lady Augusta Fane thought his appearance 'revolting. He had a fat, clean-shaven, pallid face, a head covered with long fair hair, brushed off his forehead and falling on to the collar of his velvet coat, heaving stooping shoulders, and enormous white hands ... which he waved about the whole time he was talking. If one had not seen him, and only remembered his brilliant conversations and wit, the memory would have been a rare treasure.'[17]

One afternoon Edwin Ward was invited around for tea, where, he says, '[W]e were waited on by a pretty girl about sixteen years of age, most fantastically attired, whom they called Miss Sally.'[18] 'Miss Sally' was a flower seller at Victoria Station named Sally Higgs who had caught the aesthete's eye. Struck by her beauty and charm, Miles organised a meeting with the girl's mother and managed to convince Mrs Higgs that her daughter could make a handsome living as an artists' model. Consent was given and the young girl was swept away and planted in No. 44 Tite Street as a maid and model. Guests at Keats House were greeted by 'a demure, dainty little elf recently arrived at her teens, tricked out in studio finery'.[19]

Sally quickly assimilated to life in Tite Street and proudly assumed the position of hostess at the lively gatherings of Miles and Wilde. As a 'born Bohemian' the feisty flower girl was not troubled with any so-called 'moral scruples,' and she quickly became 'one of the most sought-after models in London'.[20] When Lady Augusta Fane paid a visit to Miles's 'quaint little old house,' she was greeted by Sally 'dressed in sage-blue and holding a lily in her hand – which got very much in her way when arranging the tea-table!'[21] The 'born Bohemian' with

ELAINE.

Passing fair the face may seem,
Unknown the presence and the dream:
Tis she though of herself, alas
Less than her shadow on the grass
or than her image in the stream.

DRAWN BY FRANCIS MILES.

W. A. MANSELL & C?   COPYRIGHT,   LONDON.

Elaine by Frank Miles, *c.*1872–4, one of the many angelic faces that 'filled the windows of every stationer's shop in the kingdom'

a 'lily in her hand' would soon be making the rounds of all the most fashionable studios from Chelsea to Holland Park, her soft, feminine features appearing in Lord Leighton's *Day Dreams*, exhibited at the Royal Academy in 1882.

Miles's affinity for pubescent girls did not always end with such positive results. Scandal was never very far from Tite Street. There were darker stories behind those virginal faces. When they had been living at Salisbury Street, Wilde had returned home one night to find Miles pacing around the studio fraught with worry. Miles admitted that he was being blackmailed by a woman whose underage daughter had persuaded him to 'commit an act of extreme folly' by 'pretending that certain things were so that were not so in truth.'[22] Wilde sent Miles away and invited the blackmailer round for a meeting. At that meeting, Wilde listened sympathetically to the woman and expressed interest in supporting her case, but he explained that before he could do so, he would need to see the evidence which the woman possessed. Deceived by Wilde's acting, the woman produced the incriminating document and handed it to him. Wilde carefully read the letter, written in Miles's hand-writing.

'This is, I suppose,' asked Wilde, 'the only evidence you have?'

'It is,' she replied.

'You ought to have taken a copy of it,' he went on, 'in case you should lose it. Have you done so?'

'No,' she replied, 'but I will do so.'

'I am afraid it is too late,' said Wilde, placing the document in the fire and pressing it into the flames with a poker.

Furious, the woman called up her male accomplice from the street. However, intimidated by Wilde's imposing bulk he departed with the woman to be heard of no more. This unfortunately would not be Wilde's last skirmish with blackmailers, and future encounters would not end well.

Trouble followed them to Tite Street. On one occasion Wilde returned to Keats House to find Miles packing his bags in a state of great distress. When he demanded to know the reason for his agitation, Miles vaguely admitted having committed an offence, adding 'I am sure the parents have laid an information and that I am liable to be arrested at any moment. I am trying to get away before the police come.'[23] When the police arrived moments later and tried to force entry to Keats House, Wilde allegedly held them at bay until Miles could escape over the rooftops. With Miles safely gone, Wilde politely ushered the police inside, glibly explaining that he thought the raid was a practical joke and claiming that 'Mr Miles was travelling on the continent.' A few days after his close escape Miles returned home, but it was certainly not the last time a resident of Tite Street would be wanted by the law.

9.

PARASITE *in* TITE STREET

Shall the birthplace of art become the tomb of its parasite in Tite Street?
– James Abbott McNeill Whistler

The year 1879 was a turbulent one in Tite Street. At first everything seemed to be going smoothly – Archie and Ape were settling into No. 60, Godwin was building a house for Frank Miles, and Whistler was still glowing from his triumph over Ruskin. Tite Street had also been placed firmly on the map of fashionable destinations, playing host to the best celebrities that Victorian London could offer. In spite of all this, things turned sour very quickly. By the end of the year Whistler was bankrupt and forced to leave, Archie and Ape had split, and for a moment it seemed that the golden days of bohemian Tite Street were over almost before they had begun.

Tensions with Archie and Ape were worsening thanks in part to Whistler. Ape had fallen under the spell of his new neighbour and spent more and more time at the White House hoping he would emerge from the Tite Street cocoon a brilliant butterfly, like the great Master himself, but this was not to be. Under the influence of Whistler, Ape was convinced he should devote himself to serious portraiture. He set about trying to imitate Whistler's style and technique. Although he was able to secure a few prestigious sitters like Squire Bancroft, Ape found serious portraiture required more time, more patience and more visionary talent than his caricature sketches, which took only a few hours to complete. 'A man may caricature the people of a race that is not his own,' he later confessed, 'but it needs a native to judge them seriously' as a portraitist.[1] Whatever it required, the truth had soon become painfully clear to his friends that Ape simply lacked the 'extra "more" to make it as a portraitist'. Whistler had always championed Ape's contribution to the art of caricature. He 'taught all the others what none of them had been able to learn,'[2] Whistler said, but when it came to portraiture his 'failure lay not merely in insufficient power, but in the lack of true comprehension of the deeper qualities of character.'[3]

Artists' Houses in Chelsea in *British Architect*, 1880: Canwell House (left) and Whistler's White House (right) both by E.W. Godwin, Nos. 31–33 (centre) by Col Sir Robert Edis

The failure to secure prestigious portrait commissions was compounded by further financial troubles. Fame had gone to Pellegrini's head, and after several tantrums his position at *Vanity Fair* was precarious. He would continue as an on-again-off-again caricaturist until his death in 1889, but in the meantime the magazine's editor Thomas Bowles had found a much more level-headed, though less charismatic, artist, Sir Leslie 'Spy' Ward to continue in his footsteps, and Ape's sketches no longer regularly graced the pages of *Vanity Fair*. The added financial strain also put pressure on his relationship with Archie, who in contrast was having no difficulty in receiving commissions. Under the circumstances Ape struggled to keep up his end of the house, and now with Whistler gone, Tite Street had diminished slightly in its appeal.

Other factors complicated the delicate situation at No. 60. Ape was a boisterous and flamboyant character, the life of the party, with people coming and going from his studio at all hours of the day and night. He was loud and somewhat careless around the house. On several occasions he had set himself on fire when he dozed off with a lit cigar in his mouth. And then there was the issue of his sexuality. Ape had openly flaunted his homosexuality for years. For Archie it was a more dangerous game living with Ape. Living with an open homosexual could have devastating consequences. It was certainly not uncommon for two bachelors to live together – just a few doors away Oscar Wilde and Frank Miles were sharing a house. But people could get the wrong idea – a handsome young man and a flamboyant homosexual nearly ten years his senior, sharing a house in a street reputed for its uncanny ability to attract controversy and scandal. Even worse those whispers could reach the ear of his dying father in Yorkshire. The last thing he needed was to be disinherited as he was forging his artistic career.

Things fell apart very quickly. Both artists wished to remain in Tite Street, but to live independently. With Whistler away in Venice, Archie made an attempt to purchase the White House. When the deal fell through, he turned to Godwin to build yet another house across the street on a vacant lot he leased at No. 29, just south of the Victoria Hospital. He had decided to make a clean break and Ape agreed. Archie and Ape's studio-house went on the market and was quickly sold to the Hon. Slingsby Bethell.

Canwell House, as No. 29 soon became known, was more conventional, without any of the boldness of Godwin's other Tite Street projects. The street elevations of the house were published in the *British Architect* and show a frontage of red and yellow brickwork. The gabled roof and window fittings were reminiscent of the designs of fellow architect Norman Shaw. At the top of the house stood a studio tower with various Queen Anne trimmings and an octagonal corner cupola. The house was large for a bachelor, but Archie did not live alone for long.

Any questions hovering over Archie's sexuality were answered when he brought a somewhat unexpected guest back to his new Tite Street home. Nelly Bromley was an actress who had first come to public attention on the London stage in 1868 in a burlesque at the Royalty. She played Dolly Mayflower in the hit comedy *Black-eyed Susan* and Nimble Ned in *Claude Du Val* by Sir Francis Burnand, the editor of *Punch*. She later made her rounds of the music halls and theatres of the West End and ended up with the Richard D'Oyly Carte[4] company acting in many of Gilbert and Sullivan's best works, including *Trial by Jury*, which became a huge hit.

The young actress met Archie in the 1860s. She was already well acquainted with the Chelsea set from a friendship with William Rossetti and she knew Whistler. Wilde had also been to see her perform. Together Archie and Nelly secretly had a daughter around 1870. Archie's father was not keen on the situation, and it was swept under the carpet. Nelly moved in to Canwell House with Archie in 1880, by which point she had all but retired from the stage. Archie's work continued uninterrupted, influenced more by Millais than Whistler. In 1882 he exhibited a portrait of his sister's new husband *Major the Hon. Reginald Talbot*, and the following year he had two highly conventional paintings, *The Sleep of An Acorn* and *The Poacher's Daughter*, exhibited at the Royal Academy.

Meanwhile, on the morning of 18 September 1879 a crowd gathered in Tite Street – bailiffs, speculators, art dealers, artists and curious locals. All summer, advertisements had been announcing the auction of the White House and its belongings. Whistler was long gone, soaking up the Venetian sun at the Caffè Florian in the Piazza San Marco while a small group of loyal supporters turned out in Tite Street in the hope of procuring one of the few remaining treasures. Oscar Wilde, Charles Augustus Howell, W. Graham Robertson and William Rossetti sifted through the now mostly empty White House. Some furniture and remaining works of art would be sold at Sotheby's, but the house, itself only a year old, went under the hammer. By the end of the day it sold for £27,000. The keys were passed along to the most unlikely buyer, Whistler's arch-nemesis Mr Harry Quilter.

Harry Quilter was well known amongst the artists of Tite Street as a conservative art critic for *The Times*, a staunch adversary of aestheticism and decadence and a champion of British morality. Whistler already disliked Quilter for taking Ruskin's side during the recent trial. Like Ruskin, Quilter was a classicist, an Italophile and admirer of early Italian Renaissance painting, particularly Giotto, about whom he had written a two-volume critical monograph.

As Quilter acquired the keys to the White House, a clear division had already emerged in the art world. On one side were the aesthetes whose cause was formulated in print by Swinburne's 'art for art's sake' and Walter Pater's *History of the Renaissance*, which stated: '[A]rt comes to you proposing frankly to give nothing but the highest quality to your moments as they pass, and simply for those moments' sake.'[5] Whistler too had placed art beyond social or moral obligations. 'False again, the fabled link between the grandeur of Art and the glories and virtues of the State,' he later declared, 'for Art feeds not upon nations, and peoples may be wiped from the face of the earth, but Art is.'[6]

On the other side Quilter believed, like Ruskin, that art should serve a moral end. 'The influence over the heart of man which art has always exercised,' Quilter wrote, 'does not lie alone in the fact of the soft pleasure it gives to the sensuous portion of our natures, but in the appeal it makes to our whole being, physical, mental and spiritual and that its rank is determined, as is that of man himself, by the extent to which it can subdue its lower elements in the service of the highest qualities.'[7]

Ironically, the one event that did the most to promote Whistler's cause, that is the libel trial, also put in motion the series of events that led to Quilter purchasing his beloved White House. The year that Quilter settled into the White House was the beginning of a decade where aestheticism would take centre stage in the world of art and theatre. Within a few years of the trial and the creation of Tite Street, volumes of literature, reams of criticism and innumerable cartoons, whether parody or praise, gave the aesthetes momentum and publicity. As the *Furniture Gazette* stated in 1876, 'There has assuredly never been since the world began an age in which people thought, talked, wrote and spent such inordinate sums of money and hours of time cultivating and indulging their tastes.'[8]

Quilter was the first to express his despair that the 'morbid, uncleanly and unnatural' aesthetic craze had spread 'from painting and art criticism to poetry, fiction and drama', and

The Sleep of an Acorn by Archibald Stuart-Wortley, 1884

DESIGN FOR AN ÆSTHETIC THEATRICAL POSTER.

'Let us live up to it!' Satirising the aesthetic movement in *Punch*, May 1881

he acknowledged that the main 'protagonist in the tragedy would be the Press.'[9] In his *Gospel of Intensity* he humorously satirised the poets, painters and decorators of the aesthetic movement, which included most of the Tite Street circle. He was not alone. The 'aesthetes' had become rich pickings for the press who were keen to capitalise on the vogue for 'morbid painting' and 'sensational literature'.[10] The image of the aesthetes and artists of Tite Street was not altogether accurate, and far from flattering. They were depicted as unhealthy bodies – gaunt, emaciated faces, sunken, grave eyes and wiry frames. They replaced human nourishments with their fetish for Japanese art and porcelain pots. Effeminate mannerisms accompanied the image – they invariably clutched a lily or sunflower with limp wrists and locked knees.

George du Maurier was the aesthetic satirist par excellence. His cartoons in *Punch* both coloured public perceptions of the aesthetes and fed the movement itself. In 1882 Walter Hamilton published his sympathetic survey of the new movement in *The Aesthetic Movement in England*, the first serious and sympathetic consideration of the aesthetic movement to appear in English. In the study he tries to examine and analyse the ideals and principles of the aesthetes. Above all, Hamilton's book was the first to group this new school into a formalised movement. 'The essence of the movement,' Hamilton explains, 'is the union of persons of cultivated tastes to define, and to decide upon, what is to be admired, and their followers must aspire to that standard in their works and lives. Vulgarity ... can never be admitted into this exclusive brotherhood, for riches without taste are no avail, whilst taste without money, or with very little, can always effect much.'[11]

Yet for critics like Quilter the problem with this new exclusive brotherhood was its pretentious cult-like exclusion and rejection of mainstream trends of thought. 'The curtains are drawn closer and closer,' he argues, 'as we advance in art and mystery our voices, gradually sinking, take a tone of awe.' 'It may be seen at many a social gathering,' wrote Quilter, 'young men and women whose lack-lustre eyes, dishevelled hair, eccentricity of attire and general appearance of weary passion, proclaim them to be members of the new school.'[12] It was exactly this exclusive tendency that was picked up by Du Maurier. 'Their noble contempt for everybody but themselves envelops me,' he commented. 'They are best left to themselves like all Societies for mutual admiration of which one is not a member.'[13] Any attempt to question or subvert, Quilter believed, would be useless as the aesthetes, 'louder, shriller, and more audacious blow, day by day, the trumpets of mutual advertisement; dictionaries are ransacked for the laudatory or comminatory adjective; the puff preparatory appears for weeks and months before hand ... No flattery is too fulsome, no exaggeration too absurd to describe the merits of Art.'[14]

If Quilter had hoped to be free of these young men and women then Tite Street was certainly not the place to be. But it soon became clear that Quilter's intention was not to assimilate to the views of his neighbours. No indeed. Within weeks of purchasing Whistler's house, Quilter started implementing drastic alterations to the delicately designed interior of the White House until it was almost entirely unrecognisable. And then he started on the exterior. Less than a week after his purchase Quilter had plans drawn up to add an extra level to the facade, thus blocking out the controversial green tiled roof that Whistler and Godwin had fought so hard to get approved by the Metropolitan Board of Works.

Quilter's actions were both deliberate and effective. When he realised he could not defeat the aesthetes in print, he would resort to the only means left. Tite Street, and especially the White House, had become a symbol of Whistler himself, his public image, and his identity as an artist. His aesthetic ideologies had been manifest not only on the canvases hanging at the Grosvenor Gallery, articles in the *Pall Mall Gazette* or in the dock of the courtroom, but also in bricks and mortar. Words were difficult to destroy but houses were vulnerable. To strike at Whistler, one had only to strike at the White House.

Provoking Whistler was not in the interests of happiness or sanity. If he had expected to live a quiet and peaceful life in Tite Street then Quilter was in for a shock. In altering the White House, he had stirred a hornets' nest. The outspoken American may have been in Venice, but he would soon return with a vengeance. There was still room in Tite Street, and if he could not live in the White House itself, Whistler would live as close as possible, immediately next door in fact.

The empty double-plot of land directly north of the White House had changed hands several times in the late 1870s. Originally Godwin had drawn up a proposal for a towering multi-level scheme of studios on the plot, but the plans fell through. The lease was sold to architects Jackson & Graham who, already noted for their aesthetic furnishings, spotted a trend and snatched up the leasehold. Meanwhile Frank Dicey, a minor artist in the Whistler circle, leased the plot of land between the White House and Archie's Canwell House.

Dicey commissioned Colonel Sir Robert Edis to design a studio-house at No. 31 Tite Street, with a block of studios directly next to the White House. Edis was a comparatively conventional architect, much less daring than Godwin, a familiar, if safe, name in the Tite Street circle. Ape had sketched the 'Architecture Militant' for *Vanity Fair*, the Prince of Wales commissioned him to redesign the ballroom at Sandringham House, and he would later go on to design the Grand Central Hotel at Marylebone Station. He was a good friend and admirer of Godwin and a close friend of William Burges, but not everyone was enamoured by the Colonel. Whistler felt he was not fit to sharpen Godwin's pencils.[15] A few years after he designed Nos. 31–33 Tite Street, in 1884, Edis wrote *Healthy Furniture and Decoration* in which he declared that he had 'nothing in common with the "clap-trap" conventionalities and eccentricities of those so-called aesthetic schools which insist on certain styles of decoration and would-be quaint designs in furniture.'[16]

In contrast to other houses in Tite Street, No. 31 was rather small with only one main bedroom and a small dining room under a studio-salon. The house was finished in yellow brick with an asymmetrical front in a quasi-Tudor style. Unlike Godwin's houses, Edis used plenty of Queen Anne details in his designs and juxtaposed beside Godwin's stark white house these gave Tite Street its slightly unusual asymmetry. But the designs were safe, fashionable, and easily approved by the Metropolitan Board of Works. Indeed they were so safe that it is one of only a handful of original Tite Street buildings to have survived into the twenty-first century.

Meanwhile, Whistler had returned triumphantly to London from Venice. He successfully exhibited his 'Venice Sketches' at The Fine Art Society and early in 1881 tried to claw back his White House. Quilter had no intention of giving it back. When his pursuits failed, Whistler took a studio on the ground floor at No. 33, as close to his former house as he could legally get. When he heard the rumour that alterations were being made to the White House, Whistler flew into a rage. 'O Atlas!' he wrote in *The World*:

What of the Society for the Preservation of Beautiful Buildings? Where *is* Ruskin? And what do Morris and Sir William Drake? For, behold! Beside the Thames, the work of desecration continues, and the White House swarms with the mason of contract. The architectural *galbe* that was the joy of the few and the bedazement of

Nos. 31–33 Tite Street designed by Col Sir Robert Edis, 1880

'the Board' crumbles beneath the pick as did the north side of St Mark's, and history is wiped from the face of Chelsea. Shall 'Arry, whom I have hewn down, still live among us by outrage of this kind, and impose his memory upon our pavement by the public perpetration of his posthumous philistinism? Shall the birthplace of art become the tomb of its parasite in Tite Street?'[17]

Having spent endless months laboriously planning his beloved White House in minute detail and battling against the 'bedazement' of the Board of Works for permission to build, it is understandable that Whistler had a deep attachment to the house in which he spent less than a year. It had become an extension of the artist himself. In the process Tite Street had also become something more than just another street, it was now an ideology, a contested terrain in a battle of principles – for Whistler, Tite Street was 'the birthplace of art'. Quilter's move was a calculated offensive, and he knew Whistler's dislike of critics, made public in his trial against Ruskin, would further compound his frustration. For all his cutting wit and diatribes, there was little Whistler could do. 'He obstinately stays there in the way,' he sulked, 'while I am living in this absurd fashion, next door to myself.'[18]

10.

ALL *the* FASHIONABLES

Jeux Innocents in Tite Street

Mr Whistler's final breakfast of the year was given on Sunday last. The hospitable master has fresh wonders in store for his friends in the new year; for, not content with treating his next-door critic after the manner that Portuguese sailors treat the Apostle Judas at Easter-tide, he is said to have perfected a new instrument of torture. This invention is of the nature of a camera obscura, whereby, by a crafty 'arrangement' of reflectors, he promises to display in his own studio, to his friends, ''Arry at the White House', under all the appropriate circumstances that might be expected of a 'Celebrity at Home'.

– Atlas, *The World*, 26 December 1883

Whistler returned from Venice in a spirit of triumph. With his usual determination and stubbornness he marched back to Tite Street. The White House was a painful memory, but now Whistler turned his attention to Edis's Tite Street studio at No. 33. He immediately took up where he had left off. In April 1881, Alan Cole met a revived, brazen Whistler who was 'taking a new studio in Tite Street, where he is going to paint all the fashionables.' Tite Street was alive with 'crowds competing for sittings – carriages along the streets.'[1]

Immediately Whistler set about decorating Edis's interior with a colour scheme inspired by Japanese prints. Yellow dominated the room. When Charles Augustus Howell visited the studio he thought it was like 'standing inside an egg'.[2] Though considerably smaller than the White House next door, 'harmony' was still given primary importance. 'The whole place was sacrificed to the big studio in its arrangement,' a visitor to No. 33 commented. 'One was shown into a small dining room, with a low-pitched ceiling, walls distempered in a rather dark green-blue, with simple straight yellow curtains by the window and very plain cane-seated chairs painted a bright yellow.'[3]

The *mise-en-scène* was the ultimate in living design, wherein person and place were visually blended into one overall scheme. Whistler believed that furniture and interior design should be simple and integrate with the art on the walls. His blue-and-white porcelain and Japanese fans had all been, 'so perfectly placed as to fill its wall' that 'one did not feel the want of anything else,' rendering the need for any pictures quite unnecessary.[4] Like the White House next door, visitors to the studio at 33 Tite Street were expected to conform with the overall scheme. Every room was an arrangement and every sitter had to fit in: the men wore yellow cravats and Whistler designed little velvet butterflies for the women, who were advised not to wear black or white in case they might clash with the décor.[5]

The bankruptcy, loss of the White House and flight to Venice appeared to have changed Whistler's priorities. He now turned his focus to the world around him, particularly his studio. The living environment was of the upmost importance to Whistler. Interior decor was an extension of himself, his artistic theories and practice. He had learned all too painfully how ephemeral and vulnerable this could be. As the months of toil perfecting his White House were being quickly undone next door, he now made a point of immortalising his space the best way he knew how – in paint. The few paintings of Whistler's dating from this time, such as *The Yellow Room*, demonstrate this new priority in his work. They show an intimate connection with his domestic and creative surroundings. Maud Franklin had accompanied Whistler to Venice and was now living cheek-by-jowl in the small Tite Street quarters. In *The Yellow Room*, she casually reclines beside a fireplace ornamented with Japanese pottery against a wall of creamy yellow. Her violet blue dress was no accident. Besides offering a rare glimpse into the Tite Street studio, the picture brings Whistler's conception of interior design, fashion and spatial harmony onto the artist's canvas – a harmonious mirror of a harmonious interior.

In spite of the turbulent false start, Whistler was more determined than ever to establish his artists' quarter in Tite Street, and in fact there was very little work left to be done. If he left for Venice a martyred saint, he returned a god in the eyes of his younger admirers. No. 33 Tite Street became much more than a studio. While he was busy painting, activity buzzed all around him. He liked 'a *camarade* about the place' and thrived on attention, especially the admiration of young artists. Like the White House, his new studio became an aesthete's Mecca, a social centre packed full of visitors, sitters and devoted followers. People came to Tite Street to hear Whistler speak or watch his fascinating studio acrobatics as he 'talked and laughed and raced about all the time, putting in the touches delicately on the canvas, after matured thought, with long brushes.'[6]

When Jacques-Emile Blanche visited Whistler's Tite Street studio with Giovanni Boldini and Paul Helleu they all sat in stunned admiration as Whistler danced about the studio, singing and lunging at the canvas. 'At last with two finger-tips, whose nails were trimmed mandarin fashion, trembling with agitation,' Blanche recalls, 'Whistler pushed forward a tiny wooden panel. With a strident "Oh! Oh!" he slapped Boldini's shoulder and asked for enthusiastic approval: "Pretty, eh?" he said. The picture was a cloud over the sea, a note, a nocturne, or a "scherzo". If you said nothing, what a Philistine you seemed. "Find your way home and come no more to Tite Street," the Master appeared to say.'[7]

In the eyes of this younger generation Whistler held an immense fascination, coupled with fear and amazement. For many people he remained an enigma. While he had the makings of a social rebel, he dined at the finest tables of London and mingled with the highest of society. He may have appeared as a gentleman dandy, but he also embodied the image of the struggling 'romantic artist'. Many of these younger artists who flocked to Tite Street were themselves from respectable families and privileged backgrounds who despised their parents' more conservative outlook while at the same time recognising the economic need to attract prestigious patrons.[8]

During his year in Venice, Whistler gained a following among a group of American art students with whom he shared a building. They had been studying under Frank Duveneck, a thirty-one-year-old American who had opened a school in Munich. The 'Duveneck Boys', as they became known, all in their twenties, knew Whistler by reputation. One of the boys, Harper Pennington, thought Whistler 'first among living painters,' and believed that '[T]he rising generation understood him much better [than his own], and looked up to him.'[9]

Young, eager, bright-eyed admirers travelled from the Continent and sometimes from across the Atlantic and the furthest reaches of Australia to see Whistler and his studio. The growing 'School of Whistler' soon included not only the artists already in Tite Street, but also two American brothers Ralph and Waldo Story, along with Sydney Starr and the Canadian-born artist Elizabeth Armstrong (later Forbes). From directly across the street, Ape briefly shared the studio at No. 33 with the Butterfly, but financial strain forced him to move further afield. It was just as well. The Master preferred his disciples to be young and servile, relishing the company of 'les jeunes fous que vieux imbeciles'.[10]

The Prince of Wales, Bertie, was an early visitor to Whistler's new Tite Street abode. With Lillie Langtry he stopped in to see Whistler, who recounted smoking 'a cigar in the Studio' with the 'Royal Boy'.[11] But of all the camarades, Mortimer Menpes and Walter Sickert were the most persistent and present. These young men were 'genuine pupils', spending hours faithfully glued to Whistler's side, and drinking in his every word. Both had been students at the Slade School of Art until they fell under Whistler's influence and decided to forego academic study for the Master's more informal Tite Street atelier.

Menpes, originally from Australia, arrived in London in 1875 demonstrating a talent for the art of etching, his enthusiasm being stimulated by prominent French etcher, Alphonse Legros, under whom he studied at the Slade in 1878. The twenty-five-year-old Menpes demonstrated great artistic promise. The British Museum had accepted a gift of ten of his prints to the collection, and in October 1880 his work was included in The Fine Art Society's major exhibition *Twelve Great Etchers*, alongside established artists such as Whistler, Francis Seymour Haden and James Tissot.

It was at The Fine Art Society exhibition that Menpes met Whistler. Soon afterwards, he offered to assist with the printing of Whistler's etchings and they quickly became friends. 'The moment I saw him,' Menpes recalled, 'I realised that I had come into contact with a master. I became conscious that I was meeting face to face one of the greatest painters living. From that

The Yellow Room by James Abbott McNeill Whistler, *c.*1885

Clockwise from right: Frank Miles, the Hon. Frederick Lawless, Julian Story, Waldo Story and Whistler, 1881

hour, I was almost a slave in his service, ready and only too anxious to help, no matter in how small a way. I took off my coat and then and there began to grind up ink for the Master.'[12]

Walter Sickert also hailed from distant shores. His family moved to Britain from Munich when he was eight years old. Despite the fact that he descended from a paternal line of gifted painters, Sickert entertained aspirations of a career on the stage. In London he worked in Henry Irving's theatre company where he met and developed an infatuation with Ellen Terry. He became torn between a passion for theatre and a burgeoning talent for painting. His acting career was progressing at a painfully slow pace and he decided to embrace art. He enrolled, like Menpes, at the Slade under Alphonse Legros. But he was unimpressed by the Slade, finding it far too rigid and academic.[13] Whistler and Tite Street, he thought, had more to offer.[14]

According to legend, Sickert caught Whistler's eye one night at the Lyceum when an attempt to throw a bouquet of flowers to Terry at the curtain call almost decapitated Henry Irving. A few days later Sickert chanced to see Whistler entering a tobacconist's shop and followed him in asking if he might call at his studio. When the fateful day finally came Whistler showed Sickert 'some glorious work of his and it was of course a great pleasure to talk with [Whistler] about painting.' Whistler was 'the only painter alive who has his first

Master and pupil: Mortimer Menpes (left) with Whistler, *c.*1885

immense genius, then conscientious persistent work striving after his ideal.'[15] Sickert became a devoted follower. 'There is one God,' the young artist wrote, 'and his name is Jimmy.'[16]

In March 1882, Sickert decided to leave his stage career behind and to focus on his apprenticeship with Whistler. From the structured world of the Slade, he was cast headlong into the Tite Street maelstrom. There was no lesson plan. No workshops. No tutorials. Sickert and Menpes merely watched with fascination and imitated whenever they got a chance, but the opportunity to get any of their own work done was rare. The Master required absolute obedience and attention from his followers. The mere privilege of being in the studio was

A Little Shop in Chelsea by Mortimer Menpes, 1884–7

enough to satisfy the pupils, for the moment at least. They were expected to prepare his paints and bases, to wash his brushes and prepare props for sitters. Whistler occasionally doted on Sickert as 'Walter, dear boy' but if he ever got in the way, he would chastise him with 'Stick it Sickert' or 'Shove along, Walter, shove along.'[17]

The daily routine was taxing. 'Come at once – important,'[18] Whistler would telegram. Menpes and Sickert would rush to Tite Street. Together they would sift through post and morning papers, replying to any insults (of which there were many). Then laden with pencils and other tools, the young apprentices would follow Whistler around the Embankment and the streets of Chelsea like faithful puppies. After a few hours of sketching *en plein air*, they would then find their way back to Tite Street where Whistler would cook a lunch to be followed by an afternoon of work and chat in the studio. Other days might be spent at Whistler's hairdresser or tailor, or harassing art gallery staff in the West End before heading off to an evening at the theatre, followed by enlightening discussion and drinks at a club.

Menpes and Sickert dutifully attended to Whistler. On very rare occasions the eager pupils might even be given a specific demonstration of some technical point. But working on side projects was tolerated only as long as it did not interfere with the studio practice, and any direct question was likely to be answered with an explosion, 'Pshaw! You must be occupied with the Master, not with yourselves. There is plenty to be done.'[19]

For this new generation, belonging to the Tite Street circle was a badge of honour. 'The Whistler followers were privileged people,'[20] Menpes recalled. They filled his studio, attended exhibitions together, accompanied him on painting trips, and defended him ardently against hawkish critics. 'Our principles were [Whistler's] principles exaggerated,' wrote Menpes. They 'formed themselves into a society whose main object was to fight [Whistler's] battles.'[21] The followers would laugh at his jokes on cue and be on hand to laud or chide anyone at the Master's whim.

The followers imitated Whistler not just in art but in everything they did. They tried 'to use stinging phrases and to say cutting things,' and before long Menpes and Sickert were dressing like Whistler, adopting his mannerisms and his dandy pose. Despite their adherence to the Master – his methods, his principles and his personality – rarely were they allowed to paint in the same studio. So the group of followers took to meeting outside of Tite Street. According to Menpes they pooled their resources and found a studio in Baker Street where they could imitate Whistler's practices in their own time. '[We] were a little clique of the art world, attracted together in the first instance by artistic sympathies' wrote Menpes. '[We] were painters of the purely modern school … all young, all ardent, all poor.'[22]

Though young, ardent and poor, Sickert and Menpes did learn valuable lessons from their years of service in Whistler's studio. Whistler inspired Sickert with an abiding 'love of quality of execution,' a sense 'that paint [was] itself a beautiful thing, with loveliness and charm and infinite variety.'[23] Sickert wrote to fellow Tite Street artist, John Collier, years later saying 'Whistler inducted me into some understanding of painting.'[24]

In February 1883, Whistler was busy organising a second exhibition of his Chelsea and Venetian prints at The Fine Art Society. During the months running up to the exhibition, Sickert was in Tite Street constantly in a frenzy to get them printed. Whistler was an experienced master at the fine art of printing etchings. Through selective inking and wiping of the copper plates he was able to manipulate each print, giving it an individual texture and character. Sickert and Menpes watched and learned.

The opening of the show brought Sickert a moment of respite in which he could work on his own material. Inspired by Whistler's example he had begun a series of etchings of London scenes. Although he continued to regularly attend Tite Street, he had taken his own room in nearby Markham Square. Whistler, however, did not approve, and quickly found new projects to busy his apprentice. In April he entrusted Sickert with the task of escorting his prized painting *Arrangement in Grey and Black, No. 1: Portrait of the Artist's Mother* to Paris where it would be exhibited at the Salon. In Paris, Sickert lodged at the Hotel Voltaire as the guest of Oscar Wilde. 'Remember,' wrote Whistler in a covering note to Wilde, 'he travels no longer as Walter Sickert – of course he is amazing – for does he not represent the Amazing One?'[25]

Sickert would remain loyal to the 'Amazing One' for many years, but over time he would be replaced by newer, fresher, younger followers. Menpes too eventually tired of Tite Street. Through Whistler he was infected with 'chinamania' and travelled to Japan where he studied under the famed Japanese printmaker Kawanabe Kyosai in 1887. Menpes later confessed he slipped off 'like a naughty boy sneaking out of school'.[26] The pressure of leaving his master was so great that a confrontation was out of the question. Instead he left a note in a tobacconist in Chelsea begging the shopkeeper not to give it to Whistler until some hours later. To Whistler this was an act of betrayal, and he all but cut Menpes out of his life.

From the early 1880s, Sickert's work reflected a heavy debt to Whistler. In *The Glovemaker*, for example, he borrows directly from Whistler's *La Marchande de Moutarde*, while one of his earliest portraits of the period, *The Grey Dress*, hints of a Whistlerian portrait with the figure, painted in greys, relieved by a few monochromatic touches of black and white against a grey background, and with a radical restriction of tone and colour. Sickert was not alone in his artistic emulations. Menpes's work of the early and mid-1880s also shows strong Whistlerian influences. As late as 1887 Menpes, returned from Japan, exhibited etchings at the Dowdeswell Gallery that were characterised by vast empty spaces, spidery lines and use of plate tone to evoke impressions in the manner of Whistler.

Through their emulation of Whistler, Menpes and Sickert represented a new, fresh spirit on the English art scene. Even as 'art for art's sake' became the credo of the avant-garde, the wider public interest in art that had prevailed since the mid-nineteenth century, began to weaken. The steady balance between the social position and the form and content of painting Victorian life was coming to an end.[27]

The Grey Dress
by Walter
Sickert, 1884

II.

MASQUERADING

Wilde: 'I wish I had said that.'
Whistler: 'You will, Oscar, you will.'[1]

Of all the artists and personalities in Tite Street to come within Whistler's gravitational pull, Oscar Wilde, at No. 44 – Keats House – across the street, would develop the most turbulent friendship with the artist nearly twenty years his senior. The relationship between the two aesthetes would never be the same master-servant dynamic of Menpes and Sickert. For approximately eight months[2] Whistler and Wilde were living within yards of each other in Tite Street at the heart of 'aesthetic Chelsea'. In these crucial months the aesthetes' public personas merged in the popular imagination through caricatures in the pages of *Punch*.

For Ellen Terry, who had been introduced to both parties through her lover E.W. Godwin, Whistler and Wilde were, 'the most remarkable men [I had] ever known. There was something about both of them more instantaneously individual and audacious than it is possible to describe.'[3] This individuality and audacity made Whistler's and Wilde's relationship the most caustic of any in Tite Street. Their relationship was fuelled by a combination of admiration, jealousy, and acute narcissism. In time, this fuel would prove to be highly incendiary.

Wilde had moved to Tite Street as a lodger of Frank Miles's in August 1879, and he was in no great hurry to leave. Although he complained that Tite Street was a rather horrid address, he was at the centre of an artistic milieu that both nurtured and defined his own identity as an aesthete. In July 1877 he published a review of Whistler's *Nocturne in Black and Gold: The Falling Rocket*, describing it as 'certainly worth looking at for about as long as one looks at a real rocket, that is, for somewhat less than a quarter of a minute.'[4]

The Whistler-Wilde friendship began as swiftly and intensely as it would end. Both men had something the other admired: Whistler had a strong artistic vision, a knack for brewing controversy, and an unashamed desire for the limelight; Wilde had youthful vivacity, eloquence and intellectual wit. No doubt Whistler was somewhat flattered by the attention of the burgeoning dandy whose repartee matched his own. While most of his young followers, like Menpes and Sickert, still had a name and reputation to make, 'Wilde's name was in every man's mouth,' and he 'glittered with the glory of the work he was to do.'[5]

When Whistler returned to Tite Street from Venice in early 1881, Miles and Wilde spent more and more time across the street at No. 33. 'For two or three years Oscar Wilde was so much with Whistler that everyone who went to the studio found him there, just as everyone who went into society saw them together.'[6] The two aesthetes became the talk of London. 'At receptions the company divided into two groups, one round Whistler, the other round Wilde.'[7]

Through the paintings of one and the writings of the other, through their houses, as well as their speech, dress and mannerisms, Whistler and Wilde had become poster boys for the aesthetic movement. By 1881 the movement had already gathered momentum and publicity, helped by the Grosvenor Gallery, the Ruskin trial and the proliferation of new architectural sites like those that cropped up in Chelsea. With its Queen Anne-style buildings, the 'aesthetic craze' was beginning to ripple across Britain, but its epicentre was Tite Street. Yet few movements in history had 'provoked such a concentrated popular sneer'[8] as the aesthetic movement in the 1880s and 1890s.

The fey, whimsical aesthetes of Tite Street made ripe targets for the satirical press. *Punch* led the chorus of caricatures. In Linley Sambourne's 'Fancy Portrait of Oscar Wilde', Wilde's recognisable face sits in the middle of a large sunflower, complete with aesthetic paraphernalia consisting of Japanese pottery and an open cigarette case. 'Aesthete of aesthetes,' reads the subscript. 'What's in a name? The poet is Wilde / but his poetry's tame.'

The satirist George du Maurier knew exactly what was in a name. He had helped to evolve a new aesthetic prototype for *Punch* – the poet Maudle and the painter Jellaby Postlethwaite were later spun into Oscuro Wildegoose, Drawit Milde and Ossian Wilderness, a pathetic character mocked for his interest in lilies, the Grosvenor Gallery and blue and white porcelain. Du Maurier later said that Postlethwaite was 'the aesthetic character out of whom [I] got some fun. Postlethwaite was said to be Mr Oscar Wilde, but the character was founded not on one person at all, but a whole school.'[9] The school included not only aesthetes like Whistler and Wilde, but flamboyant personalities like Ape and lily-loving botanist Frank Miles, all of whom lived in Tite Street.

Parody and caricature of the aesthetes was not limited to print either. They made their stage debut in John Hollingshead's farce *The Grasshopper*, an adaptation of the French farce *La Cigale* by Henri Meilhac and Ludovic Halévy. Hollingshead himself was a theatrical impresario, managing the new Gaiety Theatre; he was also credited with introducing the librettist W.S. Gilbert to composer Arthur Sullivan. *The Grasshopper* had a timely debut at the Gaiety in December 1877, six months after the opening of the Grosvenor Gallery, and a few weeks after the first draft plans of the White House were being finalised.

The farce lampooned the embryonic Tite Street coterie, portraying aesthetes as flippant, self-obsessed artists accompanied by loose women. The play featured characters like Pygmalion Flippit as 'an Artist of the future', Adonis Stipple as 'his Friend and unworthy pupil' and Adelina Gushington as 'an Artist's Model, and the Pet of the Photographers'. In the play, Hollingshead takes a direct swipe at Whistler's painting style. In response, Whistler, like the fictitious Flippit who carries around a mirror to look at himself, was fascinated by his theatrical avatar. In fact, he made a point of attending the rehearsals at the Gaiety Theatre, where he was determined to paint the lead actress Nellie Farren, or the 'belle Farina' as he called her, who played the eponymous Grasshopper. Farren was invited to Tite Street where Whistler entertained the idea of doing her portrait and even made a drawing of her in performance, *Masked girl wearing a head-dress skipping* and *Souvenir of the Gaiety*.

The next farce to appear on stage was *Where's the Cat?*, adapted by James Albery from the German play *Sodom und Gomorrah*, which opened in 1880 at the Criterion Theatre. The play starred Charles Wyndham as Sir Garroway Fawne, 'an idler', and Herbert Beerbohm Tree[10] as the conspicuously Wilde-like writer Scott Ramsay, 'an Author'. The play featured this new addition in the genre of aesthetic movement caricature that was notably absent in *The Grasshopper* of 1877 – that is, the aesthetic writer. Beerbohm Tree's Ramsay took on Wilde's gestures and style of talking with famous lines such as 'I feel like a room without a dado', and 'nothing . . . seems to take romance and poetry out of a man so much as living by it.' The *New York Daily Tribune* believed that the character of Scott Ramsay 'confidentially engaged in satirizing the "aesthetic" craze as to attire, household decoration, literary taste and amatory sentiment, which has covered with absurdity and ridicule certain of the select circles of London society.'[11]

This was brought centre stage as a subject of Francis Burnand's play, *The Colonel*, which opened at the Prince of Wales Theatre in February 1881. The three-act farce features a *Tartuffe*-like plot where two wily aesthetes Lambert Streyke and Basil Giorgione, proprietors of the Aesthetic High Art Company, hope to gain control of a family fortune by manipulating the wife, Olive, in wielding their influence over her domineering mother. With their pretentious 'intensity' and 'effeminate' sneakiness, the two aesthetes have converted both the wife and her mother to dressing aesthetically, attending lectures on art, and refusing ordinary enjoyment in general, all against the wishes of her sceptical husband who, feeling excluded from the domestic sphere, has begun an affair.

Ultimately the aesthetes are thwarted in their endeavour. The sceptical, straight-speaking American Colonel saves the day by revealing the flamboyant aesthetes as artistic frauds. Once they have been exposed, the loose ends of the story are tied up – the husband returns to the arms of his wife, and the Colonel marries the mistress. Burnand delivers a clear message: Olive must 'consult [her] husband's tastes before everybody else's, and let him be master in his own house' and she should forgo any aesthetic indulgence in order to please her husband. Thus the patriarchal Victorian order is preserved.[12]

"O. W."
"O, I eel just as happy as a bright Sunflower
Lays of Christy Minstrelsy

Æsthete of Æsthetes !
What 's in a name ?
The poet is WILDE,
But his poetry 's tame.

LEFT George Grossmith as Bunthorne in *Patience* by Gilbert and Sullivan, 1881
RIGHT Fancy Portrait: Oscar Wilde in *Punch*, June 1881

The Colonel was one of the most popular spoofs on aestheticism, so popular it attracted the presence of the Prince of Wales in February 1881, and in October a command performance of the play was given for Queen Victoria at Abergeldie Castle, near Balmoral, in Scotland. With the popularity of aesthete-mocking, the *Illustrated London News* noted that the British stage was being, 'thickly sown over with a crop of lilies and sunflowers'.[13] If Hollingshead and Burnand had hoped to damage the public image of Tite Street's artists through their parody, they failed. On the contrary they served to whet public curiosity for the 'new craze'. Through the laughter, there was an element of fascination as 'the greatest aesthete of them all,' E.W. Godwin rightly noted, '*The Colonel* will make more for aestheticism than against it.' 'Mr Burnand', he continues, 'has given us the really artistic for the sham artistic to such an extent that it is hard to see why the very thing he has attempted to destroy should not acquire by his model of procedure a new lease of life.'[14]

For Wilde, *The Colonel* was nothing more than a 'dull farce', but there was something more tantalising on the horizon about which he was 'looking forward to being greatly amused'.[15] The new project was a somewhat playful operetta called *Patience,* written by Gilbert and Sullivan, and produced by Richard D'Oyly Carte. The plot centres on a village milkmaid, Patience, who must choose between two suitors: a 'fleshly poet' named Bunthorne and an 'idyllic poet' named Grosvenor. In the end, Patience prefers Grosvenor – who has, in the interim, agreed to renounce poetry and become a 'common-place young man' – while Bunthorne settles for a lily as his life companion.

Patience opened on 23 April 1881 at the Opera Comique and later transferred to the Savoy Theatre. Although based upon caricatures of Rossetti and Swinburne, the principal character Bunthorne, the 'greenery-yallery, Grosvenor Gallery, foot-in-the-grave young man,' played by George Grossmith, presented audiences with a clear amalgamation of both Wilde and Whistler. Grossmith's Bunthorne acted like Wilde in his effeminate mannerisms, but he looked more like Whistler in stature – small and wiry with the trademark white lock of hair. Wilde was intrigued and wrote to Grossmith requesting box seats on the opening night.

Wilde had become a celebrity. The art world had taken notice of this new, young apostle of art. Inspired by *Patience* and Du Maurier's caricatures, William Powell Frith put Wilde centre-stage in his *A Private View at the Royal Academy 1881* (exhibited in 1883). In the vast painting Wilde, with book in hand and a lily in his buttonhole, towers over a crowd at the Royal Academy while an entourage of eager young ladies, including Lillie Langtry and Ellen Terry, gaze at him in admiration. 'Beyond the desire of recording for posterity the aesthetic craze as regards dress,' Frith later recorded, 'I wished to hit the folly of listening

A Private View at the Royal Academy by William Powell Frith, 1881

to self-elected critics in matters of taste, whether in dress or art. I therefore planned a group, consisting of a well-known apostle of the beautiful, with a herd of eager worshippers surrounding him.'[16]

In the midst of all the parody and publicity, cracks were beginning to form in Tite Street. Between the parties at Keats House and Sunday brunches at No. 33, Wilde published a volume of *Poems* in 1881. The volume consisted of some well-exercised poems such as 'Ravenna', which had earned the young Oxonian the prestigious Newdigate Prize in 1878, alongside some newer works such as 'Symphony in Yellow' and 'Impressions du Matin' with their distinctly Whistlerian flavour:

The Thames nocturne of blue and gold[17]
Changed to a Harmony in grey:
A barge with ochre-coloured hay
Dropt from the wharf: and chill and cold

The yellow fog came creeping down
The bridges, till the houses' walls
Seemed changed to shadows and St. Paul's
Loomed like a bubble o'er the town.

The image of the immoral aesthete – corruptor of middle-class housewives – was further inflamed by the overt homoeroticism of some of Wilde's poems, including the controversial 'Charmides'. The overall reaction to *Poems* was mixed but tended towards the negative. Oscar Browning wrote a favourable review in which he exclaimed that, 'England is enriched with a new poet.' He nevertheless went on to criticise the volume for its 'irregular pulsations of a sympathy which never wearies. Roman Catholic ritual, stern Puritanism, parched Greek islands, cool English lanes and streams, Paganism and Christianity, despotism and Republicanism, Wordsworth, Milton and Mr Swinburne, receive in their turn the same passionate devotion.'[18] Few were smitten with Wilde's literary abilities, least of all Frank Miles's father, Canon Miles, who immediately wrote to Wilde, 'If we seem to advise a separation for a time it is not because we do not believe you in character to be very different to what you suggest in your poetry, but it is because you do not see the risk we see in a published poem which makes all who read it say to themselves "this is outside the pale of poetry, it is licentious and may do great harm to any soul that reads it".'[19]

Upon receiving this cutting missive Wilde burst into Miles's studio demanding to know what he thought of the letter. Miles gave a meekly neutral response and Wilde flew into a rage, 'I will leave you,' he shouted, 'I will go now and I will never speak to you again as long as I live,' and with this he tore upstairs, flung his clothes in a large trunk, and, rather than wait for help, tipped it over the banister. The case crashed down upon an antique table and smashed

Oscar Wilde reading a copy of *Poems*, photographed by Napoleon Sarony, 1882

it into fragments. He swept out of the house, slammed the door, tore off along Tite Street, hailed a cab and disappeared into the night.[20]

Wilde may have left Tite Street, but he was not homeless. He took temporary rooms at 9 Charles Street. In October a telegram arrived from Richard D'Oyly Carte in New York where *Patience* had been running successfully since September. D'Oyly Carte had ambitions to take the operetta on a tour of the United Sates, but there was a slight problem. While the aesthetes had been receiving widespread publicity in England for several years, the craze had not quite taken hold in America. The visionary D'Oyly Carte therefore decided he would have to create his own audience, and to do that, he would have to bring the aesthetic movement to America. With his usual entrepreneurial acumen, D'Oyly Carte devised a plan that would whet America's appetite for aestheticism. He hired the witty and eloquent Oscar Wilde to conduct a lecture tour in North America, giving the American public an exposure to aestheticism before the touring production of *Patience* opened at their nearest theatre.

Wilde arrived in North America on 2 January 1882, 'posing as the poseur he was supposed to be in order that the parody poseurs of *Patience* should pay off.' He used Grossmith's Bunthorne as the model both 'to imitate and to prefigure' his own image on his American tour.[21] Complete with cape, hat and knee breeches, Wilde claimed that he and his aesthetic friends did not regard his visit 'as an aesthetic mission to a barbarous clime, but our artists wish very much to have their ideas planted and growing in America.'[22] Photographs of the writer in aesthete costume reached Tite Street. His friends back home sent him their regards, 'We of Tite Street joy in your triumphs – and delight in your success – but – we think that, with the exception of your epigrams, you talk like Sidney Colvin[23] in the Provinces, – and that, with the exception of your knee breeches, you dress like 'Arry Quilter.'[24]

The tour was a success both for D'Oyly Carte and for Wilde. The tour that was only meant to last three months was stretched out to a year-long engagement. 'They are considering me *seriously*,' Wilde telegrammed Whistler. 'Isn't it dreadful? What would you do if it happened to you?'[25] 'My dear Oscar,' replied Whistler, 'that you should be considered seriously was inevitable – That you should take yourself seriously is unpardonable.'[26]

Wilde had in fact begun to take himself seriously, and he had begun to steal Whistler's limelight. To make matters worse, their public images were conflating into one stock caricature. Wilde had adopted the dress and manners of Grossmith's Bunthorne and made them his own. Through popular caricatures, the line between Whistler and Wilde had become so blurred that George du Maurier half-jokingly asked, 'Which one of you invented the other, eh?'[27] For Whistler, 'to be in danger of losing his pose before the world was bad enough, but to be mistaken for another man who rendered him ridiculous was worse.'[28] What had begun as a friendly albeit feisty relationship, whose power structure was accorded by age, soon began to uncoil.

When Wilde returned from his North America tour, he and Whistler continued on amicable terms. With Wilde no longer physically present in Tite Street, their many conversations would be conducted via telegram and recorded in various journals and periodicals. While their friendship lasted Whistler was still content to admit that Wilde 'elaborates all my best vices.'[29] Whistler would eventually lose his nerve when he saw Wilde 'befrogged and wonderfully befurred,' he exclaimed, 'How dare you! What means this disguise? Restore those things to Nathan's, and never again let me find you masquerading the streets of my Chelsea in the combined costumes of Kossuth and Mr Mantalini!'[30]

By the mid-1880s their venom would boil into full-blown public attacks and accusations of plagiarism. 'Wilde not only trifled with my shoe, but bolted with the latchet!' Whistler complained.[31]

The superficial nature of their friendship was summed up in a volley of telegrams in November 1883, when *Punch* reported that Wilde and Whistler had been discussing the relative merits of Sarah Bernhardt and Mary Anderson as actresses. Wilde sent Whistler a telegram: '*Punch* too ridiculous – when you and I are together we never talk about anything except ourselves,' to which Whistler replied, 'No, no, Oscar, you forget – when you and I are together, we never talk about anything except me.' But Wilde had the last word, 'It is true, Jimmy, we were talking about you, but I was thinking of myself.'[32]

12.

TWO LADIES

Nature is jealous of line, of hue, and even of sound; she insists that
wherever art is confronted with her, it shall partake of her own essence.
– Lady Archibald Campbell, Rainbow-Music; or, the
Philosophy of Harmony in Colour-Grouping, 1886

The parodies of the Tite Street coterie, in the pages of *Punch* or on the stage, all shared a similar narrative. Whether in *The Grasshopper*, *The Colonel* or *Patience*, a whimsical, eccentric aesthete archetype is foiled by a sturdy, trusted member of the Establishment. This popular manifestation of the aesthete as a romantic, isolated, anti-Establishment figure seeking to undermine the authority of the patriarchal power structure in Victorian society was to some extent a projection of public perceptions of real life events. The new embodiment of the aesthetic movement had almost become a craze whose adherents and disciples practised what Harry Quilter referred to as the 'gospel of intensity'.[1]

An anti-Establishment idealism did thrive in Tite Street, and society was reluctant to open its arms to Whistler, the feisty scandal-maker. During these *années de combat* it was 'an act of courage to have oneself painted by Whistler,' wrote Theodore Duret. 'One was seen as an ignorant person, devoid of artistic comprehension, and above all, a dupe.'[2] However, there were two ladies who brushed aside public opinion, seeking Whistler to paint their portraits. Lady Meux and Lady Archibald Campbell came from remarkably different backgrounds. One had been a barmaid while the other had been a ward of the Duke of Argyll. Their portraits would become the best known Whistler portraits to emerge from Tite Street in the 1880s.

As was to be expected from someone who had climbed further up the social ladder than most ladies of the age, Lady Meux was no stranger to controversy. From a small fishing village in south Devon, Susan Valerie Langdon moved to London with her brothers after the death of her father. A dazzling beauty with blue violet eyes, dark golden hair and a striking figure, she found herself singing and dancing in various bars, casinos and dance halls until she met her Dorian Gray-like Prince Charming in the form of Harry Meux, heir to a vast brewery fortune.

The life of Harry Meux, though padded by enormous wealth, was no less turbulent than Susan's. Shortly after he was born, Harry's father, the 2nd Baronet, developed a mental illness, and his wife Louisa Brudenell-Bruce abandoned him and their son to live out her life as an exile in France. Harry was returned to England where he spent his childhood in boarding schools. On reaching his majority in 1877, Harry was granted an enormous allowance of £28,000 a year (at a time when £5,000 a year was considered wealthy and a professional man might earn around £500 a year).

At some point in the mid-1870s Harry met Susan, most likely at the Casino de Venise opposite the brewery in Holborn and they eloped in 1878. *Truth* wrote that in marrying Susan, Harry had 'abandoned all idea of Parliamentary career', but Susan, by marrying well, had 'landed the biggest fish which has floated in the matrimonial waters for some time.'[3] Harry's estranged mother, on hearing the news, conceded that her son was 'quiet and a perfect gentleman' which is why she was so astonished that 'he should be mad enough to marry any lady of that class.' It was true that Susan had been 'knocking about London for ten years' and that she was five years older than Harry, but in an ill-advised attempt to make amends, she admitted to Harry's grandmother, the Dowager Marchioness of Ailesbury, that all her 'sins were committed before marriage and not after.'[4]

A good marriage would not save Susan Langdon from trouble, however. Indeed it plunged her further into a life of controversy and social ostracism. Polite society refused to associate with the former barmaid with a questionable past. Simply associating with Lady Meux meant running the risk of being tainted. When she interviewed the young Margaret McMillan, later to become an important figure in the Labour movement, for the position of secretary, Lady Meux warned her that she was 'a woman not received' in society. 'Men come here,' she said, 'distinguished men, but not their women. I am outside … It is only right to tell you, that it isn't a good thing for you to come here. You might not get another post.'[5]

Despite the precarious social position of his wife, Harry was determined to shower his bride with an enviable wardrobe of Parisian dresses and diamonds worth £10,000. The family were appalled at the lavish and flamboyant manner in which young Harry was doting upon his new wife and they took legal action to limit his stake in the brewery business. Undaunted, the smitten young heir decided that he would commission a painter to complete three portraits of his wife. When it came time to choose a painter Lady Meux chose Whistler.

London was full of portrait painters in the 1880s. With her money Lady Meux could easily have chosen one of hundreds of well-known and respected portrait artists or Royal Academicians. Instead, she spurned the Academy 'without troubling herself with the opinions of others' in favour of another outsider.[6] No doubt she would have felt at home in the rogue group of Tite Street bohemians, themselves the subject of so much controversy, scandal and public ridicule. 'You and I,' she later wrote to Whistler, 'always get on well together. I suppose we are both a little eccentric and *not* loved by *all* the world. Personally,' she continued, 'I am glad of it as I should prefer a little hate.'[7] Whistler likewise welcomed the commission, an opportunity of colluding with the bold and vivacious Lady Meux in constructing an image that would confirm through art a status that was denied her in real life. On a more practical level for Whistler the commission for three portraits at 500 guineas provided some much-needed capital after his devastating bankruptcy.

The famous trio of portraits began with sittings in the summer of 1881. Lady Meux arrived almost daily at No. 33 where she would stand upon a dais twenty feet from the artist who 'held in his left hand a sheaf of brushes, with monstrous long handles. His movements were those of a duellist fencing actively and cautiously with the small sword.'[8] By October, the first portrait, *Arrangement in Black: Lady Meux,* was completed. Whistler called it his 'beautiful Black Lady' while Theodore Duret, who saw the artist at work on it, found in the effect '*quelque chose de mystérieux et de fantastique.*'[9] Turned slightly to the right, but facing the viewer straight on, Lady Meux is depicted from below, erect, luxuriously attired and unabashedly dripping with diamonds. The painting itself is a testament of elegance, grandeur and authority. It was, as Thomas Way declared, Lady Meux's 'state portrait'.[10] The year after it was completed, the painting was sent to the Paris Salon, where Henri Rouart described it to Edgar Degas as 'an astonishing Whistler, excessively subtle but of such quality!'[11]

One sketch (attributed to Menpes or Charles Brookfield) shows Whistler in his Tite Street studio with three long brushes working on three separate portraits of Lady Meux at once. The second portrait was a stark contrast from the first. *Harmony in Pink and Grey: Portrait of Lady Meux* depicts the subject in almost exactly the same position as before, displaying her voluptuous form to full advantage and with a bold outward gaze conveying her seductive confidence. What has changed in the second portrait is Whistler's colour palette. While the first portrait is dark, hardly differentiating where the subject ends and the background begins, *Pink and Grey* gives a more virginal portrayal of Lady Meux in a feminine pink dress against a slightly darker pink background. In contrast to the low-cut, sleeveless dress of the previous portrait, *Pink and Grey* shows a fully covered Lady Meux complete with a hat and floor-length dress, a far more respectable depiction of a Victorian lady.

While Whistler was working on Lady Meux's portraits, his Tite Street studio was graced by another notable sitter – Lady Archibald Campbell. Unlike Lady Meux, Lady Archie was a respected socialite, intellectual and sophisticated, moving in the most elite circles of society. She was also one of the most important, unsung heroes of the aesthetic movement. One Parisian newspaper later described her as '*la Grande dame esthétique de Londres*'.[12] Lady Archibald Campbell was born Janey Sevilla Callander in Scotland, but when her father died she became a ward of the Duke of Argyll. In 1868 she married Lord Archibald Campbell, the second son of the Duke of Argyll, who had made considerable money in banking.

Whistler first met the Campbells at the opening of the Grosvenor Gallery, and they became keen patrons of his work. Around 1882 Lord Archibald Campbell commissioned a new portrait of his wife. While Whistler was finishing *Pink and Grey*, Lady Archibald

'Whistler's Lady Meux' attributed to Mortimer Menpes or Charles Brookfield

Campbell came to the Tite Street studio to stand for her first portrait. According to Theodore Duret, 'she was a tall woman of great distinction, svelte, blond, and also intelligent and independent in spirit . . . [She] was an ideal model for a painter.'[13] This must have been the case. Between 1881 and 1882 Lady Archie came to Tite Street almost daily.

Whistler started two portraits of '*la Grande dame esthetique*'. First he painted *Portrait of Lady Archibald Campbell in Court Dress* followed by *The Grey Lady: Portrait of Lady Archibald Campbell*. From his lecture tour in America, Wilde wrote to Whistler, 'And the Moon-Lady, the Grey Lady, the beautiful wraith with her beryl eyes, our Lady Archie, how is she?'[14] If he had had time to respond to Wilde's telegram, Whistler's answer might have been, 'not happy!' The artist had already started working on a third portrait progressing with unprecedented speed, and within just a few sittings he had produced a life-sized portrait. But the third and final portrait was not quite what Lady Archie had in mind.

In *Arrangement in Black*, Lady Archie is seen with a raised skirt deliberately exposing her ankles, but perhaps more insulting was her seductive backwards glance, demurely looking out at the viewer. For Lady Meux this pose might have worked, but for Lady Archibald Campbell it was a step too far. When *Arrangement in Black: La Dame au brodequin jaune – Portrait of Lady Archibald Campbell* was displayed it failed to impress the sitter's family. W. Graham Robertson reported that 'the Campbell family rejected it with the delicate remark that it represented a street walker encouraging a shy follower with a backward glance.'[15]

In both sets of portraits, Whistler manipulated image to ironic effect. With Lady Meux, he depicts a strong and respectable yet virginal woman (at least in *Pink and Grey*) a far cry from

LEFT *Arrangement in Black: Lady Meux* by James Abbott McNeill Whistler, 1881
RIGHT *Harmony in Pink and Grey: Portrait of Lady Meux* by James Abbott McNeill Whistler, 1881–2

the real life of the subject, a former barmaid. On the other hand, Lady Archibald, a highly respectable woman of society, is depicted in a pose suggestive of a prostitute. The joke did not amuse everyone. One afternoon while he was working on another portrait of Theodore Duret, Lady Archibald Campbell barged into the Tite Street studio. Pacing around the studio, frantic and excited, she demanded that Whistler change everything. Before the artist had a chance to respond, however, she had stormed out of the studio, jumped in her carriage and sped off out of Tite Street.[16] It was only after several days of intense begging by Theodore Duret that Lady Archie decided she would return to complete the painting. Whistler later conceded that he would change the name of the portrait to preserve her reputation. When it was exhibited in Paris in the painting anonymously appeared as *Arrangement in Black: La Dame au brodequin jaune.*

Lady Archie was not the only lady to lose her temper in Whistler's studio. That same summer of 1884, Whistler was working on the third and final portrait of Lady Meux – *Portrait of Lady Meux in Furs (Harmony in Crimson and Brown).* Whistler selected a fur wrap with the subject standing in a full-frontal position, draped in warm, brown sable furs, with her face the only part of her body exposed. The portrait was the most gruelling of them all and was still in progress as late as 1886. Sittings grew more and more tense. Lady Meux was restless and agitated having to sit under the furs for hours on end in the hot, stuffy studio. Whistler likewise had grown furious when his sitter sent her servant woman in her brown furs to model. He sent her a telegram on 30 July 1886, 'cannot struggle with melting maids in altered furs ridiculous prefer to pay back money though as always charming will paint you quite a new portrait new arrangement if you promise to stand for it yourself.'[17] She returned obediently to Tite Street, but after just a couple sittings she snapped, 'See here Jimmy Whistler! You keep a civil tongue in that head of yours or I will have in someone to finish those portraits you have made of me!'[18]

While Whistler was finishing her portrait, Lady Archie brought a new face to Tite Street, an American actress named Eleanor Calhoun. Calhoun had been born and raised in the distant wilderness of California, a descendant of former Vice President of the United States John C. Calhoun, and was once engaged to the future tycoon William Randolph Hearst.[19] With her good looks, charm and social connections Nelly became a successful actress and eventually moved to England where she became a darling of London society. In 1882 she was performing at the Haymarket Theatre and had become good friends with Lady Archie, spending her afternoons at the Campbells' house in Coombe Wood, Surrey.

Coombe Hill Farm was an Elizabethan farmhouse 'on the gentle, southern slope of a low hill'. 'One summer day,' Calhoun later recalled, 'when the sun, a somewhat exclusive god in England, deigned to show forth in full power, and splash the forest with splendor, flaming on the trees and between their dark velvety masses of shadow, making more vivid still the crimsons and purples and rose-colors of the stretches of rhododendrons, it seemed to me that in such an English forest must the vision of Rosalind have first come to Shakspere [sic]. In

Arrangement in Black: La Dame au brodequin jaune – Portrait of Lady Archibald Campbell by James Abbott McNeill Whistler, 1882

Note in Green and Brown: Orlando at Coombe by James Abbott McNeill Whistler, *c.*1884–5

an impulse at the thought, I threw off my wrap and began to speak Rosalind's words. Lady Archibald stood far back as audience, while I acted through the scenes. As I heard the words I was speaking ringing through the woods, the idea flashed upon me, "Why not give the play so, here, on this very spot?" I called out to my friend, "I want to act this play right here among these trees." I ran to her and began to expound the matter. "What if I bring actors and realise Shakespeare's own dream out here in the forest itself!"'[20]

In Tite Street, Calhoun and Lady Archie divulged their idea to E.W. Godwin who was immediately recruited into the scheme. They set about planning the spectacle. As well as designing houses, Godwin was a stage director, producer and costume designer. He had in fact designed numerous costumes for his ex-lover, Ellen Terry. Just a year prior, in 1882, he founded The Costume Society and had published a manifesto *The Costume Society, or Society for promoting the knowledge of Costume, by copying and publishing Historical Costume from Contemporary Sources only.*[21] He went to great trouble to achieve archaeological correctness in his work. When Henry Irving commissioned him to design costumes for *Hamlet* he travelled to Denmark to see the original Elsinore Castle.

Lady Archie's theatrical accomplishments however were slightly more amateur. She had performed in a few smaller roles but had the passion, determination and, more importantly, the money to make her vision a reality. A financial agreement was signed between Godwin as director and Lady Archibald as president, which specified that, for managing the plays in the open air, Godwin would receive a salary as a theatrical manager.

Calhoun, along with the Grey Lady and the Wicked Earl set to work in the autumn of 1883 and spring of 1884 to create one of the most lavish spectacles of the aesthetic movement in Britain – an open-air production of *As You Like It*. Lady Archibald 'entered with heart and soul into the plan' and set about establishing a small theatre company of amateur actors to perform in open-air private theatricals. The eager thespians were able to recruit a number of 'interesting personalities' into their ranks including seasoned actor Herman Vezin, 'the finest speaker of Shakespearian verse' as Jacques.[22] Besides Calhoun, the rest of the cast was comprised of amateurs, including Lady Archie as Orlando.

The troupe had managed to find a bit of 'fine old forest, silent but for its own denizens,'[23] about an hour's drive from Tite Street where they were determined to launch their theatricals. The production however was not without a few hitches. One afternoon Lady Archie wrote a frantic telegram to Eleanor. 'It's all over, the royal George is furious. Come.'[24] It would seem that the plot of land the idealistic aesthetes were using did not actually belong to them. Indeed they had ventured somewhat beyond the boundaries of the Campbell's gardens. At some point they had intended to contact the Duke of Cambridge and ask his permission to use his land, but in their flurry of creativity it had slipped their minds. For a moment it seemed that their aesthetic venue was doomed. After much tribulation, however, another spot was secured in a part of the same forest belonging to another estate, 'a peaceful setting in the woods behind Coombe Hill Farm'. Finally, after several months of careful preparation and rehearsals, on a mild July afternoon in 1884, their creative collaboration came together. Performed as the London Season was in full swing, it gave people an opportunity to escape to the country for an early evening entertainment. The very elite of society represented by the Prince and Princess of Wales, Princess Louise, the eccentric Duke of Saxe-Meinengen along with numerous other 'statesmen, diplomats, poets, painters, sculptors and the finest of the world of fashion' thronged to the private production.

Max Beerbohm aptly called it 'the very Derby Day of Aestheticism'.[26] The entire Tite Street circle of artists and bohemians was in attendance. Whistler had been attending rehearsals and painted a small oil portrait *Note in Green and Brown: Orlando at Coombe* while Oscar Wilde wrote the lines, 'Through an alley of white hawthorne and gold laburnum we passed into the green pavilion, the air sweet with the odour of lilac and with the blackbird's song'.

A grove of lime trees formed a natural stage separated from a tiered 300-seat 'auditorium' with a sage-green curtain. This sheltered grove formed the main acting area, with natural 'wings' made out of clumps of low bushes and piles of small sticks. A 'proscenium' was created by a green curtain strung between two trees, which was dropped by a pulley (operated by two men dressed as foresters) into a narrow trench at the start of the performance and raised again in the interval. The trench itself was camouflaged by a narrow belt of moss planted with ferns which also marked the end of the stage.

Godwin's costumes were a successful experiment in harmonizing the natural surroundings to Lady Archie's 'freedom of mood'. In *The Truth of Masks* Oscar Wilde vividly described the scene: 'The Duke and his companions were dressed in serge tunics, leathern jerkins, high boots and gauntlets, and wore bycocket hats and hoods. And as they were playing in a real forest, they found, I am sure, their dresses extremely convenient.'[27]

Beyond the elements of design, the acting was also praised for its 'impression of absolute reality'. Realism was carried to extreme lengths with the introduction of real deer, real stag-heads and even real goats, bells tinkling in a perfect pre-determined harmony. The foresters entered singing, their voices gradually increasing in volume; at one stage a slain deer was seen in the distance being carried towards the fire. At the close of the performance the cast wandered away, singing, so that they were soon lost behind the trees and only their voices could be heard, until finally even their voices were no longer audible and the curtain was slowly raised, blotting out the scene.

'All the conventional symbolism,' wrote *The Era*, 'the "make-believe" of the ordinary stage, everything which is conveniently summarised in the phrase *optique du theatre*, the asides, "stage-whispers", the actor taking the audience into his confidence, and so forth, became in the open-air either impossible or un-needed, and the performers were able to abstract themselves from all reference to the spectators, thus producing a sense of illusion so perfect as almost to make the audience feel like a body of eavesdroppers.'[28]

13.

SHELLEY THEATRE

A private theatre in a country mansion is unquestionably an
advantage where the tastes of the owners lend themselves to such
entertainments, and not a few notable residences in England
contain more or less complete arrangements of the kind.
– 'A Private Theatre at Chelsea', *Building News*, 16 May 1879

While the characters of Tite Street were being mimicked on the stage in the West End and
performing their own theatricals in the woods of Coombe, within their own street stood
a 229-seat private theatre belonging to Sir Percy Shelley, the only son of Romantic poet
Percy Bysshe Shelley and writer Mary Wollstonecraft. Shelley already had a country house
at Boscombe Manor with its own private theatre. He came to Chelsea in 1878 when he
purchased two plots of land from the Metropolitan Board of Works along the newly built
Chelsea Embankment and commissioned architect Joseph Peacock to design a house
overlooking the river. The end product was an eclectic mix of Queen Anne and late Tudor
style with the front in red brick, and window quoins and other details in Tisbury stone.

Shelley was well aware of the bohemian enclave just around the corner. Only a year after
his arrival in the neighbourhood he was himself the subject of a caricature by his Tite Street
neighbour Carlo 'Ape' Pellegrini for an 1879 *Vanity Fair* edition entitled 'The Poet's Son'.
Despite his literary heritage, Shelley did not publish a single line of poetry in his life. He
did however have an interest in theatre, and for nearly four years he produced a handful of
amateur plays in his own private Tite Street theatre. Just a year after his house was built, Sir
Percy's solicitor contacted the Board of Works about leasing an empty site in Tite Street in
which to build a theatre. A special contract would be necessary stating that he would not use
the property as a 'Public Theatre, Music Hall, Lecture Hall, Circus Amphitheatre, Aquarium,
Skating Rink, Dancing Saloon, or as any other place of entertainment, amusement,
exhibition, or for any public purpose of a like nature.'[1]

Shelley had no intention of using the space for public purpose. Instead he intended to
stage his own private theatricals with a selected guest list on particular nights, with proceeds

going to charity. So he signed the contract in May 1879, paying £880 for the site, and commissioned Joseph Peacock to design the theatre. A month after Archie and Ape's house next door was finished, construction began on the Shelley Theatre.

Facing Tite Street, Peacock's theatre was finished in the Queen Anne style, carried out in yellow stock brick, with red brick dressings enriched in the central feature by stone pilasters and rusticated quoins. The overall shape of the theatre building was almost perfectly square. From the street there was no indication that a theatre existed in that spot with the exception of an inconspicuous awning over the main door. At the rear of the building was a green room, with accompanying dressing rooms along with offices and even a carpenter's shop, which had its own entrance from Paradise Row behind.

The interior of the theatre was spacious, with a high ceiling painted 'subdued bluish green, and ornamented with a few golden stars.'[2] The auditorium was a semi-circular shape with tiered seating from the orchestra pit and plenty of plush red chairs. Above the stalls was a semi-circular balcony supported by slender iron columns adorned with graceful wooden rails and ornamented with carved wood. The proscenium arch was also ornamented in the same carved wood, and on each side of the stage cosy private boxes, shaded with Japanese curtains. In front of the stage was an open orchestra pit separated from the stalls by a screen of carved wood work 'simple yet elegant in design, and a similar arrangement conceal[ed] the footlights.'[3]

Like a giddy schoolboy, Shelley supervised every step of the theatre's construction with an almost childlike fascination in everything from the hot water apparatus and stage lighting to battens, floats, orchestra rails and dressing rooms. He even helped to paint the proscenium borders and drop scenes. The Shelley Theatre opened its doors for the first time at the end of May 1881, just a few months after Whistler returned to Tite Street from Venice. For the opening night Shelley selected Wilkie Collins's play *The Lighthouse*, in which he played a minor part as the Pilot. The play was followed by Planche's *A Romantic Idea*. Horace Wigan, head of the London School of Dramatic Art, was called in to stage manage the productions. Performances continued in March the following year with a production of *Two Loves and a Life* by Charles Reade and Tom Taylor. In December 1882 the *Morning Post* announced that the Prince and Princess of Wales and other members of the royal family would attend the opening of the newest play, *The Cousins*, preceded by a shorter piece, *Après le Bal*, with tickets sold for one guinea each in aid of the London School of Dramatic Art. Again in January performances of *Parvenu* and *My Turn Next* were given in aid of the Victoria Hospital for Sick Children, located at the top end of Tite Street.

Shelley's private theatre was doing well, but its fate was determined by other events in Tite Street. Shortly after the theatre was built, its neighbours Archie and Ape had decided to move. Archie relocated to a new house across the street, but their old house on the corner of Dilke Street, designed by Godwin, was purchased by the Hon. Slingsby Bethell, an amateur artist. Bethell immediately set about altering the interior of the house by uniting

Theatrical cartoon by Sir Percy Shelley

the previously divided studios on the top floor, and it was around this time that the building became known as Chelsea Lodge. Godwin's interiors were not the only thing that Bethell sought to change in Tite Street.

Less than a year after moving to Tite Street, Bethell complained to the Metropolitan Board of Works that Shelley's theatre had caused him 'serious inconvenience and annoyance,' and that operating his private theatre was 'contrary to the Theatre Act.'[4] Bethell held that the keeping of a theatre or musical hall in Tite Street would be detrimental to the 'high-class property in the locality' which would be 'prejudicially affected.'[5] The matter went to the Westminster Police Court in January 1883. Shelley was outraged at the complaint and protested that the courts should not be able to 'stipulate what an Englishman did in the privacy of his own home.'[6]

Horace Wigan, a witness in the case, rose in support of Shelley with a letter to *The Era*. 'The performances commenced between eight and nine o'clock, and were over soon after eleven,' Wigan stated. He argued that the annoyance these caused could not have differed from 'that caused by balls and evening parties to which the sojourner in Belgravia is subject during the season.' He went on to say that 'when the theatre was built, Mr Archibald Stuart-Wortley was the owner, and resided in the house of which Mr Bethell is now the occupier, so that, in point of fact, Mr Bethell sought the neighbourhood of the theatre, which was constructed before his arrival.'[7]

Bethell struck back, protesting that the reason he was filing the complaint 'was not on the nuisance caused by a great assemblage of carriages and cabs at the theatre next to my residence but the fact that Shelley had breached his contract with the Board of Works by staging public theatricals in Tite Street. By June 1882, the theatre, unknown to me, had been placed in the hands of Mr Mitchell of Bond-street, and was hired by Sir Charles Young for the sum of £50, who gave two public performances and sold tickets. In November, 1882, it was still offered for hire at £25 per night by the same agent. Mr Aide's performances then followed – three in one week, with sale of tickets; after these, a performance in January last for the Victoria Hospital, also with sale of tickets.' Futhermore he expressed a concern that the value of his property may be 'depreciated very considerably on adjoining a public place of entertainment.'[8]

After hearing various witnesses, Judge D'Eyncourt ruled that after reviewing the facts of the case he was bound to impose a nominal penalty in spite of the fact that Shelley's performances had 'benevolent motives.' Bethell may have emerged from the case victorious but was thenceforward seen as nothing more than a thankless curmudgeon. Although Shelley was supported by his neighbours, the royal family, the courts and the public, he had violated the terms of his contract with the all-powerful Metropolitan Board of Works and was forced to pay the fine.

Sir Percy himself wrote the final word in a letter to *The Era* published on 3 March 1883:

Sir,

Mr Bethell's attempts to justify himself rests on two grounds – (1), that I have used my theatre otherwise than as a private theatre; (2), that I have so used it to the annoyance of my neighbours.

As to the first I deny I have so used it, and this is a pure legal question for the Judges of the Queen's Bench to decide. As to the second, with the exception of Mr Bethell, all my neighbours, residents in Tite-street, have assured me since these proceedings that not only is the theatre no annoyance to them, but they have also expressed their sympathy for me in the annoyance to which I have been subjected by Mr Bethell's action.

I will not occupy your space by pointing out the numerous inaccurate statements in Mr Bethell's letter. The shorthand notes of the proceedings before the magistrates will shortly be published, when any one who cares can see for himself the true state of the case, and the desire on the part of Mr Bethell to dictate how those who live near him are to enjoy their own property.

Both for the sake of the public and myself I regret that 'a very humble part' especially 'without lines' has not been assigned to Mr Bethell in every performance at my theatre: for if it had, 'my successor,' about whom Mr Bethell seems so desirous, with whose wishes he appears so familiar, and whose advent by my decease he so kindly anticipates, would then have had the uncongenial task of dealing with this question and with Mr Bethell.

Sir Percy Shelley, Chelsea Embankment[9]

Around 1884 the Shelleys left their home on the Embankment and moved to Wetherby Gardens and lived there until Shelley's death in 1889. Bethell continued to live at the Chelsea Lodge, but would himself later be taken to the Westminster Police Court, in a case presided over once again by Judge D'Eyncourt, on charges of assaulting a shoemaker's apprentice in the Queen's Road at the top end of Tite Street. The apprentice claimed that when he arrived at Bethell's home in Tite Street to deliver a pair of boots, Bethell had refused to pay for them and then proceeded to assault the young man with a thick malacca cane.

The Shelley Theatre remained intact but empty and unused until 1899 when it was torn down to make way for a block of flats called Shelley Court. In 1912, Shelley's old house on the Embankment was also pulled down. Although the Shelley Theatre met its demise prematurely, Tite Street's theatrical dominion would be secured in the coming decade, by one of the greatest playwrights of the British stage, Oscar Wilde.

14.

JOHN COLLIER
& the WILD WOMEN

Tite Street is, as far as its externals go, somewhat dark and shut
in by its tall houses; but it more than atones for any outside
dullness by the excessive light and learning of its interiors.
– *Highways and Byways*, 1902

On 9 May 1871 one of the most sensational trials of the century opened at Westminster
Hall. At the defendants' table sat Frederick William Park and Ernest Boulton, otherwise
known as 'Fanny' and 'Stella', two cross-dressing homosexual men charged with 'conspiring
and inciting persons to commit an unnatural offence' – the unnatural offence being the then
illegal act of sodomy. At the prosecuting bench sat Sir Robert Collier, the Attorney General
in charge of prosecuting the alleged sodomites. After nearly six days of gruelling testimonies
about the altogether sordid lives of the two young men and their various debaucheries with
other young men, Sir Robert remained unable to prove that any unnatural offence had taken
place, and Fanny and Stella were found not guilty. While the verdict was a triumph for
the young men, the trial exposed the absence of legislation needed to convict sodomites.
This problem would soon be solved. The ripples made by Fanny and Stella's trial would
eventually be felt in Tite Street, when one of its famous residents would be prosecuted for a
new crime known as 'gross indecency'.[1]

With the scandal of the Fanny and Stella case behind him, Sir Robert Collier moved
his family to the newly built Chelsea Embankment on the borders of the artistic enclave in
Tite Street. In just a few short years the entire Chelsea riverfront had developed beyond all
recognition. By the early 1880s a row of tall Queen Anne houses fronted the Embankment,
ornamented with gothic gas lamps along the elegant promenade. The Embankment was
deemed a triumph of Victorian civil engineering as the 'unpleasant mud banks' of the Thames
were replaced by 'pleasant drives and ornamental gardens'. 'In designing these works,' wrote
the Metropolitan Board of Works, an endeavour had been made 'to render them not only

useful, but agreeable, by giving some architectural embellishment . . . laying out the surplus ground as ornamental gardens, and planting trees on either side of the road, in imitation of the Boulevards of Paris [to form] a thoroughfare not unworthy of the great capital.'2 Three Embankment houses were designed by E.W. Godwin adjacent to Tite Street, and others were quickly built. One by one they were snatched up by a host of Victorian grandees such as the Viceroy for India and Sir Percy Shelley. Sir Robert Collier was one of these grandees, commissioning architect Phené Spiers to build a house at No. 7 Chelsea Embankment.

When he was not prosecuting cross-dressers in court, Sir Robert was an amateur painter of Alpine landscapes, which he exhibited annually at the Royal Academy. He also had two sons destined for success. The elder son served as Under Secretary of State for War and later became the Chairman of the London County Council, while the younger son took quite a different path. After four years at Eton, John Collier approached his father and announced his desire to become a painter. The idea was greeted with support. With his considerable social standing, Sir Robert was able to arrange a meeting for his son with the Royal Academician, Sir Lawrence Alma-Tadema.

Alma-Tadema was already a prominent figure in the London art world. He had given up private tutoring to focus solely on painting, but he did agree to give the young artist some advice.3 Advice, however, could only go so far. Collier felt he needed more formal artistic training, and to this end he went to study under another great Victorian painter, Sir Edward Poynter, head of the Slade School of Art, predecessor to Alphonse Legros. He then went to Paris to train at the Académie Julian under the classical painter Jean-Paul Laurens, whose influence, along with Alma-Tadema's, would remain prevalent in Collier's art for decades to come. Sir Robert decided to further aid his son's artistic development by commissioning Spiers to build a studio extension at the rear of his house facing Dilke Street at the corner of Tite Street.

A decade before the landmark Boulton and Park case, another controversial event had shaped the development of the modern world. When *The Origin of Species* was published in 1859, Charles Darwin had created an earthquake in Victorian religious evangelism. The theory of evolution had already been incubating in Britain for nearly a quarter of a century, but it was with Darwin's writing that it finally hatched. *The Origin of Species* met with fierce criticism from both the Church and the scientific communities on an international scale. But Darwin also had many staunch friends, not least the anatomist and biologist Thomas Huxley.

Huxley, a President of the Royal Society, was a prominent and outspoken member of the Victorian scientific community. The stern, forthright figure was caricatured by Ape for *Vanity Fair* with his commanding presence, famous mutton-chop sideburns and determined gaze. Huxley coined the term 'agnostic' to describe his religious beliefs and founded the famous X-Club, a dinner club of scientific minds who gathered to debate the newest theories of the day. Although he disagreed with Darwin on many points, Huxley soon became known as 'Darwin's Bulldog' for his stoic support of his colleague's unorthodox theories.

John Collier by Marian Collier, c.1882–3

In the same year that *The Origin of Species* was published, Huxley had fathered the third of eight children. Marian Huxley was a shy and sensitive girl, a stark contrast to her brazen father. At a very tender age she demonstrated a precocious talent for painting, and at the age of twenty Marian was already exhibiting at the Royal Academy. Her first picture, *The Sins of the Father*, was a quixotic portrait of her two sisters Ethel and Nettie as children playing cards. Marian's talent earned her a place at the Slade Art School where she subsequently met the astute and determined John Collier. In 1879 Collier had asked Huxley for Marian's hand in marriage and he readily agreed. Just a few weeks before the marriage, Collier visited the Huxleys with his brother and his sister-in-law, the future Lord and Lady Monkswell, where they found Marian to be 'quite the artist's wife, her hair comes down, she forgot the band to her dress, she is always wanting pins.' In spite of her rather dishevelled appearance they still found her 'a dear child full of brightness and life'.[4]

The young couple were married in June 1879 and shortly after the wedding their thoughts turned toward building a studio-house of their own. Tite Street seemed like an obvious location for two blossoming artists to make their mark, with a thriving artistic quarter literally on their doorstep. Collier toyed with the idea of using the favoured Tite Street architect E.W. Godwin or his father's architect Phené Spiers, but in the end decided to use Frederick William Waller, husband of his new sister-in-law, Jessie Huxley (Marian's older sister).

A plot was selected in the middle of Tite Street, between the Shelley Theatre and Frank Miles's Keats House. The Tite Street house was designed in the popular Queen Anne style and consisted of three storeys, with attic and basement, the exterior designed in yellow brick with red brick dressings, large Flemish gables and a tiled roof.

On the first floor was an enormous studio that ran the depth of the house. The studio was both airy and elegant but reached by a rather steep and angular staircase which made it nearly impossible to move large pictures out of the house. Eventually a trap door was cut into the studio floor so that canvases lowered through it could slide directly out of the side door. The studio's tall main bay window faced north-east with a wide arch opposite the main door, which opened into an inglenook with a fireplace, similar to the one in Frank Miles's studio. Just to the south of this, a staircase led up to a rooftop platform with a view over the garden.

The Colliers' first few years in the new Tite Street house were incredibly productive. Collier had submitted three portraits to the Royal Academy in 1878 and three again in 1879. But it was his painting in 1881 that would attract the most attention and give him a foothold in the professional art world. *The Last Voyage of Henry Hudson*, painted with faint Pre-Raphaelite influences of Millais, is Collier's first narrative painting. The subject of the painting is Henry Hudson, the great navigator of the seventeenth century whose voyage to the Arctic was thwarted by a mutiny of his crew. The painting shows a desolate man helplessly adrift in a small boat with his two sons amidst a sea of imposing icebergs. *Henry Hudson* attracted considerable attention at the Royal Academy and was purchased for the Tate through the Chantrey Bequest.

On the heels of his success with *Henry Hudson*, Collier completed a number of other portrait commissions, mostly from friends of his father or father-in-law. In 1881 he painted the famous botanist Sir Joseph Hooker, and Dr James Joule the following year. One such portrait was of Huxley's friend and fellow evolutionary scientist, George Romanes. When the Linnean Society commissioned a portrait of Darwin, Romanes recommended young Collier for the job, writing that Collier was 'sure to do the work well' and adding that 'he is such a pleasant man to talk to, that the sittings are not so tedious as they would be with a less intelligent man.'[5]

The ageing Darwin was unable to travel far, so Collier journeyed from Tite Street to Down House in Kent over the course of a few sittings in late July and early August 1881, completing the last portrait of one of the most influential figures of the nineteenth century. Darwin later wrote to Romanes thanking him for the suggestion: 'All my family who have seen it think it the best likeness which has been taken of me, and, as far as I can judge, this seems true. Collier was the most considerate, kind, and pleasant painter a sitter could desire.'[6] Darwin wrote to John Collier in February 1882 to thank him for the completed portrait, 'Everybody whom I have seen and who has seen your picture of me is delighted with it. I shall be proud some day to see myself suspended at the Linnean Society.'[7]

Standard portrait commissions were an excellent way of earning income for any artist. Though he was an artist of considerable means, Collier had building costs to recoup from his Tite Street house, not to mention a new wife to support. But there was an itch Collier could not help scratching, and the early success of *Henry Hudson* gave him a taste of his true calling. While profitable portraiture kept him busy, at his core Collier was a storyteller. As *Darwin* was drying and in reality dying in 1881, Collier returned to the Royal Academy with his chilling, life-sized *Clytemnestra* and the following year with *Circe*.

In *Clytemnestra*, Collier demonstrated his powers of artistic storytelling much more in line with his mentors Alma-Tadema and Frederic Leighton in both subject and style, invoking a figure of classical antiquity in a highly dramatic moment of crisis. In his rendition of the classic Greek tragedy, a fearsome Clytemnestra draws aside a curtain to appear before the Elders of Argos with her right hand resting upon a long inverted axe, its blade dripping with blood. The features of her stony face are hardened and inflexible, and an eerie light radiates from behind the drawn curtain, while the evil flare of her eye betrays a brewing madness within.

Madness was something which Collier would become only too familiar with as an unwelcome but unavoidable guest at his new Tite Street studio-house. In 1884 Marian had given birth to the couple's first daughter, Joyce, but the happy occasion was soon marred by a grim shadow. In the months following the birth of her daughter, Marian had begun to suffer from acute post-natal depression. Once 'a dear child full of brightness and life,'[8] Marian Collier had now all but given up painting. Entire weeks were spent in bed where she refused

Clytemnestra by John Collier, 1882

Marian Collier (née Huxley) by John Collier, 1882–3

to take food or water. The situation became so severe that Collier hired a full-time nurse and two attending maids who specialised in melancholia.

The ensuing months in were tortuous and bleak, but slowly Marian recovered and returned to the studio where husband and wife painted portraits of each other. Collier's painting meanwhile had continued unabated. Stiff and formal portrait commissions such as *Daughters of Colonel Makins* and *The Rev Dr Ferrers* (Vice Chancellor of Cambridge University) were punctuated with fleshy Greek goddesses and sumptuous femmes fatales. In *Circe,* Collier paints the nude goddess from behind coyly glancing over her left shoulder and resting against a pensive tiger in an inhospitable woodscape. Circe was the ultimate femme fatale of Greek mythology. Having murdered her husband she became a master of alchemy and potions, befriending the more exotic creatures of the world. Collier's fixation on wild women developed further with the *Maenads* the following year depicting a troupe of lusty Dionysian revellers dressed in leopard skins, waving thyrsi aloft, rattling tambourines and leading a pack of leopards.

Collier's depictions of 'wild women' became part a larger dialogue about gender that was raging in the late Victorian period. Anti-feminist writer Elizabeth Linton famously decried the work of independent women in her essay, 'The Wild Women as Social Insurgents' published in *Nineteenth Century* (1891). In it she claims that feminists were hard at work 'obliterating the finer distinctions of sex', arguing that the feminists' 'idea of life for herself is absolute personal independence coupled with a supreme power over men'.[9]

Yet Collier's wild women and femmes fatales may have also been evoked from a personal, much darker motivation. They came from the imagination of a man who was trying desperately to understand the perceived 'madwoman' with whom he shared a bed. Marian had fallen back into her depression, and Collier could do nothing but watch and paint as his wife withered before his eyes. Desperate to save her, Collier sent Marian to various doctors around the country, but nothing seemed to be working. For all his belief in the power of science Professor Huxley was helpless. He paid regular visits to his daughter in Tite Street, but there was nothing he could do. One evening he went to see her 'when she knew she was going mad and I knew it too by her look of melancholia'.[10] After near three years of torment, in the autumn of 1887, Collier took his wife to Paris to see a world-renowned specialist, Dr Charcot, in the hope he might affect a cure. But by that point there was nothing to be done. Before any treatment could start Marian had contracted pneumonia and died in November 1887.

If Collier was devastated by the death of his wife, it was not reflected in his studio output. Throwing himself into work Collier spent more time in the studio than ever before. But the memory of Marian Collier haunted Tite Street. The studio they had shared, the happy optimism of their first house together, and the tragic loss, were all too much for Collier, and shortly after his wife's death he decided to leave Tite Street behind.[11]

15.

LOVE LOCKED OUT

'Art for art's sake' is only the gabble of vacant minds
who have learned how to paint without having to say anything.
– Anna Lea Merritt

'One of the loveliest of the Landmarks in the realms of Art has been discovered within the lifetime of most of us,' wrote Sir Wyke Bayliss, President of the Royal Society of British Artists. 'I mean the formal, authoritative recognition of the fact that women can paint pictures.' For most of the nineteenth century the position of female painters in Britain had been precarious. They faced hurdles at every stage of their career, from art school admission and renting studios to finding appropriate sitters and patrons for their work and being taken seriously by critics. With the exception of a small handful of women artists such as Elizabeth Thompson, who painted 'masculine' battle scenes, women artists were expected to paint domestic and feminine subjects: paintings of young children, portraits of women, domestic scenes and flowers. For Bayliss, the 'discovery' that women could paint 'has been made not too late for me to have seen the painting *Love Locked Out*.'[1]

Love Locked Out was one of the most popular works produced in Tite Street in the 1880s. It was painted by Anna Lea Merritt. The success of the painting was significant for being the first work by a woman to be purchased by the Chantrey Bequest for the Tate Gallery. Merritt was part of an ever-growing community of American expatriate artists working in London. Anna Lea was raised from an early age with a healthy diet of classics, languages, mathematics and music with private tutors in her native Philadelphia. In the dark years of the American Civil War she studied anatomy at the Women's Medical College in Philadelphia where she trained to be a nurse. Though it was not her desired profession, her medical studies gave her a solid foundation in the nuances of anatomical structure which would later aid her artistic work.

In 1865 her medical studies were cut short when her family moved to Europe. There, in the great European capital cities, she took art lessons wherever she could. While the Accademia in Florence refused to admit women as students, Lea managed to get private

Love Locked Out by
Anna Lea Merritt,
1890

lessons from the famous Italian painter of history scenes, Stefano Ussi, one of the few classically trained artists to give private tutorials to female students. From Florence, Lea and her family moved to Paris, but with the outbreak of the Franco-Prussian War, they were forced to relocate to London in 1870.

Taking rooms at 54 Devonshire Street, Anna Lea met a man living in the same building who would have an enormous impact on her career as an artist. Henry Merritt was a well-known art conservator and art history scholar. Lea and Merritt quickly became close friends. 'Let me advise you next time when your picture is begun,' he told her. 'In the first place, choose something of human interest, only a head or a portrait.' Lea later wrote, 'From that time he assumed the direction of my studies . . . how he scolded me; how ruthlessly he rubbed out again and again the work of days, bidding me do it better; what pains he took to make me appreciate true points of excellence!'[2]

In Devonshire Street a romance was kindled. Anna Lea and Henry Merritt were eventually married in April 1877, but three months later Henry died of cancer. Devastated by the loss, Anna Lea Merritt moved to Chelsea which 'seemed like a village in those days for kind people came to call upon me as they do on strangers in country villages'. At first she took a 'tiny house at 95 Cheyne Walk, far away from all familiar streets'.[3] Through her studio window overlooking Whistler's garden at Lindsey House, she watched him laying out canvases to dry.

With her husband now dead, and with very little independent income, Merritt was keen to find suitable sitters, but men generally did not want portraits by women. Even when they did, women could not charge the same rates as their male counterparts. While her male colleagues could expect to receive £1,000 for a portrait commission, Merritt and her female colleagues only received about £100 to £300 for a portrait, depending on its size.

When her lease at Cheyne Walk expired, Merritt began looking for something more substantial. She found an empty studio in Tite Street. But Merritt would face rejection at every turn on the basis of her sex alone. 'The owners would not let any flat to any lady,' she later recalled, 'only *men* were allowed the comfort of small dwelling rooms, a large studio and most especially a janitor-cook!' 'Not wishing to leave the picturesque neighbourhood' of Chelsea, she managed to obtain the lease of a newly built house next door to John Collier. Led by sheer determination to make her way as a female artist, Merritt invested all her funds 'in building the house at No. [50] Tite Street'.[4]

The Tite Street location was ideal for Merritt. 'Although before the days of taxis it was considered very far away' Tite Street proved strategically sound as 'portrait painters must live conveniently near their patrons' who were quickly populating the up-and-coming areas of Chelsea, Belgravia, Knightsbridge and Kensington nearby. Tite Street also had a unique arrangement. In those days, she wrote, it 'had only a few detached houses, not numbered but named.'[5] It was almost obligatory that any house had a name, in keeping with those that already existed – White House, Chelsea Lodge, Keats House, Canwell House – Merritt determined that 'the only one appropriate for mine was Work House but my friends absolutely refused to visit me at such an address; therefore it was called the Cottage, which suited its lowliness.'[6]

The studio-house at No. 50 Tite Street was designed by Frederick Waller and Sons who had initially designed it as a speculative extension to John and Marian Collier's More House. It was considerably smaller than any other house in the street with only two floors and a basement but with a spacious studio. For a widow, the small, quaint house was a perfect fit. 'Every room was small and cottage-like,' she wrote, 'except the studio – that was indeed spacious.' 'For artists understand the necessity of space to secure atmosphere. Our work should be seen at a distance of at least three times the height of the painting; an artist ought to step back after every touch to look at his sitter side by side with the painting.'[7]

Once the studio was set up for portraits, Merritt invited her first Tite Street sitter, a fellow American, James Russell Lowell. Lowell was an American poet, friend and contemporary of Ralph Waldo Emerson. In 1880 he had been appointed United States Ambassador to the United Kingdom and had befriended Merritt. In supporting his compatriot, Lowell commissioned the eager artist to paint his portrait. He came to her studio and sat for 'about an hour at a time while one cigar lasted'.[8]

Merritt's arrival in Tite Street heralded an age when London witnessed a large migration of wealthy American artists to its shores. The American contingent in Tite Street reflected an overall demographic in Europe. Whistler and Merritt lived in Tite Street and Mark Twain briefly lived at the top of Tite Street in Teddington Square. Other American artists – Edwin Abbey, Romaine Brooks and John Singer Sargent – would also come to make Tite Street their home. Indeed some of the best American art of the late nineteenth century had been created in France and Britain. And many notable American paintings were made in Tite Street itself.[9]

Merritt maintained strong connections with her American roots. In 1876 she had successfully submitted her work to the American section of the Pennsylvania Exposition in Philadelphia. To Philadelphia she sent two paintings, *Saint Genevieve* and *The Patrician Mother*, both of which were well received and earned her Centennial medals. The *Nation* praised the two paintings as being 'rich and aristocratic models, painted with restrained force, colored with tender splendour, and in type reminding us of those women in society who seem born to fill panels in family portrait galleries.'[10] Another critic found a 'degree of daring in this artist's work so far removed from the ordinary conventional portraiture of the period as to be quite startling. There is not the slightest effort obvious in her execution, but there is such a defined purpose and such evidence of grasp manifest in the handling, as to evince the possession of absolute genius. Details are indicated in such a way as to seem to be clearly defined, while ruling everything there is a forceful mastery of technique which causes this painting to quite stand out from among the rest in special prominence.'[11]

In 1881, the year before she moved to Tite Street, Merritt was asked to help organise an exhibition, *American Artists at Home and in Europe*, for the Pennsylvania Academy of Fine Arts in Philadelphia. The Academy was quite keen to secure Whistler's *Arrangement in Grey and Black, No. 1: Portrait of the Artist's Mother* for the exhibition, and the task fell to Merritt to liaise with her neighbour. In time Whistler agreed for his painting to be sent to America, though Merritt later lamented the fact that the painting was not secured for America and instead went to the Luxembourg in Paris.

Naturally, Merritt had many encounters with her Tite Street neighbours. 'In Chelsea, Whistler was much talked of,'[12] and it was not long before she had an introduction. Like Collier next door, and Quilter across the street, Merritt had little time for Whistler, Wilde and the aesthetic movement. They kept a distance, and whenever their paths did cross, their interactions were strained. At a dinner party at Mansion House, Whistler approached Merritt and indicated that he liked her eyeglasses which she always wore. They made a humorous comparison to his own monocle. '[M]ine are for looking,' she said, 'Yours are for looks.'[13] For Merritt, the aesthetic movement was all look and no substance.

Merritt was also dismissive of the Pre-Raphaelite school. The Pre-Raphaelites, she believed, had 'set the example of minute exactness. In every portion of a picture they required equal exactness, even in corners where Turner or Romney would have obliterated details in order to focus attention on the important central motive, they persisted in representing minutae.'[14] Though she dismissed the Pre-Raphaelites, she had in fact relied on their methods and techniques as inspiration for her own work as it developed in the 1880s. As a young girl Merritt had seen William Holman Hunt's oil painting, *The Light of the World*, which was included in his first major show of British art in America in New York, Philadelphia and Boston in 1857-8. Hunt's painting made a lasting impression, and its influence can be seen in Merritt's benevolent Christ-figure in *I Will Give You Rest*.

In her Tite Street studio 'the light and space were just what [I] needed and the benefit was at once evident in [my] work.'[15] With the success of her two paintings in Philadelphia, Merritt was able to attract enough attention in England for portrait commissions to start rolling in. The editor of the *Etcher* requested that Merritt etch a portrait of Ellen Terry as Ophelia, the role Terry 'was then playing with wonderful success at the Lyceum'. One evening, at Terry's invitation, Merritt called at her backstage dressing room. When Terry came off the stage Merritt saw 'tears on her cheeks, still feeling the reality of Ophelia's sorrows. Her emotion was even more impressive than it had been from the front – my admiration was entirely captured. Miss Terry gave me another sitting in my studio.'[16] In 1879, a youthful Ellen Terry sat for Merritt in the role of Ophelia.

Like Collier, Merritt occasionally turned her brush away from portraiture. In one such venture she produced *War*. Despite the decidedly masculine association of the title, the painting was remarkably feminine. Instead of an epic battle scene or a victorious celebration as one might expect, the painting simply portrays a group of soldiers' wives and a single

Ellen Terry as Ophelia by Anna Lea Merritt, 1880

War by Anna Lea Merritt, 1883

child. That same year she exhibited *Camilla* at the Royal Academy. The painting was not a triumph at the Academy; however, in 1889 she sent it to the Exposition Universelle in Paris where she was awarded Honourable Mention.

Unlike Whistler and Collier's *femmes fatales*, Merritt's women were altogether more natural, depicting vulnerability, futility, determination and strength simultaneously. In 1885 she attracted considerable attention with *Eve*, depicting the biblical Eve in the moment after she has bitten the forbidden fruit. Eve sits on the ground, her undraped figure in profile, her head bent on her knee in evident alarm and amazement; her reddish-golden hair makes a veil around her and cuts a far too yellow reflection on her bosom, while the apple-tree, laden with golden russets, hangs enticingly over her, and the one bitten apple rolls at her feet.

While *Camilla* was receiving praise in Paris, a new Merritt painting was being celebrated at the Royal Academy. *Love Locked Out*, painted in memory of her husband, was widely deemed the best painting of 1889. 'The thought had been inspired years before as a monument to my dead husband,' Merritt wrote. 'In my thought the closed door is the door of the tomb. Therefore I showed the dead leaves blowing against the doorway and the lamp shattered.'[17] The *Standard* praised the brushwork as 'suggestive of ... facility and spontaneity' writing that, 'the draftsmanship is extremely expressive – nothing can be better than the regretful and plaintive attitude of the Cupid at the closed and golden gate.'[18]

With the success of *Love Locked Out*, Merritt found a seat at the table of the successful artistic circles of London, still male-dominated by Holman Hunt, Lord Leighton, Watts, Frith, Rossetti and Burne-Jones. The road to success had not been easy for Merritt and she would have to work twice as hard as her male colleagues in order to achieve success. Above the door of the Tite Street studio she hung a terracotta panel that read, 'Whatever shall be, every circumstance, must be overcome by endurance.'[19]

Merritt used her hard-won fame and success to draw attention to the obstacles facing women artists. As an aspiring young artist Merritt had found it almost impossible to find tuition as it was relatively uncommon for women to be accepted into a reputable atelier. Despite her credentials Merritt was never invited into the Royal Academy as so many of her male neighbours and colleagues had been. 'I always think that the Committees of the Royal Academy show impartiality and fairness in the hanging of women's pictures,' she wrote, 'but when one not connected with the Academy was proposing many artists as suitable for election, it would have been pleasant to find such names as Mrs Butler's, Miss Montalba's and Miss Rae's[20] among those of Mr Collier, Mr Whistler and Mr Weguelin.'[21]

Alongside Merritt in Tite Street there were only a handful of practising women artists. When Archie Stuart-Wortley finally left Tite Street in 1886, the prolific Scottish sculptor Mary Grant took his place in Canwell House. Grant's career had no doubt been helped by her uncle, Sir Francis Grant, President of the Royal Academy from 1866 to 1878. She began sculpting in the 1850s and in the early 1860s studied first in Florence under the renowned Italian sculptor Odoardo Fantachiotti, and then in Rome with the Welsh neoclassical sculptor John Gibson. Grant finally established herself with a studio at 64 Great Titchfield Street in the late 1860s and took private lessons from John Foley, an Irish sculptor who had spent most of his career working in London and was best known for his statue of Prince Albert on the Albert Memorial.

Under the direction of such notable men, Grant had made a name for herself as a portrait painter and sculptor in London. By the time she arrived in Tite Street in 1886, she was already considered 'one of the busiest of lady-sculptors'[22] with a number of major commissions under her belt including busts of the Duke of Argyll, Sir Francis Grant, R.A. and Georgina, Lady Dudley. One of her most prestigious commissions came from the Raja-i-Rajgan of Kapoortala who asked for a colossal marble bust of Queen Victoria (1871, now in the Metropolitan Museum of Art, New York).

At Canwell House, Grant was a 'bright and amusing neighbour' who had filled the two large studios on the ground floor full of her own 'works in progress'.[23] In 1886, the same year that she arrived in Tite Street, she exhibited a relief of her neighbour, the Hon. Mrs Slingsby Bethell at the Royal Academy. One of the other works in progress littering her Tite Street studio was a majestic bust of poet laureate Alfred, Lord Tennyson for the National Portrait Gallery (of which she was a Trustee), after the Thomas Woolner relief in the Tate. Her final Royal Academy exhibit in 1892 was a bust of the late Charles Parnell, MP, one of the great leaders in the drive for Irish Home Rule, along with Prime Minister William Gladstone, of whom Grant also made a bust in 1902.[24]

In 1900 Merritt published a controversial article for *Lippincott's Monthly Magazine*. 'A Letter to Artists: Especially Women Artists' highlighted the specific pitfalls and extra dedication needed to become a professional woman artist. The article was developed from Merritt's lecture, 'Art as a Profession for Women,' which she had presented to the Women's Art Congress and to the Cambridge Discussion Society earlier that year. In the lecture she asks, 'Can women really paint as well as men?' 'It is time to ask this question and I think we may say that while a great many men are inferior to some women, there are some men, in the more difficult branches of art, very far ahead of all. We certainly can think of women who are not surpassed in their line, but it is not the greatest. I see no reason why they should not, when they recognise that the great strength of their work will be its feminine quality.' This 'feminine quality' was precisely what set Merritt's work apart from that of her male colleagues. Feminine not only in style – soft, subdued tone, smooth, gentle lines but also in subject and content.

Merritt never remarried after the death of her husband. She lamented that '[T]he chief obstacle to a woman's success is that she can never have a wife,' and admitted that 'the inequality observed in women's work is generally the result of untoward domestic accidents. Just reflect what a wife does for an artist: Darns the stockings; Keeps his house; Writes his letters; Visits for his benefit; Wards off intruders; Is personally suggestive of beautiful pictures; Always an encouraging and partial critic. It is exceedingly difficult to be an artist without this time-saving help. A husband would be quite useless. He would never do any of these disagreeable things.'[25]

By the late 1880s, a combination of repeated asthma attacks and a lack of funds meant Merritt would have to leave Tite Street. The times were 'very hard for artists,' she wrote. '[F]or ten years, with great expense, I had held on successfully, but anxiously depending entirely on portrait painting, always *uncertain* of the next month.' For most women artists, especially women artists working and living independently, work was always 'uncertain,' making it even harder to survive. So it was that the cost of maintaining a house in Tite Street became too much of a burden. 'At last I found a tenant for No. [50],' she wrote, 'and decided to busy myself in the real country.'[26]

16.

WILDE'S CLOSET

Lady Stutfield: There is nothing, nothing like the beauty
of home-life, is there?
Kelvil: It is the mainstay of our moral system in England, Lady Stutfield.
Without it we would become like our neighbours.
– Oscar Wilde, *A Woman of No Importance*, 1893

'We have been looking at a house in Tite Street, which I think we are likely to take,' wrote the affianced Constance Mary Lloyd to a friend in March 1884.[1] Less than two months later, the 'grave' and 'mystical' Constance with her 'wonderful eyes and dark brown coils of hair,' would be married to Oscar Wilde. Nuptial festivities commenced. The couple were given a special party by Whistler at No. 33 a few weeks before their wedding. In spite of her husband's gushing adoration, Constance remained sceptical of Whistler. 'She does not think Jimmy the only painter that ever really existed,' Wilde wrote to Waldo Story. 'However, she knows I am the greatest poet, so in literature she is all right.'[2] When their big day finally arrived on 29 May, the couple received a telegram from their Tite Street friend, 'Fear I may not be able to reach you in time for ceremony – Don't wait.'[3]

When it came time to find a place to settle in London, Wilde turned almost immediately towards Tite Street. Constance had acquired a modest dowry from her recently deceased grandfather's estate, and it was enough to help them lease their first home. By 1884 most of the empty plots in the street had been filled, so there was no hope of a grand, new White House or Keats House endeavour. Wilde, however, entertained no ambition of being an artist, so a spacious studio-house was not necessary. Instead the Wildes managed to find a four-storey red-brick terrace on the west side of the street, built as a speculative venture by the architectural firm Butler & Beeston between 1877 and 1880. The house seemed just about adequate for the Wildes, although a sketch by Godwin shows a planned extension to the rear of the house, which would have reduced the garden to almost half its size and added at least another two rooms. But for lack of money, time and planning, the extension never came to fruition.[4]

Sketch of an interior, possibly Oscar Wilde's drawing room by Beatrice Godwin, *c*.1884

Upon return from his North American lecture tour, Wilde had begun three years of travelling around Britain giving lectures on the 'House Beautiful' and 'Dress Reform'. He had preached to his audiences 'that beautiful and rational designs are necessary in all work'. He believed that the ability to create 'noble and beautiful designs' was a gift that could only come 'as the accumulation of habits of long and delightful observation' and only 'by those who have been accustomed to rooms that are beautiful and colours that are satisfying'.[5] So when it came to his own home, it would have to be a perfect demonstration of the 'noble and beautiful'. In his lectures Wilde had lauded his neighbour, Whistler, as 'the greatest artist of his day'.[6] But when asked to help decorate the new Tite Street house, Whistler replied, 'No, Oscar, you have been lecturing to us on the House Beautiful; now is your chance to show us one.'[7] Wilde was determined to do just that and commissioned their mutual friend E.W. Godwin to design the 'House Beautiful' in Tite Street.

As with Whistler's White House across the street, the creation of Wilde's new home was not without its dramas. Godwin had employed a builder, named Green, who was apparently already under contract from the landlord of No. 34 to do some minor repairs. Trouble started, however, when Wilde, on discovering Green's work was less than adequate, fired him and then refused to pay him, at which point Green began seizing some of the furniture until payment was made. Godwin then hired a second builder named Sharp. Meanwhile, Green was suing Wilde for non-payment. Sharp took much longer than expected to complete

Tite Street from Royal Hospital Road, with terraced houses where the Wildes lived, 1905

the work. Not only did the Wildes have to settle out of court with Green,[8] but Sharp's bill finally came in around £250 more than they had expected. With all this the house was still uninhabitable nearly nine months after their wedding.[9]

Despite the burden of rising costs and the stress of building, Wilde enthused about his new house when it was finally finished just after the New Year 1885. Godwin, ever the champion of Japanese design, had invented 'new uses for whites'. 'I have,' wrote Wilde, 'a dining room done in different shades of white, with white curtains embroidered in yellow silk: the effect is absolutely delightful, and the room is beautiful.'[10] He pronounced to Godwin that his interiors were imbued with poetry, 'Each chair is a sonnet in ivory, and the table is a masterpiece in pearl.'[11]

The Wildes' Tite Street house was spread over four floors with a basement. Entering the house from the front door to the right was Oscar's study with pale yellow walls and the woodwork in red enamel. In a corner of the room was a red plinth upon which stood a cast of the Hermes of Praxiteles. Most of the wall space was occupied by bookshelves filled with copies of the Greek and Latin classics, French literature and works of contemporary authors.[12] Also on the ground floor at the rear was a dining room painted in white blended with pale blue and yellow. The Chippendale chairs were painted white and upholstered in white plush with white carpet throughout. A bow window looked out over the garden behind the house and into Paradise Walk behind.[13]

On the first floor 'Pre-Raphaelitism was given free rein.'[14] In the drawing room the walls were painted a buttercup yellow. Godwin and Whistler had decorated the ceiling in blue, with painted dragons and two bright peacock feathers. An enormous grand piano sat in one corner, several black and white bamboo chairs alongside tall Japanese vases filled with bulrushes sat in another, while etchings by Whistler filled the walls. Above the mantelpiece stood a life-sized portrait of Wilde, painted by the American artist Harper Pennington.

To the rear of the first floor, off the drawing room, was Wilde's smoking room. Here the walls were covered with William Morris patterned wallpaper of dark red and dull gold. The room was decadently North African with plush divans, ottomans, Moorish hangings and lanterns filling the room, and a glass beaded curtain covering the window. Up another floor was the Wildes' bedroom at the front of the house and Oscar's dressing room at the rear while the entire top floor was reserved as a nursery and playroom.

'There was an air of brightness and luxury' about No. 34 Tite Street, wrote the Comtesse de Brémont, 'A smart maid opened the door and I found myself in the wide hallway towards the dining room. There tea was served in the most delightfully unconventional manner from a quaint shelf extending around the wall, before which white enamelled seats – modelled in various Grecian styles – were placed . . . I presently found myself sitting in one of the white Greek seats, drinking tea out of a dainty yellow cup that might have been modelled from a lotus flower, and being talked to by a young poet.'[15]

Although it was less than ten years old, Tite Street held many glorious and troubled memories for Wilde. Three years previously he had lived with his friend, the artist Frank Miles, at No. 44. But the idealistic, young man who stormed out of Tite Street in 1881 was transformed into a matured gentleman by the time he returned three years later. Upon his arrival back from the American lecture tour, Wilde had cut his hair short, remarking 'the Oscar of the first period is dead'.[16] But his hair was not the only thing about his appearance that had changed. Even Whistler noticed that 'Oscar is awfully fat.'[17] If his wanton flamboyance had once ruffled society feathers, his new 'domestication' was altogether a shock. Everyone noticed a change. 'There was Oscar Wilde,' reported *The Bat* upon seeing him one afternoon at the theatre, 'subdued, meditative, married'.[18]

Any conjugal quietude was shattered on Friday, 5 June 1885 when Constance gave birth to their first child, a baby boy whom they named Cyril. A year later she went into labour for the second time, on a bleak November day in 1886. The family doctor was called from his home in Mayfair but had difficulty finding Tite Street through the thick fog blanketing the city. Eventually the baby arrived, but in the mêlée, the flustered couple forgot to register their second son's birth until several weeks later, by which point they had forgotten the exact day of his birth. They eventually compromised on 3 November 1886. His name was given as Vyvyan.

Tite Street was a perennially interesting place for the two boys. Along with their father's riveting bedtime stories, the street itself also fed their fertile imaginations. Beyond the white door of No. 34, the boys bowled hoops and rode tricycles along the pavements with other children of the neighbourhood. In the nearby Royal Hospital, Cyril and Vyvyan made friends with some of the resident Chelsea Pensioners who allowed the boys to dig in their gardens. They were invited up to the dusty, old rooms for tea 'out of thick mugs and slabs of bread and butter and cake' and then entertained with stories of the battlefields from one old man, nearly a hundred years old, who had been a drummer boy at Waterloo, and had sailed back to England in the same ship as the Duke of Wellington. The boys shared a nursery at the top of the house which overlooked the Children's Hospital on one side and Paradise Walk on the other. From the balcony of the nursery the boys would watch horrific 'processions' to and from the hospital. One night they saw a woman being admitted with a blood-soaked shawl around her head after she had been stabbed by her husband in a drunken rage.[19]

The sound of fighting was all-too familiar in Tite Street. Paradise Walk was one of the most forbidding slums in Chelsea. 'It was', recalled Vyvyan, 'a row of small tenement houses with wretched, filthy back yards, from which the sounds of brawling rose nightly.' The row held a horrid fascination for the young boys and the brothers grew up 'terrified' of the narrow lane in the shadows of their own house. In their imaginations they had 'peopled it with dreadful creatures that crawled up the wall' of their house at night and 'scratched at the nursery windows to get in'.[20] In an attempt to blot out the eyesore of Paradise Walk, the Wildes had constructed a decorative lattice over the rear window of their first-floor drawing room.

No. 34 was not only a family home, it was a fashionable salon. With the dramas of interior decor now past, and with two healthy, attractive boys begot, Constance was free to pursue new hobbies, and she threw herself into the role of a society hostess. Invitations to Mrs Wilde's 'at homes' in Tite Street were highly prized tickets for the London season. Like Whistler at No. 33, the Wildes exercised a comprehensive harmony as Constance entertained 'in a cream-tinted dining room, of which walls, furniture, and all things are in unison.' Everything was in perfect harmony, 'even the guests,' wrote one observer 'who are of course the crème de la crème of society'.[21] The greatest artistic and literary figures of the age passed through the famous white door. 'To my mother's receptions came people of such widely different interests,'[22] Vyvyan later recounted. 'I was not prepared for the crush of fashionable folk that overcrowded the charming rooms of the unpretentious house in Tite Street,' wrote Anna, Comtesse de Brémont. Whistler attended along with Walter Sickert and Mortimer Menpes.[23] The guest list also included eminent artists such as Sir William Richmond, Edward Burne-Jones and his fellow Pre-Raphaelites; renowned actresses such as Sarah Bernhardt and Lillie Langtry; and of course the greatest poets and writers of the age – Algernon Swinburne, Robert Browning, and even Whistler's bitter rival, John Ruskin.

Constance diligently kept a visitors' book to record the various Tite Street guests. Oliver Wendell Holmes, Walter Pater, Ellen Terry, William Morris, Robert Browning and Mark Twain are among the many to have signed. The artist George Frederic Watts, who had refused to divorce his child-bride Ellen Terry, ironically wrote, 'Our greatest happiness

Constance and Cyril Wilde, 1889

should be found in the happiness of others.' Walter Crane, who illustrated a volume of Wilde's children's stories, wrote, 'From your book I take a leaf, By your leave to leave and take; Art is long if life be brief, Yet on this page my mark I'll make.' Swinburne scribbled some lines of verse on childhood, while George Meredith wrote a poem 'Love Is Winged for Two',[24] George Percy Jacomb-Hood, Charles Ricketts and Charles Shannon lent their artistic skills with a series of decorative sketches.[25]

The public perception of No. 34 was carefully controlled and manipulated. For the twice monthly 'at homes', the house would be transformed with scenery and costumes, all meticulously planned. Both Oscar and Constance took great care to live up to their reputations. If Constance was a successful hostess she was always somewhat overshadowed by her husband, the ultimate 'talker'. Katherine Bradley and Edith Cooper were rather critical of Constance on a visit to a Tite Street soirée: 'Received by Mrs Wilde in turquoise blue, white frills and amber stockings. The afternoon goes on in a dull fashion till Oscar enters. He wears a lilac shirt and heliotrope tie.'[26]

Constance was Oscar's most devoted follower and along with her husband she had thrown herself behind the banner of Dress Reform. The couple carefully planned their outfits when hosting parties in Tite Street or parading the streets of Chelsea. When the Countess of Brémont came to a party at their home, she saw Constance 'arrayed in an exquisite Greek costume of cowslip yellow and apple-leaf green. Her hair, a thick mass of ruddy brown, was wonderfully set off by the bands of yellow ribbon. The whole arrangement was exceedingly becoming to the youthful, almost boyish face with its clear colours and full, dark eyes.'[27]

Constance, the two children and Oscar, 'wonderfully befrogged and befurred,' quickly sewed themselves into the Tite Street tapestry. All in all, No. 34 seemed the perfect family home – a reasonably sized house for a family of four, fitted with a 'noble and beautiful' design. Yet with its Tite Street locale, it was far from ideal. The street had been a bohemian Babylon for Wilde in his younger days. Here it was that he had enjoyed the freedom of a bachelor lifestyle compliments of Frank Miles. Things were different now. He had responsibilities, a house to maintain, and a family to provide for. Wilde may have changed, but Tite Street remained the same. There were still artists, soirées and plenty of mischief to be found.

Surrounded by this fresh and vibrant bohemian scene, Wilde gradually grew bored with the domesticated life of marriage and family. Ghosts from his past were never far away. One of these ghosts was a young Cambridge student, Harry Marillier. Wilde had known the young man as a schoolboy five years previously. Shortly after Cyril's birth, Marillier had written to Wilde asking if he would like to attend a student performance of *The Eumenides* at Cambridge. Wilde went to the performance where he was greeted by 'bright young faces, and grey misty quadrangles, Greek forms passing through Gothic cloisters'.[28]

The flirtation between Wilde and Marillier continued for several months. 'I had been thinking a great deal about you,' Wilde wrote, 'There is at least this beautiful mystery in life, that at the moment it feels most complete it finds some secret sacred niche in its shrine empty and waiting. Then comes a time of exquisite expectancy.'[29] Wilde asked him to write, 'long letters to Tite Street,' and in January 1886 Marillier was invited to No. 34, 'Come at 12o'c on Sunday and stay for lunch . . . Let us live like Spartans but talk like Athenians.'[30] Marillier accepted the invitation and brought a handsome Oxonian, Douglas Ainslie, along with him. Ainslie was a twenty-one-year-old undergraduate at Oxford, who at the age of sixteen, had fallen in love with Constance.[31] 'We must have many evenings together,' Wilde wrote to Ainslie, 'and drink yellow wine from green glasses in Keats's honour.'[32] Marillier and Ainslie were not the only young men to pass through the white door of No. 34 at Wilde's invitation. A host of eager and admiring, handsome twenty-somethings followed in their footsteps.

Meanwhile, across London in the House of Commons during the summer session of 1885, Section XI of the Criminal Law Amendment Act was introduced by Henry Labouchère. Labouchère, a Liberal MP for Northampton, had been a distant supporting character in the Chelsea arts scene of the 1860s and 1870s. He had been instrumental in launching Lillie Langtry's stage career, and was also a friend and patron of Whistler's. In the 1870s he purchased Whistler's *Harmony in Yellow and Gold: The Gold Girl – Connie Gilchrist* which he later returned to the artist with the instruction for Whistler to 'work on it'.[33] While on his lecture tour of North America, Wilde had praised him as the 'best writer in Europe'.[34] In return Labouchère criticised Wilde as nothing more than an 'epicene youth' and an 'effeminate phrasemaker' who lectured to 'empty benches'.[35]

Labouchère's amendment to the Act effectively criminalised any homosexual acts between men. The act of sodomy had been illegal in Britain since the seventh century and had been punishable by death since the days of Henry VIII (until 1861). However, proving that the act of sodomy had been committed was in many cases impossible. From Labouchère's amendment a new crime was created called 'Gross Indecency', which came to cover a multitude of homosexual 'sins', and was punishable by up to two years' hard labour. The amendment stated that:

> Any male person who, in public or private commits or is a party to the commission of, or procures the commission by any male person, of any act of gross indecency with another male person, shall be guilty of a misdemeanour, and being convicted thereof shall be liable at the discretion of the Court to be imprisoned for any term not exceeding two years, with or without hard labour.[36]

The Act was passed through Parliament in August 1885. A year after the passage of the Criminal Law Amendment Act, Wilde met a young Canadian who was a student at Oxford. Wilde later described Robbie Ross as having the 'face of Puck and the heart of an angel,'[37] while later Alfred Douglas described him as 'a rather pathetic-looking little creature, in appearance something like a kitten and a slender, attractive, impulsive boy.'[38]

When they first met, Ross had only just turned seventeen. Though he was considerably younger, he was more sexually experienced and has claim to providing Wilde with his first full homosexual experience. Wilde and Ross became great friends, sharing interests in the arts and literature and the 'seedier' side of life. Ross was able to give Wilde the catharsis of physical intimacy in a way that the other young visitors to Tite Street had not. As Franny Moyle aptly surmises, '[I]f Marillier had revealed to Oscar that there was an empty niche in his life, Robbie was the young man who actually filled it.'[39]

During the summer of 1887, Ross came to stay at Tite Street as a paying guest while his mother was travelling on the continent. Constance adored Ross and they gradually became quite close friends. While he was staying at Tite Street, Wilde and Robbie were practically inseparable. After dinner they would close themselves away in Oscar's smoking room where they would spend endless hours talking and laughing the night away while Constance disappeared to her bedroom. For the moment this frivolity was hidden beneath the veneer of the domestic life behind the closed doors of No. 34 or in amorous letters.

Life for the Wildes in Tite Street was not all tea parties and 'at homes'. While Constance was raising the two children and managing the housekeeping, Wilde was put to work. In November 1887, he was appointed Editor of *The Woman's World*, a magazine that aimed 'at being the organ of women of intellect, culture and position'.[40] The new working man would rise every morning and walk from Tite Street up to Sloane Square. From there he would take the underground train to Charing Cross, and then walk up the Strand to the office just off Fleet Street.

Having a full-time job did little to curb Wilde's growing appetite for the company of handsome young men. Marillier and Ross were just two faces in a series to be invited to Tite Street with or without Constance present. There were poets like Richard la Gallienne, whose poem 'With Oscar Wilde: A Summer Day In June '88' opens, 'With Oscar Wilde, a summer day / Passed like a yearning kiss away'.[41] There was also the young French writer Marc-Andre Raffalovich with whom Wilde had many 'nice improper talks'.[42]

Though it started with the best intentions, Wilde could not completely hide his inner desires, and it was not long before No. 34 became his closet, a public front of domesticity. If there was a doubt or question over his exploits with the entourage of young men, Wilde could simply point to No. 34, where a wife hosted parties for London's elite, and two healthy boys listened to wholesome bedtime stories by the hearth. Wilde put on the mask of the heterosexual husband and father while he harboured 'unspeakable' desires inside. William Rothenstein later spent many happy hours with 'Wild Oscar' at his home in Tite Street which was 'white within and black without, like his own soul'.[43] There were some secrets that the bricks of Tite Street could not conceal and the closet in Tite Street would not remain free of skeletons for long.

17.

A PRINCE
in PICCADILLY

To die before being painted by Sargent is to
go to Heaven prematurely.
– Saki

From the window of his study at No. 34 Oscar Wilde enjoyed a panoramic view of Tite Street. Whenever he grew bored with writing at Carlyle's desk or musing over his extensive library, Wilde could simply look out to see his friends and neighbours come and go. One foggy morning in January 1889, Wilde looked from his window to see the actress Ellen Terry exit No. 33 dressed as Lady Macbeth. Wilde thrilled at living in 'the street that on a wet and dreary morning . . . vouchsafed the vision of Lady Macbeth in full regalia magnificently seated in a four-wheeler.' He captured the sense of promise that awaited the witty aesthetes and decadent artists of Tite Street, declaring that the street in which they lived 'can never again be as other streets: it must always be full of wonderful possibilities.'[1]

In 1884 Whistler left No. 33 for a larger house in The Vale, just around the corner. His studio was taken over by artist Henry Arthur Fane and then by Bernard Edward Cammell. Cammell was the son of a wealthy steel industrialist near Sheffield.[2] After studying at Eton and Trinity College, Cambridge, Cammell moved to London and Tite Street. He proved a highly conventional painter in the wake of Whistler, and his work *A Derbyshire Laddie* and *Waiting* failed to garner any enthusiasm from the Royal Academy.

The 'wonderful possibilities' of Tite Street were renewed in 1886 with the arrival of one of the most promising young artists of the age, thirty-year-old John Singer Sargent. Like Whistler, Sargent had American roots, had trained in Paris and later moved to London to start his career. Sargent was born to culture-loving and peripatetic American expatriates who had permanently relocated to Europe. As a child he had demonstrated an aptitude for drawing, painting and music, and he spent disciplined days at various museums and churches around the great capitals of Europe copying old masters.

Sargent came to live in Tite Street by a long and turbulent path that started in Paris where he was trained in the atelier of renowned French society portraitist Carolous Duran. By 1884, the young artist had already achieved considerable success at the annual Paris Salon with his *En Route pour la Pêche* in 1878, *El Jaleo* in 1882, and again with *The Daughters of Edward Darley Boit* in 1883. He had hoped to repeat the success in 1884, but when he returned to his studio in the boulevard Berthier on the night the Salon opened, he was confronted by a distraught Madame Avegno. The woman stood in the middle of the studio with tears streaming down her face and pleaded with Sargent to remove his portrait of her daughter, *Madame Gautreau*, from the exhibition.

For nearly two years Sargent had been planning and working on a portrait of Madame Avegno's daughter, an American expatriate socialite, Virginie Amélie Avegno Gautreau. The full-length portrait shows a pale-skinned Virginie in a black sleeveless dress, with her body angled forward and her head to the side, but with ample amounts of cleavage and shoulder exposed. The painting opened as a sensation that by midday had escalated into a scandal as a mixture of criticism both good and bad swirled in the Parisian press. The latter prevailed. 'My daughter is lost' cried the sitter's mother. 'All of Paris mocks her. My family will be humiliated. She will die of a broken heart.'[3]

With the scandal of Madame Gautreau (the painting was exhibited at the Salon as *Madame xxx*, as was common, but came to be known as *Madame X*) still fresh, Sargent turned his gaze across the Channel to London. 'Just now I am rather out of favour as a portrait painter in Paris,' he wrote 'I have been coming to England for the last two or three summers and should not wonder if I someday have a studio in London.'[4] The writer Henry James championed the ambitious young artist and thought Sargent a 'genuine painter'.[5] With all his powers of persuasion, James tried to convince Sargent to settle in London, where James sat at the centre of a vast coterie of American expatriate writers and artists. 'I want him to come here and live and work,' wrote James, 'there being such a field in London for a *real* painter of women.'[6] Sargent seemed to be taken with the idea. 'There is perhaps more chance for me there as a portrait painter, although it might be a long struggle for my painting to be accepted,' he wrote. 'It is thought beastly French.'[7] His prediction was correct.

During the winter of 1885-6 Sargent roamed around London, working from the studios of his friends, and only after months of searching eventually found a suitable studio-flat on the ground floor at No. 33 Tite Street, the very same studio that Whistler had vacated. In September 1886 he moved into Tite Street and nine months later signed the lease for 'the Studio and two rooms with Dressing Room' at an annual rent of £140. In addition he agreed to pay £35 per year for 'the services of the Housekeeper to answer the door and take messages and use of the Kitchen fire'.[8]

On 5 November Sargent unveiled his new studio-flat to his close friends. 'It was a great success,' wrote Lucia Millett to her parents. 'The rooms are large and beautifully decorated.

Madame X (Madame Pierre Gautreau) by John Singer Sargent, 1883–4

Then too he has many wonderfully beautiful things.'[9] For the most part Sargent left what remained of Whistler's decor untouched. However, it became clear that 'covering a surface with forms and lines in a definite pattern was beyond Sargent's powers.'[10] While Whistler had meticulously decorated the flat in yellow, with the 'flights of fans' and porcelain adorning the walls in perfect harmony, Sargent instead 'invoked the aid of the dressmaker and the florist and filled in holes with the help of pieces of furniture; satin and velvet flowed in cascades, cushions bulged like Zeppelins on sofas, azaleas moved from vases to urns, and arum lilies added a white note to a park-like background.'[11]

In contrast to the combative, swashbuckling figure of Whistler and the gregariously outspoken Wilde, Sargent was shy beyond the intimate comfort of a select group of friends. If he was more modest than his neighbours, Sargent was no less bold and revolutionary in his art. With his numerous Salon successes and his daring portrait of *Madame X*, he had already established himself as an artist of exceptional skill and vision, but also as an artist who was prepared to take risks and to push conventional boundaries.

Sargent's life was 'as orderly as that of a bishop'.[12] He approached life in the studio with professional gravitas, wearing a collar and tie, waistcoat and jacket whilst working. Yet his formality of dress did not deter him from the same studio gymnastics practised by Whistler. With the contents of the studio lined against the walls, with a brush in one hand, palette gripped by the other, and a cigar slowly burning away in his mouth, Sargent would back away from the sitter and canvas with slow but deliberate steps, eyes fixed, and then would stop and lunge at the canvas. Sir George Sitwell later enjoyed the spectacle of Sargent 'rushing bull-like … and shouting,' and covering 'about four miles a day in the studio'.[13]

Sargent was not publicity-seeking in the manner of Whistler and Wilde, but his approach to art was no less progressive and advanced in forging a new style. Whatever Sargent felt or believed about art, he kept it among his intimate circle of friends. He may not have been as boastful with the same outgoing, self-important style of his other neighbours, yet he maintained a youthful confidence, having an 'air of a conquering hero about him'.[14] As Henry James wrote, 'It is difficult to imagine a young painter being less in the dark about his own ideal, having from the first more the air of knowing what he desires.'[15]

Although he was little known by society at large, many of Sargent's paintings had already been seen by his artist neighbours in Tite Street and Chelsea, both at the Paris Salon and the Royal Academy in London. When Sargent told his parents that he was moving from Paris to London, his father wrote that his son seemed 'to have a good many friends in London, and appears to be very favorably known there'.[16] Sargent certainly was 'favorably known' amongst a certain intimate group of friends, and indeed his arrival in Chelsea 'caused quite a stir among the local painters, for he had quite a reputation in Paris.'[17]

Sargent was already acquainted with his Tite Street neighbour Oscar Wilde and his new bride Constance. During their honeymoon in Paris, Sargent had given the newlyweds a dinner at his studio in the boulevard Berthier.[18]

Sargent's relationship with Whistler, however, was slightly more delicate. The two artists had originally met in Venice after Whistler's bankruptcy. Almost seven years later, Sargent was now on Whistler's home ground, and the Butterfly watched the newcomer with cautious acknowledgement. Whistler dismissed Sargent's paintings as 'no better than the rest'.[19] Over time, however, the two artists would grow into a peaceful friendship, relatively unblemished by jealousy or competition. Sargent's studio was always open to Whistler, whom he found immensely entertaining and quite 'a scream'. The brash, outspoken Whistler would come bursting into Sargent's Tite Street studio unannounced, as if he himself still held the lease, and 'would go on to tell his story of his most recent run-in with some other more or less notable, and how the other chap had offended him, or how he had taken a rise out of the other fellow.'[20]

Despite his early successes at the Paris Salon, Sargent did not receive such a warm welcome in England. Although in 1887 he was represented at the Royal Academy by *Carnation, Lily, Lily, Rose* (which Whistler jokingly called *Darnation, Silly, Silly Pose*), the reserved English critics were not forthcoming in their praise of his work. Instead, opinions were decidedly mixed. The *Magazine of Art* confessed to finding Sargent's work 'somewhat unpleasant in colour', but it acknowledged 'their veracity and the infinite cleverness, and they scintillate with sunlight,'[21] while the Royal Academy considered his pictures 'the most brilliant, the most defiantly original'.[22] At the White House, Sargent's neighbour and Whistler's arch-nemesis, Harry Quilter, wrote that Sargent had 'succeeded in painting a picture which ... is purely and simply beautiful as a picture ... how is it possible to describe in words that subtle rendering of brilliance and shadow that united mystery and revelation, which render this composition so admirable?'[23]

The art scene that Sargent found in London was decidedly more conservative than the one he encountered ten years previously in Duran's Paris studio. For the new generation of British art students, Paris had a tempting appeal as the world centre for art training. It became a cradle of the avant-garde movement where academism had all but lost any real authority or influence. The same could not be said of London, although the Grosvenor Gallery continued to challenge the orthodoxy of the Royal Academy.

As Sargent was arriving in Tite Street, another event was taking place in London that would have far-reaching impact for the larger art world. 'The time is passed of its authority in matters of art,' William Henley, editor of the *Magazine of Art*, complained of the Royal Academy, 'and though to be rejected is still a serious disappointment, it is no longer a disgrace ... as an educational institution it has little or nothing to teach; and its students, as soon as they have passed the curriculum it imposes on them, make hast to betake themselves to France, to learn not only how to paint and draw, but to forget as much as they can of the theory and practice acquired in its schools.'[24] In April 1886, a new group of artists came together. Initially calling themselves the Society of Anglo-French Painters, they eventually came to be known as the New English Art Club. This group of artists (not necessarily 'New' or 'English') sought to establish their own exhibitions outside the dogmatic constraints of the Academy. In doing so they effectively 'introduced a new sensibility into English art, which swept away the current emphasis on the work of the High Victorian classicists and the painters of illustrated anecdotes and domestic genre.'[25]

Though Tite Street would remain his base for the rest of his life, it was in America, not in Britain, that Sargent first tasted high acclaim for his art. In September 1887, just a year after arriving in Tite Street, Sargent set sail for the first of many trips across the Atlantic. To herald his arrival in America, Henry James wrote glowing reviews of Sargent in *Harper's*. 'Those who have appreciated his work most up to the present time emit no wish for a change,' he wrote, 'so completely does that work seem to them, in its kind, the exact translation of his thought, the exact 'fit' of his artistic temperament.'[26]

In December, a Boston exhibition of Sargent's work featured *El Jaleo* and portraits of *Mrs Marquand*, *Mrs Inches*, *Mrs Boit*, *Mrs Gardner* and *The Daughters of Edward Darley Boit*. Though Sargent had never lived in America, they immediately claimed him as one of their own. 'No American has ever displayed a collection of paintings in Boston having so much of the quality which is summed up in the word *style*,' wrote the *Daily Advertiser*. 'Nothing is commonplace; nothing is conventional. The personal note is always felt at first and at last it is what impresses. This style is generally, and in the best examples invariably, elegant and distinguished. One is conscious of being in good company.'[27]

The Americans praised Sargent's style, and his lack of 'commonplace' conventionality in a way that contemporary critics in England were not prepared to do. In America, he was 'able to start at the very top, as he had not done in France or England,' and whatever damage had been done to the artist's confidence by the *Madame X* scandal was steadily undone by his ecstatic reception in his ancestral homeland. After a year of high praise in America, Sargent returned to Tite Street with more confidence, 'He had come into port, under full sail, with flags flying and a cheering crowd on the wharf to greet him.'[28]

If portrait commissions were slow to materialise Sargent would actively seek out subjects for the canvas. On the evening of the 27 December 1888, recently returned from his trip to America, he met Joseph Comyns Carr, and the two men went to see Henry Irving's new production of *Macbeth* at the Lyceum, starring Ellen Terry as Lady Macbeth. After separating from E.W. Godwin, Terry had made her celebrated return to the stage as Portia in *The Merchant of Venice* at the Prince of Wales Theatre in 1875, a performance that inspired Wilde to compose the lines 'No woman Veronese looked upon / Was half so fair as thou whom I behold'.[29] She had since become a star of the West End, and when she swept on stage as Lady Macbeth in Act I, Scene V, Sargent was captivated, leaning forward in his seat and muttering under his breath, 'Oh my! Oh my!' The artist could not contain himself and after the performance asked Terry if she would allow him to paint her in her costume as Lady Macbeth.[30]

Ellen Terry as Lady Macbeth by John Singer Sargent, 1889

Sargent wrote to his patron Isabella Gardner in America: Terry 'has not yet made up her mind to let me paint her in one of the dresses until she is quite convinced that she is a success,' yet he still fantasised about the endeavour. 'From a pictorial point of view there can be no doubt about it,' he wrote, 'magenta hair!'[31] Terry eventually consented to being painted in full stage costume designed by Mrs Alice Comyns Carr.[32] In January 1889 Terry arrived in Tite Street by four-wheeler carriage which sat parked outside No. 33. The sittings were quick and painless. Sargent experimented with a number of poses until he finally chose one that was not actually in the play.

The painter Edward Burne-Jones stopped by the Tite Street studio and gave Sargent some tips on the final colouring of the portrait, which he adopted. The result was a fearsome Lady Macbeth, holding a crown aloft with a look of greed and terror in her eyes. Terry was thrilled with the result and thought the finished portrait 'magnificent' and Sargent himself a 'saint'. 'The green and blue of the dress is splendid,' she wrote, 'and the expression as Lady Macbeth holds the crown over her head is quite wonderful.' Sargent decided to submit the painting to the New Gallery where it immediately garnered attention. 'Sargent's picture,' wrote Terry, 'is talked of everywhere and quarrelled about as much as my way of playing the part.' *Lady Macbeth* soon became 'the sensation of the year,' and the New Gallery had 'dense crowds round it day after day.'[33]

If Whistler's passion had been Japanese pottery, Sargent's was the piano, and it served as a potent distraction and therapeutic muse throughout his life. On any given day, a passerby might be treated to the sound of a tune coming from No. 33. 'Music', wrote Percy Grainger, 'seemed to be less a recreation to him than a sacred duty.'[34] His manservant Nicola later wrote that Sargent cared little for theatre, 'but he loved music and was … happiest in the company of musicians'. He played the piano 'like a professional, was particularly keen for the guitar and as a matter of fact would play almost any instrument.'[35]

In instances where he was stuck on a painting or getting the right effect, Sargent would turn to music for inspiration. Above all Sargent had a 'strong predilection' for the French composer Gabriel Fauré. A close friend of Sargent suggested that 'it was perhaps Gabriel Fauré who was his greatest friend and who knew him best.'[36] While painting the composer George Henschel one afternoon, Sargent was stuck when it came to finishing some details on the eyes. He stood back from the canvas. 'Let's play a Fauré duet,' he said, and together with the sitter they played to the end of the piece. Then Sargent suddenly jumped up and went to the portrait, and with a few strokes of the brush accomplished the eyes.[37]

This love of music and an eye for character would lure Sargent to the exotic Spanish dancer Carmencita in Paris and then in New York, where he painted her portrait. He had invited the dancer and her band of guitar-playing gypsies to perform in Tite Street for a select group of friends and neighbours. At first it seemed like a good idea but soon Sargent discovered that his studio was a bit too cramped and he agonised over who would be invited.

On the night of the performance the Tite Street studio was packed with people crammed against the walls. The sensuous Carmencita and her band took the middle of the floor. 'The scene in the dimly lit studio was a Sargent picture or an etching by Goya,' W. Graham Robertson recalled, 'the dancer, short-skirted and tinsel-decked, against a huge black screen, the guitarist, black against black, and their white shirts gleaming.' Sargent's guests stood in the dark periphery and corners of the room while Carmencita 'postured and paced . . . ogled . . . flashed her eyes and her teeth.' 'From the guitarist behind her came a low thrumming, a mere murmur and softly, under her breath, Carmencita began to sing. Old folk songs she sang, mournful, haunting, with long cadences and strange intervals, and as she sang she clapped her hands, softly swaying to the rhythm.'[38]

At this party Sargent's neighbour from the Chelsea Embankment, Lady Monkswell (whose brother-in-law John Collier built More House in Tite Street) found herself sitting next to Sargent's newest sitter, the 'pretty Lady Agnew'. Lady Agnew was born Gertrude Vernon and had married the wealthy Andrew Noel Agnew, a barrister who had inherited the baronetcy and estates of Lochnaw in Galloway. The Agnews met Sargent through their mutual friend Helen Dunham, whose portrait the artist was also painting. Having recently inherited his father's wealthy estate, Noel Agnew decided to commission Sargent to paint his wife. The beautiful young 'Gertie' first sat in Tite Street in June 1892, and the painting was completed swiftly in just six sittings.

In the portrait Gertie is painted in one of the famous bergère chairs that Sargent favoured. The portrait was a triumph in composition, character and colour. Lady Agnew is shown reclined, but not quite in repose, gripping the arm of the chair, a mildly pensive agitation present in her eye, highlighted by a slightly raised eyebrow. Sargent also demonstrates a mastery of colour technique. In contrast to the standard chiaroscuro style inherited from Carolous Duran, with Lady Agnew there is very little black used except on the shadows of the chair. Instead, Lady Agnew's pearl-white dress is complimented by a cream-coloured chair and a topaz screen behind. The picture was categorically well received. One reviewer wrote that Sargent:

> . . . has shirked no difficulty in the problem before him of modelling the actual form and nuancing the real colour as light models and shades it. He has sought refuge in no cheaper solvent of tonality, whether brown, blue, or gold. His brushwork boldly challenges you by presenting a definite tone for every inch of surface . . . he never permits some pleasantly warmed juice to veil his view of air, colour and form. He puts all straightforwardly to the touch of right or wrong, content sometimes to lose a superficial beauty of colour or of elegance in the steadfast pursuit of true improvement.[39]

The picture of Sargent's escalating success in London was becoming clearer and his 'pursuit of true improvement' was never more evident. In 1889 there had been three

Carmencita by John
Singer Sargent, 1889

successful exhibitions of his work. At the Royal Academy he exhibited the portrait of *George Henschel*, and at the New Gallery he had *Lady Macbeth*, drawing in huge crowds. By the dawn of the 1890s, Sargent's career in London was in full bloom. A friend wrote to Vernon Lee that London was at Sargent's feet. 'There can be no two opinions this year. He has had a cracking success.'[40] Another commentator noted that Sargent's increasing popularity made him '[A] Prince in Piccadilly, an Emperor in Regent Street.'[41]

Through the 1890s, after a decade of 'concentrated experiment' in portraiture Sargent had, as Elaine Kilmurray points out, 'developed a form of bravura realism crossed with Impressionism, painting with an eye for the realities of light and colour in powerful and succulent brushstrokes so that his sitters were presented as real people. His vision and technique was introducing something new to the English portrait tradition and was beginning to stamp an exciting authority on the English art world.'[42]

Since his arrival in London, Sargent had perplexed the Royal Academy. He was an outsider – an American, trained in Paris, and painting in the French style, and a card-carrying member of the New English Art Club – yet he could no longer be ignored. The Americans adored him and the French recognised him with the award of Chevalier d'honneur in March 1889. The English art establishment was slowly beginning to realise that the young artist standing in their midst was becoming a force to be reckoned with. In 1894 he was elected as an Associate of the Royal Academy.

His ascension into the establishment was seen by some as a betrayal of the avant-garde principles that had defined Tite Street artists, particularly Whistler. The *New York Times* observed that 'The Royal Academy has been passing over painters of the orthodox Academic routine to elect revolutionaries like Sargent … In their present fit they may be quite capable of electing even J.M. Whistler if they did not feel certain he would laugh at them.'[43] They were quite right. 'No my dear Sargent!' exclaimed Whistler upon hearing the news, 'you cannot '*go in there*' and expect 'irony' to follow you! Tell me one thing only – did you? In the face of great temptation / Chuck up the t'other nation / To become an English man!? – However *you* are all right – for you have at last proved that a man is not to be judged by his Associates!'[44]

Sargent had little choice. The door to the Royal Academy had been opened. The days of the *Madame X* scandal were long past, and now Sargent tasted official, institutional recognition for his work from one of the world's most notable authorities in art. With the light of success and future glory shining through, Sargent, in spite of Whistler's protestations, took a step forward. He did not look back.

Lady Agnew of Lochnaw by John Singer Sargent, 1892–3

18.

AESTHETIC RIVALRIES

It is ten o'clock.
Thus we may see how the world wags.
'Tis but an hour ago since it was nine,
And after one hour more 'twill be eleven.
And so, from hour to hour, we ripe and ripe,
And then, from hour to hour, we rot and rot,
And thereby hangs a tale.
– William Shakespeare, *As You Like It*, Act II, Scene 7

In October 1886, just a month before Constance Wilde gave birth to her second son Vyvyan, Edward William Godwin, Tite Street's chief architect and designer, died. The robust fifty-three-year-old had shown no signs of fading health until a few weeks before his death. After a brief funeral service his coffin was hoisted on to an old wagon. Whistler, accompanied by Godwin's widow, Beatrice, and their mutual friend Lady Archibald Campbell, all huddled together on the back of the wagon and eased their grief over an alfresco lunch on the architect's coffin as it clip-clopped to the graveyard.

After the White House, Chelsea Lodge, Canwell House, and Keats House, Godwin's last creation in Tite Street was a tall block of artists' studios simply called Tower House. As late as 1884 there was still an undeveloped plot of land opposite Edis's studios at No. 33, whose lease was held by an old Admiral's widow named Eleanor Bagot.[1] As it appeared the widow had no intention of building on the vacant site, Godwin presented her with proposals for a tower of studio-flats comprised of four double-height studios with mezzanines for living and a communal kitchen in the basement.

Bagot was sympathetic to Godwin's scheme and the plans were submitted to the Metropolitan Board of Works. The Board were still indignant over earlier Godwin collaborations and the plans were swiftly rejected. But Godwin and the old widow had a clever plan to bypass the Board's rejection. It was agreed that Bagot would buy the freehold of the site outright, which then released any developments from the Board's control. Godwin's plans were given to the firm Denton, Son & North who built the Tower House at No. 46 in 1884. It would become the last Godwin building in Tite Street.

Godwin's sudden death left his widow Beatrice to raise their son Edward alone and in debt. Beatrice was the second of ten children born to John Birnie Philip, the Scottish sculptor famous for designing the frieze around the Albert Memorial in Hyde Park.[2] After the death of her father, Beatrice married Godwin, recently split from Ellen Terry, and worked in his studio workshop. Beatrice was herself a fledgling artist, and her work had attracted the attentions of her husband's good friend, Whistler. 'Mr Whistler called last Sunday,' wrote Godwin, 'and was quite enthusiastic about a little figure painting' by Beatrice. Godwin remarked that Whistler was 'thoroughly proud and told me she was worthy to be anyone's pupil.'[3] Upon Godwin's death Whistler had campaigned for an annuity fund for the widowed Beatrice so that she might train as an artist and earn her own living. The Duke of Argyll and Alfred, Lord Tennyson also petitioned successfully for her to be granted a pension from the civil list.

Beatrice was acknowledged to be 'very handsome' but also 'looked very French' with 'a delightful devil-may-care look in her eyes.'[4] Whistler found her 'charming to look at'[5] and that winter he started a portrait of Beatrice, *Harmony in Red: Lamplight*, which he exhibited at the Society of British Artists in 1886. The following year Whistler encouraged Beatrice to submit her paintings *Lamplight*, *The Muslin Gown* and *The Novel* to the Society exhibition, but under the masculine pseudonym 'Rix Birnie' for fear they would be prejudicially overlooked as works by a female artist.

Whistler's model and mistress Maud Franklin also exhibited her work at the same exhibition under the pseudonym 'Clifton Lin'. As Whistler and Beatrice spent more and more time together at his studio in The Vale, a romance was kindled, and Maud was eventually pushed out of the picture. Despite being mother to two of his children, she had no choice but to leave, seeking refuge in Paris. She would later marry a wealthy American and live in the south of France until she died at her villa in Cannes in the early 1940s.

Beatrice herself was already smitten with Whistler, and many years later, on her deathbed, she would confess to having loved him 'always even from the Peacock Room days.'[6] But their romance was slow to develop. Whistler's friend, Henry Labouchère, remembered that Beatrice 'was a remarkably pretty woman, and very agreeable, and both she and he were thorough Bohemians. . . . They were obviously greatly attracted to each other, and in a vague sort of way they thought of marrying.'[7] Along with artist Louise Jopling, Labouchère persuaded Whistler and Beatrice to fix the day for a wedding.

In 1888 Whistler returned to Tite Street, leasing a studio at Godwin's Tower House. That same August, he married Beatrice. The wedding was held at St Mary Abbots Church in Kensington. Afterwards the bride, groom and their guests went to breakfast at the Cafe Royal and then came back to Tite Street. Among moving boxes, pallets, crates and unfinished canvases the guests had to make themselves comfortable until eventually even the wedding cake was banished to the sofa.

Harmony in Red: Lamplight
by James Abbott McNeill
Whistler, 1884

Beatrice arrived in Tite Street with nothing but a toothbrush and a sponge as her trousseau. She already knew the street well. Shortly before re-marrying she lived briefly in a studio flat above Whistler's at Tower House. If anything that experience gave her a glimpse into the eccentricities of her future husband, who was 'a great nuisance.' His artistic acrobatics had continued unabated, and 'he was trotting all day long across the floor of the studio, putting a few touches on his canvas and trotting back to see the effect.'[8]

As usual, it was not long before Whistler put his own stamp on Tower House, decorating his new studio in varying shades of white, and introducing a butterfly scheme on everything including 'his house linen'.[9] The arrangement was not terribly spacious, but Whistler had become used to cosy quarters since leaving his spacious White House. On the top mezzanine he and Beatrice shared a tiny bedroom while the whole of the main floor served as a studio-cum-drawing room.

Despite his many absences, Tite Street had remained Whistler's domain, his natural habitat and the street where he created some of his most memorable work. But for Beatrice it was a slightly more complicated location. First, it had haunting memories of her recently deceased husband, whose creative signature was clearly stamped on a number of its houses. For nearly two years she lived with Whistler, her deceased husband's friend, in a building he had designed. Moreover, she could not tolerate Oscar Wilde, living only a few doors away. Beatrice had known Wilde from the days when Godwin had decorated No. 34. In a rather unflattering caricature she had revealed her true feelings when she portrayed him as a portly, conceited pig. But Beatrice was not the only one in Tite Street with a loathing of Wilde. Relations between her new husband and Wilde had grown sour long before the Butterfly returned to Tite Street.

Back in 1881 Wilde dashed out of Tite Street and went to America to lecture on the 'Aesthetic Movement in England' wearing knee-breeches and flamboyant costumes. Upon his return he decided to continue his lecture tour around the provinces of Britain. Whistler consistently mocked him for 'masquerading' the streets of Chelsea in his outrageous costumes. Wilde however remained unflappable and continued to hold Whistler in reverence, praising him as the man who 'unites in himself all the qualities of the noblest art, whose work is a joy for all time, who is, himself, a master of all time.'[10]

Whistler clearly nurtured some resentment for Wilde, which eventually blossomed into full-blown accusations of plagiarism. Twenty years older than Wilde, Whistler had never quite accepted that his young friend had genius too and perhaps felt a sting of jealousy that Wilde could succeed in the world without his direction. Wilde had unknowingly rubbed salt in the wound when he began to put his name on aesthetic theories that Whistler believed were his own.[11] Perhaps more troubling was the fact that Wilde had begun to draw attention away from Whistler, and nobody encroached on Whistler's spotlight without a fight.

By early 1885, Whistler felt it was finally time to take ownership of his theories and an elaborate plan was hatched to give a public lecture. In usual bold fashion Whistler scheduled the lecture at the unheard-of time of ten o'clock in the evening at the Prince's Hall in Piccadilly. Preparations for the big event consumed the artist. Friends and neighbours were kept awake, roused in the middle of the night by a double-knock, followed by Whistler with a page or paragraph of the lecture for approval. The streets of Chelsea became a rehearsal space with Whistler pacing 'up and down the Embankment . . . repeating sentences' to his dutiful and obedient pupils.[12]

When it came to the lecture itself, nothing was left to chance. A strategic seating plan was carefully drawn up, and Whistler had a dress rehearsal the day before to smooth over any technical blips. On 20 February 1885 the Prince's Hall was sold out. The press speculated whether the artist 'was going to sketch, to pose, to sing, or to rhapsodise,' and were perplexed when the 'amiable eccentric' chose to appear simply as 'a jaunty, unabashed, composed, and self-satisfied gentleman, armed with an opera hat and an eyeglass.'[13] His Tite Street neighbour Anna Lea Merritt took some delight 'to remember that actually once Mr Whistler was really shy,' and that 'when he came before his puzzled and distinguished audience there were a few minutes of very palpable stage-fright.'[14]

Whistler cleared his throat. 'Ladies and Gentlemen!' he began. 'It is with great hesitation and much misgiving that I appear before you, in the character of The Preacher.' 'Art is upon the Town!' he declared with gusto, 'to be chucked under the chin, by the passing gallant! – to be enticed within the gates of the house-holder – to be coaxed into company, as a proof of culture and refinement! If familiarity can breed contempt, certainly Art, or what is currently taken for it, has been brought to its lowest stage of intimacy!'[15]

The 'Preacher' was relentless but disorganised, skipping from one topic to another 'with charming ease and much grace of manner.'[16] He dispelled the popular principle that art was a social mechanism with the power to improve the human condition. 'Beauty is confounded with virtue,' he said, 'and before a work of Art, it is asked, "What good shall it do?"' and as a result the art-consuming public had become accustomed to looking not 'at a picture, but through it, at some human fact, that shall . . . better their mental or moral state.'[17]

For Whistler, art existed outside the confines of time and place, irrelevant to any larger social context, and he disagreed with Wilde over the idea that once society decayed, art decayed too. 'It is fallen, this teaching of decay. The Master stands in no relation to the moment at which he occurs – a monument of isolation . . . having no part in the progress of his fellow men.'[18] Art was, or at least should be in his opinion, indifferent to social change or the world-at-large, yet in the same breath he then reaffirmed statements that Wilde had already touched upon, that 'there never was an artistic period' and 'there never was an Art-loving nation'.[19]

Whistler then went on the offensive. He begrudged writers and critics for interfering in the work of the painter – a core issue in his libel trial wherein he argued that 'none but an artist' could comment upon art. 'For some time past,' he said, 'the unattached writer has become the middleman in this matter of Art, and his influence, while it has widened the gulf between the people and the painter, has brought about the most complete misunderstanding as to the aim of the picture.' The craft of painting and the craft of writing were fundamentally opposed, according to Whistler. Writers were trained to organise plots and therefore saw paintings as nothing more than 'symbol of story.' The very form of painting and literature are incompatible – literature being concerned with narrative and 'literary climax'. The painting on the other hand is focused on 'mere execution' only.[20]

As he jumped from point to point, Whistler agreed somewhat with Wilde's past lectures. Both agreed that 'art' was superior to 'Nature'. 'Nature contains the elements, in colour and form, of all pictures, as the keyboard contains the notes of all music,' said Whistler. 'But the artist is born to pick, and choose … that the result may be beautiful – as the musician gathers his notes, and forms his chords, until he brings forth from chaos glorious harmony.'[21] When it came to art, however, Whistler claimed that, 'Nature is rarely right. Seldom does Nature succeed in producing a picture.'[22] Wilde would take this a step further when he later said that it was 'Life that imitated Art.'[23]

Wilde listened patiently while his friend and neighbour openly drove the knife in deeper and then twisted it, attacking him personally, and striking down his own aesthetic theories. Though he never mentioned Wilde's name, it was perfectly clear who Whistler was referring to when he spoke of the 'unattached writer' who 'paraded in costume'. That evening Wilde went home to his study in Tite Street and wrote a letter to the *Pall Mall Gazette*. His language was highly alliterative and mildly antagonistic, calling Whistler 'a miniature Mephistopheles, mocking the majority!' who made a 'holocaust of humanity'[24] in his lecture.

Wilde wrote that the 'Artist is not an isolated fact' but is instead the result of a 'certain milieu' and a 'certain entourage,' such as the one that was flourishing in Tite Street. Next Wilde took Whistler to task over assertions that the 'unattached writer' had become the 'middleman in this matter of art' intruding into the realm of the artist. 'The poet is the supreme Artist,' Wilde argued, 'for he is the master of colour and of form, and the real musician besides, and is lord over all life and all arts; and so to the poet beyond all others are these mysteries known; to Edgar Allen Poe and Baudelaire, not to Benjamin West and Paul Delaroche.'[25]

Whistler took the bait. He replied to Oscar's letter in the *World*. 'Nothing is more delicate, in the flattery of "the Poet" to "the Painter", than the naiveté of "the Poet" in the choice of his Painters – Benjamin West and Paul Delaroche! You have pointed out that "the Painter's" mission is to find "*le beau dans l'horrible*" and have left to "the Poet" the discovery of "*l'horrible*" *dans* "*le beau*"!' Wilde shot back, 'By the aid of a biographical dictionary, I made the discovery that there were once two painters, called Benjamin West and Paul Delaroche, who rashly lectured upon Art. As of their works nothing at all remains, I conclude that they explained themselves away. Be warned in time, James; and remain, as I do, incomprehensible. To be great is to be misunderstood.'[26]

The dialogue cooled between the two aesthetes. Each went his own way pursuing his own aesthetic ends. But the wound was not allowed much time to heal. A year later an article appeared in the *Art Journal* announcing that an 'organisation having for its object the foundation of a "National Exhibition of the Arts" has been established.'[27] It was described as an 'anti-Academy movement', with an interest in reforming the Royal Academy itself. The National Exhibition had been championed by leading figures of the day and Whistler was invited to join, which he would have gladly done, until he learned that his *bête noire*, Harry Quilter, and his newest rival, Oscar Wilde, had also been asked to join.

Whistler shot off a letter to the *World*, 'What has Oscar in common with Art? except that he dines at our tables, and picks from our platters the plums for the pudding he peddles in the provinces. Oscar – the amiable, irresponsible, esurient Oscar – with no more sense of a picture than of the fit of a coat, has the courage of the opinions – of others. With 'Arry and Oscar you have avenged the Academy.'[28] Whistler sent a copy of the letter to Wilde in Tite Street with a note, 'Oscar, you must really keep outside "the radius".' Wilde refused to rise to the provocation and simply wrote back to the *World*, 'Alas, this is very sad! With our James vulgarity begins at home, and should be allowed to stay there.'[29] Whistler replied, 'A poor thing, Oscar – but for once, I suppose your own.'[30]

Wilde held his tongue. The days when he had been dependent on his feisty neighbour for inspiration in matters of art and taste, along with his notoriety, were long gone. Wilde was creating his own brand of aesthetic decadence from No. 34. His pen remained ever busy. In the same year that Whistler returned to Tower House in Tite Street, Wilde published a collection of short stories, *The Happy Prince and Other Stories*, illustrated by Walter Crane and George Percy Jacomb-Hood. The collection contained five short stories, each containing a moral relating to the effects of extreme selfishness, egotism and betrayal, all characteristics rife in Tite Street, and which had burnt Wilde on numerous occasions.

In the past, Wilde made no attempt to hide his perceptions of Whistler's selfishness. 'Mr Whistler always spelt art, and we believe still spells it with a capital "I",'[31] he once wrote. *The Remarkable Rocket* tells the tale of a proud Rocket who was one of many intended to be let off at the wedding. The pompous Rocket denigrates all the other fireworks, eventually bursts into tears to demonstrate his 'sensitivity,' but being wet he then fails to ignite and is thrown away into a ditch. There he still believes that he is destined for success and treats his companions – a frog, dragonfly and duck – with snobbish disdain. Two boys eventually find him and decide to use him for fuel on their campfire. But when the Rocket finally explodes, nobody sees him except a frightened goose who gets hit with his falling stick.

In the story, the Rocket tells his companions, 'You should be thinking about me. I am always thinking of myself, and I expect everyone else to do the same. That is what is called sympathy.' 'You forget that I am very uncommon and very remarkable … The only thing that sustains one through life is the consciousness of the immense inferiority of everybody else, and this is a feeling I have always cultivated.' In these words are strong echoes of Whistler, commanding his pupils in Tite Street to be 'occupied with the Master, not with yourselves.'[32] And then there was his frank assertion that when he and Wilde were together they never

Illustration from Oscar Wilde's *The Remarkable Rocket* by Walter Crane, 1888

talked about 'anything except *me*.'[33] The rocket is highly symbolic in this instance as a rocket (or firework) was the subject of Whistler's *Arrangement in Black and Gold* which precipitated his libel trial against Ruskin and eventually led to his bankruptcy.

The jewel in the crown of Wilde's collection was the eponymous 'The Happy Prince,' being perhaps the most autobiographical of all the stories in the collection and revealing the unspoken life behind the walls of No. 34 Tite Street. Wilde presents a story of duplicity, desire and secret love, significantly, between two male characters. In 'The Happy Prince' a Swallow, who 'began to tire of his lady-love,' leaves and flies to a city where there is 'a statue of the Happy Prince' standing 'gilded all over with thin leaves of fine gold, for eyes he had bright sapphires, and a large red ruby glowed on his sword-hilt.'

Like Wilde, whose study looked over Tite Street, the Happy Prince, 'perched above the city,' with feet 'cemented in place,' and confesses 'there is no Mystery so great as misery.' With the help of the Swallow, the Prince gives away pieces of his gilded armour. One recipient of his benevolence is a struggling writer, 'leaning over a desk covered with papers, and in a tumbler by his side there is a bunch of withered violets. His hair is brown and crisp, and his lips are red as a pomegranate, and he has large and dreamy eyes. He is trying to finish a play for the Director of the Theatre, but he is too cold to write any more.'

The story not only carries hints of Wilde's life in Tite Street, it also forecasts the ruinous years to come. When at last the Prince has given away everything that he can, left completely exposed and penniless, he tells his love, 'I am glad that you are going to Egypt at last, little Swallow.' '[Y]ou have stayed too long here; but you must kiss me on the lips, for I love you.' When the Swallow kisses the Happy Prince on the lips, he falls down dead at his feet. 'At that moment a curious crack sounds inside the statue, as if something has broken. The fact is that the leaden heart had snapped right in two. It certainly was a dreadfully hard frost.'

For Christmas of 1888, Oscar invited the young Irish poet, William Butler Yeats, to spend the holiday at No. 34 Tite Street. Originally from Dublin, Yeats had only vaguely known Wilde through their Irish connections. The poet was at first surprised by Wilde's sensible appearance writing that 'his past of a few years before had gone completely' and that 'the perfect harmony of his life' in Tite Sreet, with 'his beautiful wife and his two young children, suggested some deliberate artistic composition'.[34]

Both Oscar and Constance had expended vast quantities of time, money and energy to develop this 'deliberate artistic composition,' even if it was slightly brittle. In the 'perfect harmony' of No. 34, Yeats and the Wilde family shared a wholesome yuletide dinner accompanied by generous helpings of banter. 'We Irish are too poetical to be poets; we are a nation of brilliant failures,' Wilde boasted, 'but we are the greatest talkers since the Greeks.'[35] After dinner Yeats put this theory to the test as he entertained the family with a fireside story about a monster. Both Cyril and Vyvyan had vivid imaginations but Yeats's story was more severe than their father's tales of handsome princes and faeries. They burst into tears, and it fell to their father to invent a cosy bedtime tale to restore normality to No. 34.

When the children were finally sent off to bed, Wilde and Yeats retired to the smoking room where they discussed early proofs of a polemical duologue, 'The Decay of Lying,' which was to be published the following month in a journal called *Nineteenth Century*.[36] In the essay Wilde expands upon Whistler's own ideas offered in his ten o'clock lecture. 'All bad art comes from returning to Life and Nature, and elevating them into ideals,' Wilde argues. 'Life and Nature may sometimes be used as part of Art's rough material, but before they are of any real service to art they must be translated into artistic conventions.' Indeed he even echoes Whistler when saying, 'the only beautiful things are the things that do not concern us.'[37]

Wilde further evolves his own thread of Paterian and Whistlerian theory which would henceforth constitute the backbone of his credo. 'Life imitates Art,' he writes, 'far more than Art imitates Life. This results not merely from Life's imitative instinct, but from the fact that the self-conscious aim of Life is to find expression, and that Art offers it certain beautiful forms through which it may realise that energy.' Wilde continues that Nature itself also imitates Art. 'The only effects that she can show us are effects that we have already seen through poetry, or in paintings. This is the secret of Nature's charm, as well as the explanation of Nature's weakness.'[38]

Wilde concludes that 'Lying, the telling of beautiful untrue things, is the proper aim of Art.' Wilde, aware of his own divergence from Whistler and Pater and writes that, 'it is a theory that has never been put forward before, but it is extremely fruitful, and throws an entirely new light upon the history of Art.'[39] Wilde's work as an art theorist and critic would soon give way to writing for the stage, and the ideas that he nurtured in his essays would manifest themselves in one of the most sensational novels of the decade.

Tensions between the two Tite Street aesthetes had receded somewhat by the end of the 1880s. Wilde received an invitation to a show of Whistler's work at the Suffolk Gallery in 1887, but the fissures in Tite Street would never completely heal. In 1890, Whistler and his bride departed Tite Street for the last time and embarked for Paris where a further decade of controversy, social climbing, and a periodic court case awaited. For Wilde the coming decade dawned full of promise, and the 'wonderful possibilities' of Tite Street were alive, but its end would prove otherwise. 'Life goes faster than Realism,' Wilde once wrote, 'but Romanticism is always in front of life.'[40] In the decade that lay ahead Realism would catch up with Life, and with very dire consequences.

19.

DORIAN GRAY
& TITE STREET

Most of our modern portrait painters are
doomed to absolute oblivion. They never paint
what they see. They paint what the public sees,
and the public never sees anything.
– Oscar Wilde

'I have invented a new story,' wrote Oscar Wilde to Joseph Stoddart, editor of *Lippincott's Monthly Magazine* in December 1889. 'I am quite ready to set to work at once on it. It will be ready by the end of March.'[1] A month before his letter to Stoddart, Wilde had given up his day job as editor of *The Woman's World* and settled into his study in Tite Street to begin a career as a fiction writer. The story would become Wilde's first and only novel, *The Picture of Dorian Gray*, and it appeared in *Lippincott's* July 1890 issue.

By the time Wilde sat down to write *Dorian Gray*, two institutions had risen in popularity in Britain: honorary societies and portraiture. All over London, clubs and societies were being formed, and nearly every famous writer, artist, thinker or politician, every theory and every region of London seemed to have a club or society dedicated to its advancement and understanding. There were general clubs for artists like the New English Art Club and the Royal Society of British Artists. There were societies for painters in pastels and painter-etchers, alongside reformed and unreformed watercolour societies. Together with these new societies were specialised exhibitions which focused attention on a particular medium like 'black and white' etching, as well as shows of specialised subjects like 'fair children' or 'fair women'.

Meanwhile, portraiture had come to dominate the walls of most London galleries, and in portraiture, Tite Street was the leading force. Year by year new faces in half-length, full-length and groups spilled forth from Tite Street in multitudes. There were Whistler's harmonies and arrangements, and Sargent's *Lady Agnew, Mrs Hammersley, Earl of Dalhousie, Graham Robertson, Ellen Terry* or *Lord Ribblesdale*. For almost half a century, British portraiture had been a rather neglected art. High Victorian grandees had preferred not to flaunt their wealth and prestige in portraits, but by the last quarter of the nineteenth century attitudes towards fame had changed. As early as the 1870s John Everett Millais had encouraged young Archie Stuart-Wortley to take up portraiture as a means of earning income. But by the 1890s, with the help of Whistler's *Arrangement in Grey and Black, No. 1* and *Harmony in Grey and Green: Miss Cicely Alexander*, along with his portraits of Lady Meux and Lady Archibald Campbell, portraiture had taken on a new prestige for artists, imbuing it with aesthetic as well as commercial interest.[2] It was only a matter of time before the art of portraiture would have its own dedicated society.

In the spring of 1891, the newly founded Society of Portrait Painters met at the home of Archibald Stuart-Wortley, a former Tite Street artist, now living in Westbourne Terrace. Of the sixteen founding members, almost half were based in Tite Street.[3] This was no mere coincidence. The emergence of portraiture and the emergence of Tite Street were linked by historic forces. In the 1860s London was sitting at the heart of a vast Empire, and the wealth that it brought home led to projects like the construction of the Chelsea Embankment, which in turn led to the creation of Tite Street. Around the same time, the children of the great Empire-builders and captains of Industry – the Meuxs and Agnews – were coming of age and were inclined more and more to enjoy the fruits of their parents' ambition. With ample leisure time this generation of beautiful young things found new and stimulating ways to indulge in self-glorification and gratification. Portraiture met the demand of an image-conscious age obsessed with looking at itself.

The Society of Portrait Painters was a necessary product of the growing number of portrait artists filling London's studios. Its *raison d'être* was simply to promote portraiture as a respected art form. On a more practical level it sought to provide publicity for the diversity of artists now practising in the field. The Society's first exhibition, held in 1891, was a testament to this range and diversity of portraiture. The exhibition included a mix of portraits by Whistler, accompanied by some from older Royal Academicians like Millais, Watts and Leighton.

The juxtaposition of the standard academic portrait and more modern portraits ignited a new debate at the heart of the art world – whether a portrait should be a mere likeness, exercising honest degrees of verisimilitude, with the artist virtually absent, or whether it should be a work of art in itself, an interpretation, an active dialogue between artist and sitter. The debate was given a fleshly face by one of Tite Street's most notable personalities, in a novel which would soon add a fascinating but bloody angle to the relationship between portraiture, artist and sitter – a complex relationship at the very heart of Tite Street.

From his study on the ground-floor at No. 34, Oscar Wilde had an unimpeded view of the famous, and most infamous, faces of the age as they came and went: Ellen Terry, Lady Meux,

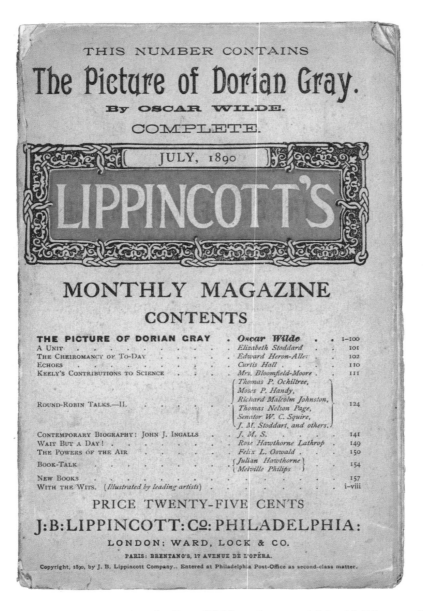

THIS NUMBER CONTAINS

The Picture of Dorian Gray.

By OSCAR WILDE.

COMPLETE.

JULY, 1890

LIPPINCOTT'S

MONTHLY MAGAZINE

CONTENTS

PRICE TWENTY-FIVE CENTS

J:B:LIPPINCOTT:C̱O̱:PHILADELPHIA:

LONDON: WARD, LOCK & CO.

PARIS: BRENTANO'S, 17 AVENUE DE L'OPÉRA.

The Picture of Dorian Gray by Oscar Wilde in *Lippincott's Monthly Magazine*, July 1890

Lady Archie Campbell, W. Graham Robertson, the Prince of Wales and Lillie Langtry. He worked in the shadow of the old Victoria Children's Hospital, where victims of domestic violence were taken wrapped in bloody shawls, and just metres away from a 'wretched' little street where the sound 'of brawling rose nightly'.[4] In short, Wilde had unfettered access to a street where bohemians, aristocrats and vagrants all co-mingled, where artists and poets lived in the arms of their models and mistresses, and where madness had already stolen the promising lives of Marian Collier and Frank Miles. So when Wilde sat down to write his first novel, it was inevitable that it would be informed by life in the street around him.

Dorian Gray is the story of a youthful London dandy who has his portrait painted by the artist Basil Hallward, falls in love with it, and wishes that the picture should grow old and he remain forever young and beautiful instead. As he embarks on a life of pleasure and experience under the corrupting influence of Lord Henry Wotton, Dorian discovers that his wish has come true. He remains eternally youthful in outward appearance while his portrait grows old, wretched and corrupt in the attic of his Mayfair mansion.

In *Dorian Gray* the line between portrait, painter and sitter are fantastically transcended, and within its pages 'life imitates art'. The portrait painter Basil Hallward could have been any of a handful of Tite Street artists. Dorian Gray was recognisable in almost any of the wealthy dandies with their 'rose-red cheeks and rose-red boyhoods' who had come strolling into Tite Street. While Wilde was working, new debates about portraiture were arising and in the same year that Wilde's novel was published in book form, the Society of Portrait Painters was being established by some of his neighbours with the hope of elevating portraiture to a new level. Wilde beat them to the task.

Sewn into the fabric of the novel are details and evocative clues that pertain to the sordid, often scandalous, lives of those living nearest in Tite Street. Locations certainly play a central role in the novel, ranging from artists' studios and Mayfair drawing rooms to Euston Road slums and opium den in the docklands. Taking account of where the novel was written, it is hardly surprising to find that it opens in an artist's studio. The resemblance between Hallward's studio (in Half-Moon Street, Mayfair) and Frank Miles's studio-house in Tite Street, where Wilde once lived, is clear.

Miles was a keen botanist and took particular pleasure in cultivating his garden in Tite Street. Wilde takes great pains to evoke a certain botanical element in his descriptions of Hallward's studio with his garden full of laburnums, lilacs, roses and even a pear tree. Godwin had designed the inside of Miles's studio 'to meet the taste of a lover of flowers'.[5] Even when Jacomb-Hood moved in several years after Miles' departure, there remained 'a fine vine, jessamine, a Japanese cherry ... and a syringa which fills the air with perfume in the summer.'[6] Godwin had decorated the studio in the Anglo-Japanese style with 'blue cretonne curtains in a Japanese bird pattern with a thin blue lining over the windows,'[7] much like the description of Hallward's studio, where 'the fantastic shadows of birds in flight flitted across the long tussore-silk curtains that were stretched in front of the huge window, producing a kind of momentary Japanese effect.'

Other locations play a vital role in the novel. Written from Wilde's own library, it is unsurprising to find that most of the major dialogue scenes are set within libraries. Wilde's library was the most sacred room in the entire house, 'the Holy of Holies', 'a place of awe', recalled his son Vyvyan, and 'it was sacrosanct; a place in the vicinity of which no noise was to be made, and which must only be passed on tiptoe.'[8] Lord Henry's 'little library,' described at length, with its 'high-panelled wainscoting of olive-stained oak, its cream-colored frieze and ceiling of raised plaster-work, and its brick-dust felt carpet' bears a strong resemblance to Wilde's. Lord Henry even has a 'tiny satinwood table' upon which sat a 'statuette by Clodion.' Wilde's library had a motif of red and yellow, the walls being painted pale yellow and the woodwork enamelled red and a 'table once owned by Carlyle,' while on a red column in one corner stood a cast of the Hermes of Praxiteles.[9]

As the story of *Dorian Gray* progresses its connections with Tite Street grow deeper. Seeking a taste of Lord Henry's 'new hedonism', Dorian goes out 'in search of some adventure', and from Trafalgar Square wanders eastward losing his way in 'a labyrinth of grimy streets and black grassless squares', until he stumbles upon an 'absurd little theatre, with great flaring gas-jets and gaudy play-bills', where he first sees the 'greatest romance' of his life in the form of the actress, Sybil Vane. Dorian falls madly in love with Sybil and eventually proposes marriage to her.

The story of a young, wealthy dandy meeting and falling in love with an impoverished actress was an already familiar tale in Tite Street by the time *Dorian Gray* was written. Back in 1875, Wilde's one-time neighbour, Archibald Stuart-Wortley, like Dorian, a handsome, golden-haired youth fell in love with, impregnated, and eventually married the actress Nelly Bromley. Yet from the clues given in the novel it is more likely that the fictional romance in *Dorian Gray* was inspired by the real-life romance of Harry and Valerie Meux. In 1881, Whistler had started the first of three portraits of Valerie, Lady Meux in his Tite Street studio. At a time when Wilde was 'so much with Whistler',[10] it is unlikely that he would not have been at least vaguely familiar with Lady Meux and her sensational story.

Harry Meux was the heir to a vast brewery fortune. Like Dorian, he was a young man of means whose father had died when he was young. His mother had lived as an exile in France, effectively abandoning her son to the care of relatives, not unlike Dorian's mother, Margaret Devereux, who dies when he is still a boy. Harry came into a fortune when he inherited the Meux brewing dynasty whose headquarters happened to be located between Holborn and Tottenham Court Road, a stone's throw from the famed Casino de Venise.[11] It was in the Casino that Harry met his future wife Valerie, or Val Reece, formally known as a barmaid, but who was in all likelihood a prostitute.

The 'gaudy, gilded' entrance to the Casino bears a similarity to the fictional Theatre Royal, Holborn, with its 'gaudy play-bills'. Yet if Harry and Valerie Meux were indeed the inspiration for the characters in the novel, Wilde took some artistic licence in eloquently disguising the vulgar burlesque Casino for a theatre performing a repertoire of Shakespeare. Harry and Val married, against the wishes of his family, and it would be several decades before the former barmaid would be accepted into society. A similar fate may have awaited Sybil Vane, had she not killed herself instead.

Having written the magazine story in just three months (though it was considerably extended for the 1891 book edition) it seems highly likely that certain ideas for the story and its characters had been germinating for some time in Wilde's mind. It is likely that they were derived from the very world that surrounded him in Tite Street. Wilde certainly did not need to go too far to find material for his new story. There was nothing in the 'labyrinth of grimy streets' in the East End that could not be found by glancing out of his window into Paradise Walk. There were no millionaires of Mayfair that he had not met at one of Constance's fashionable 'at homes' in Tite Street. The inspiration for *Dorian Gray* could be found, quite literally, on his doorstep.

At the heart of the novel Wilde explores the complex relationship between artist, sitter and work of art – a poignant topic in a street dominated by portrait painting. 'Portraits supplant the individuals whom they represent,' writes Kenneth McConkey. 'They function as analogues, existing in parallel to their subjects. They fix a moment within a lifetime, within an era. They therefore provide communication with the past of a most significant kind. At a certain juncture, the artist and sitter collude in the production of an image which, to some extent, becomes a substitute for a living being. It is taken from the sitter and cannot be reclaimed. It becomes the possession of others for whom it acts as a cue to imaginative consciousness. Recognising the being within its frame, the spectator partakes of an illusion. The image becomes an aesthetic object, living yet distanced from normal experience.'[12]

With *Dorian Gray*, Oscar Wilde ushered the Nineties into Tite Street. It would prove to be one of the most turbulent decades in the street's already rocky history. Tite Street would become a factory, producing illusions that were, as McConkey writes, 'living yet distanced from normal experience.' The most prominent of these were a host of post-hoc prototypes of Dorian Gray who would flock to Chelsea in the 1890s.

Wilde may have created Dorian Gray in Tite Street, but Whistler was the first to paint him. A year after the first edition of *Dorian Gray* was published, Robert, Comte de Montesquiou, the leading exponent of French aestheticism, who would later become the decadent protagonist in Marcel Proust's *Remembrance of Things Past*, commissioned the Butterfly to paint his portrait. Whistler accepted the commission, and sittings began in Cheyne Walk, where Whistler was based for a short time, in July 1891 and continued for many months working 'all through the day and night on the portrait'.[13]

In 1894, a few years after *Dorian Gray* was published, the actress Ada Rehan was sitting to Sargent in Tite Street. Rehan wrote to the handsome, refined twenty-eight-year-old W. Graham Robertson, writer and illustrator, 'I have something particular to tell you about Sargent . . . he's very anxious to paint you . . . he says you are very paintable.' The portrait began in the summer of 1894. As with the Comte de Montesquiou, sittings were long and laborious. One afternoon, in the heat of the studio, the exhausted sitter, who had been standing upon the dais for his portrait for several hours, suddenly began feeling faint and recalled that 'Sargent glanced at me. "What a horrid light there is just now," the artist

W. Graham Robertson
by John Singer
Sargent, 1894

Arrangement in Black and Gold:
Comte Robert de Montesquiou-
Fezensac by James Abbott
McNeill Whistler, 1891–2

remarked. "A sort of green," – He looked more steadily. "Why it's you!" he cried and seizing me by the collar, rushed me into the street, where he propped me up against the door-post. It was a pity that Oscar Wilde opposite was not looking out of the window: the "wonderful possibilities of Tite Street" were yet unexhausted.'[14]

When Sargent eventually saw Whistler's Comte de Montesquiou on display, he fretted that he would be accused of imitation. Sargent's portrait of W. Graham Robertson was suspiciously close to that of Whistler's Comte de Montesquiou. The painting was also an illusion, as Sargent made his sitter younger and slimmer on canvas than he was in reality. In both portraits clean, handsome dandies are dressed in chic, well-tailored black coats. 'The picture deserves study,' wrote George Moore of Graham Robertson's portrait, 'for in it Mr Sargent has realised once and for ever the type of fashionable young man of artistic tendencies of this end of the century . . . his face wears an expression of perplexed dissatisfaction, and if you asked him why he was unhappy he would answer, "I never was happy except on the rare occasion when I believed myself to be a great man."'[15] The 'fashionable young man of artistic tendencies', created in print by Wilde and painted by both Whistler and Sargent, would embody the spirit of Tite Street in the 1890s.

20.

The CHARMED CIRCLE

Imagine a man of genius following in the wake of Whistler!
– *The Oracle*

'Of course you will settle in Chelsea,'[1] Whistler told the young artist, William Rothenstein when he returned from training in Paris. By the 1890s Chelsea was an undisputed artists' colony with its headquarters in Tite Street. 'We have the curious contrast of artistic splendour in a blazing brand-new quarter, of which the sacred centre is Tite Street,' wrote Benjamin Ellis Martin in 1889. 'Here amid much that is good and genuine in our modern manner, there is an aggressive affectation of antiquity shown by the little houses and studios obtruding on the street, by the grandiose piles of mansions towering on the embankment: all in raging red brick, and in the so-called Queen Anne style … mighty swells dwell here, and here pose some famous farceurs in art and literature.'[2]

Whistler left Tite Street for the last time in February 1890, moving briefly to Cheyne Walk, and then to Paris with his wife, Beatrice. In his wake, a wave of burgeoning talent arrived. Rothenstein was certainly not unique in Chelsea, being an artist recently returned from France. Most aspiring English artists trained in Paris and spent their summers in one of the many picturesque artist colonies like Pont Aven or Grez-sur-Loing before returning to London to begin their professional careers.

Once back in London the artists gathered in one of the only parts of the modern capital that retained the feeling of a village, nestled by the river, and set apart from the rest of the city. With the emergence of new rival galleries and clubs such as the Grosvenor Gallery, the New Gallery, the New English Art Club, the Pall Mall and the Grafton Galleries, there was a growing call for the Royal Academy to reform its old-fashioned system, and it would start with the Royal Academy Schools. In Tite Street, Frank Miles, who had studied at the Academy's school, added his voice to the cry, 'In the Academy there is a teacher in each room. He is miserably paid, and the result is that he is sometimes not so much better an artist than his pupils.'[3]

Beyond its schools, the Academy had 'not done its work,' according to Miles, in encouraging other forms of art beside oil painting – such as etching or sculpture – in its exhibitions. Each exhibition should have 'far fewer pictures' and have them 'all well hung.'[4] He recommended rotating the pictures frequently to give better attention to some that had been overlooked. In selecting works for the exhibitions, Miles would insist that all Academicians voted instead of a select 'hanging committee'. For instance, those who had voted Sargent's *The Misses Vickers* to be the worst picture of the year,[5] writes Miles, 'would crush out all real talent, which is invariably novel, and creates its own ever-widening circle of appreciators.'[6]

Miles's pleas resounded in Chelsea where many artists found a community with the same values and camaraderie that they had shared in Paris. By the 1880s, the area of Chelsea where the King's Road met Church Street had become known as London's 'Latin Quarter'. Here vast studios were being built. The largest group of studios were in Manresa Road, then a cul-de-sac directly off King's Road. Some of these had been built as workshops for the metal workers and other craftsmen who created the Great Exhibition of 1851 in Hyde Park.[7] On the western side of Manresa Road stood Merton Villa Studios, a ramshackle group of buildings, around an empty workyard entered by a narrow lane littered with old carts.[8] Empty lofts and warehouses soon became the workshops and studios of Chelsea, providing adequate and cheap (with a rent of £40 per year) space for artists to work.

Artists in Chelsea developed a unique identity that set them apart from the rest of the capital. They dressed casually, sometimes disreputably, without their collars or perhaps smoking clay pipes. 'The man who talked impressively about "Art" and who goes in for silk ties and gold studs,' soon removed himself to the more respectable realm of Hampstead.[9] This bohemian crowd looked for somewhere nearby to meet, talk, eat and drink like they had in the boulevards of Paris.

In the 1860s and 1870s the small circle of artists and aesthetes in Chelsea met at Rossetti's Tudor House in Cheyne Walk. In the 1880s the studios of Tite Street had served as gathering points. By the 1890s, however, Chelsea was flourishing, and Tite Street could not contain the artistic energy arriving in the new creative quarter. The artists of Chelsea began to merge themselves into a somewhat cohesive and organised group, meeting at the studio of American artist Stirling Lee on King's Road. Here in September 1890 they discussed the formation of an exhibiting society for Chelsea artists. In October a second meeting was held with Whistler in the crowd. Artist Theodore Wores proposed that 'A Club be formed of Chelsea artists, under whose auspices an annual exhibition be held.' His suggestion was greeted by the chants of, 'Club, club, club!' Whistler rose and the crowd was silenced, 'Gentlemen, let us not start our club in any beer hotel,' he said in earnest. 'Let us start our club clean.'[10] The following month a constitution was agreed:

Rule No. 1: That the Club shall be called the Chelsea Arts Club.

Rule No. 2: That the Club shall consist of professional Architects, Engravers, Painters and Sculptors.

Rule No. 3: That the object of the Club shall be to advance the cause of art by means of exhibitions of works of art, life classes and other kindred means and to promote social intercourse amongst its members.

Rule No. 4: That its affairs shall be managed by a Council of 13 members with Treasurer and Secretary. Ten of these would be elected by vote and this committee would have the right to choose the remaining three.[11]

The club became a centre of parties and festivities, lectures and meetings, dinners and fancy balls where social (and no doubt other forms of) intercourse were promoted. 'Every now and then we had an evening of music and recitations and story-telling.'[12] Artist George Percy Jacomb-Hood recalled the Club's 'intimate and convivial life' and the evenings after dinner 'when Whistler was in the habit of strolling round ... always charming and amusing and Sargent for a time would come to lunch at the long table.'[13] When Whistler's portrait of his mother was purchased by the Musée du Luxembourg for 4,000 francs in 1891, the Chelsea Arts Club held a reception in his honour. At the reception the artist was presented with a parchment of greetings signed by a hundred Club members as 'a record of their high appreciation of the distinguished honour that has come to him by the placing of his mother's portrait in the national collection of France.'[14] For Whistler the purchase was a personal victory and a recognition that his hard-fought aesthetics were now being taken seriously at an institutional level. 'It is right at such a time of peace, after the struggle, to bury the hatchet – in the side of the enemy – and leave it there,' Whistler proclaimed. '[T]he congratulations usher in the beginning of my career, for an artist's career always begins tomorrow.'[15]

Meanwhile, back in Tite Street a new vacancy had opened at No. 44. Frank Miles had found success as a society portraitist and as artist-in-chief to *Life* magazine but by the mid-1880s, Miles had begun to show more interest in his garden than his studio, becoming all but a recluse gardener in Tite Street, renouncing the idea that 'art is for art's sake'.[16] Interest in his 'prettily drawn heads' had also declined. Even Ruskin, when asked 'what he thought of' Miles's work allegedly responded, 'I think nothing of them.'[17]

The handsome, golden-haired Miles, suffering from syphilis, admitted himself in to the Brislington House asylum near Bristol and died there two years later in 1890. The studio-house in Tite Street remained empty and unloved for over six years until the artist and illustrator George Percy Jacomb-Hood came to the rescue. Miles's Trustees had tried to sell the house, but the reserve had never been reached at auction. Jacomb-Hood, who had been crammed into nearby Merton Villas in Manresa Road, convinced his father to buy the lease outright, which he did, and then rented the house to his son.[18]

Jacomb-Hood's new property, empty since 1888, was more Miss Havisham than Mr Miles, and in much need of repair. He was sensitive to Godwin's designs which had remained mostly intact. He also found numerous surprises in the house from the days of Miles's occupancy. He uncovered a 'concealed staircase' that 'led down from the studio to a room opening on to the main staircase,' which later served as a 'convenient bolt-hole for a sitter from any unwelcome visitor,' and was no doubt used by Miles, and Wilde, on many occasions.[19]

Other secrets emerged too. One day a visitor to Tite Street introduced herself as Sally Higgs, Miles's former model. Higgs had been discovered by Miles working as a flower girl at Victoria Station and was later trained by him as a model and installed in the Tite Street studio where 'she acted as attendant at his "studio teas", dressed in a Japanese kimono.'[20] Now, several years after Miles's death, she returned to Tite Street and called at the house that she might 'be allowed to see again the scene of her triumphs and happiness'.[21] Higgs told Jacomb-Hood many 'tales' about Frank Miles and Oscar Wilde, who had lived with him briefly almost fifteen years before.

George Percy Jacomb-Hood was a founding member of the New English Arts Club and Honorary Treasurer of the newly formed Chelsea Arts Club. He had studied at the Slade with Marian Huxley, wife of John Collier. Collier later recommended Jacomb-Hood to study with his former tutor, Jean-Paul Laurens, in Paris. Jacomb-Hood had worked with Walter Crane to illustrate Oscar Wilde's *The Happy Prince and Other Stories*, published in 1888. A steady and regular income was earned working as an illustrator for numerous publications. He started his professional drawing career for the *Illustrated London News*, later worked for *Black and White,* and was finally enlisted into William Luson Thomas's *Graphic* army.

Working as an illustrator for *The Graphic* meant that Jacomb-Hood spent extended periods away from Tite Street, often being sent on commissions to the far-flung corners of the Empire with his sketch-pad and pencils. While away on one such expedition, Jacomb-Hood offered William Rothenstein the exclusive use of his Tite Street studio. For the first time since the early days of Miles and Wilde, Keats House was once again a hive of artistic activity.

Rothenstein settled in to Keats House in the few short weeks he was resident in Tite Street. A visitor to the studio recalls the impressions of 'two candles, a great luminous twilight and the curly cub of an artist, chattering incessantly as a bird sings.'[22] Rothenstein was 'blessed in his poverty, lunching on an egg and some marmalade and then taking a box for *The Second Mrs Tanqueray*.'[23] Rothenstein infiltrated the dynamic coterie of Chelsea artists. 'The men who counted most for me lived [in Chelsea],' he wrote, 'Sickert, Steer, Ricketts and Shannon. The name itself, soft and creamy, suggested … Whistler's early etchings, Cremorne, old courts and rag-shops.'[24]

Years earlier Rothenstein had met Oscar Wilde in Paris and when he eventually arrived in Chelsea, Wilde introduced him to local artists Charles Ricketts and Charles Shannon who were publishing their art journal the *Dial* and lived in the same house that Whistler had occupied in The Vale, around the corner from Tite Street. Ricketts and Shannon were

William Rothenstein by John Singer Sargent, 1897

considered more 'austere' in the Chelsea arts community, and they preferred to operate independently of the New English Arts Club circle. They had strong connections with Tite Street, designing or illustrating a number of Wilde's works, including a volume of his short stories, *Lord Arthur Savile's Crime and Other Stories* and *The Sphinx*.

The Climax, illustration from Oscar Wilde's *Salomé* by Aubrey Beardsley, 1893

In Paris, Rothenstein had met and befriended the Anglo-Australian artist Charles Conder and Max Beerbohm. At No. 44 Tite Street, they all came together in Rothenstein's borrowed studio, together with a host of other artists including Philip Wilson Steer, Charles Wellington Furse, Walter Sickert and D.S. MacColl.

In the 1890s, Chelsea, and Tite Street, became the spiritual centre of a new religion of decadent 'New Hedonism'. Begun in Paris with the work of Théophile Gautier, Charles Baudelaire and more recently Joris-Karl Huysmans' *A Rebours*, French decadence was manifest on British shores in Swinburne's *Poems and Ballads*, Walter Pater's *Renaissance*, and Oscar Wilde's *The Picture of Dorian Gray* and his newest play, *Salomé*. Experience and pleasure were celebrated over pragmatic toil and almost always with a homoerotic undertone. The characters of Tite Street were not a far cry from Huysmans' decadent Des Esseintes or Dorian Gray, who lived for experience alone as Pater recommended, 'to burn always with this hard, gem-like flame, to maintain this ecstasy, is success in life.'[25]

After *Dorian Gray*, Wilde attempted a decadent drama, *Salomé*, in which he depicts a famous femme fatale as a cold and seductive virgin lusting for the head of John the Baptist so that she can kiss it on the mouth and gratify her desire. A new print edition of the play was to be published by John Lane in 1894, and a tall, gaunt, hook-nosed illustrator named Aubrey Beardsley was selected to illustrate it. Beardsley was born in Brighton but later moved to London, and in 1892 went to Paris where he befriended Rothenstein, whose work he praised. In Paris, Beardsley, much like Whistler several generations before, acquired a taste for Japanese prints and the work of Toulouse-Lautrec which would come to influence his future work.

Beardsley had already illustrated a number of well-known works, including Thomas Malory's *Le Morte d'Arthur*, with his unique style of black and white illustrations. Beardsley also helped to co-found the *Yellow Book*, published between 1894 and 1897 by Elkin Matthews and John Lane. Along with Ricketts and Shannon's *Dial*, the *Yellow Book* became one of the leading journals of the aesthetic movement in the 1890s with artistic contributions from Charles Conder, Rothenstein, Sickert and Steer.

In this milieu of the decadent Nineties, Jacomb-Hood and Rothenstein were drawn to Tite Street to live and work in the shadows of great giants like Whistler, Wilde and Sargent. Though Rothenstein was not as accomplished as his neighbours he was inclined to think he and the other young artists 'had qualities that somehow placed us among the essential artists'.[26] Jacomb-Hood regarded Sargent with complete reverence. When Sargent mentioned to Jacomb-Hood that he admired a picture by Rothenstein, Jacomb-Hood arranged an introduction so that the praise could be heard 'from his own lips'.[27]

Sargent invited Rothenstein to his studio. After lunch they both started working on sketching a nude, Sargent monitored the younger artist's work but noticed that his neighbour was 'insufficiently trained' and set about to help him. Rothenstein 'was glad enough of the chance to see Sargent at work,' he later admitted, but 'Sargent's reticence

Diana of the Uplands by Charles Wellington Furse, 1903–4

prevented his telling me how bad my painting was, and I was too stupid and conceited to see that here was a chance of acquiring the constructive practice I lacked, and above all, a scientific method of work.'[28] Younger artists were often intimidated by Sargent, and many, including Jacomb-Hood and Rothenstein, put him on a pedestal. Despite this, or perhaps because of it, Rothenstein believed that Sargent 'remained outside the charmed circle' of 'great artists' in Chelsea.[29]

At the centre of this charmed circle of great artists in the 1890s was the 'boisterous' painter Charles Wellington Furse, who used Sargent's studio at No. 33. Furse was already friends with fellow Tite Street artists before he arrived as one of the founding members of the New English Art Club. With Furse, the studios at No. 33 came to life again. Like Whistler before him, Furse loved an audience and enjoyed having people coming into the studio while he was painting, to discuss his work and make suggestions. Whenever he at work, the studio would be full of 'generals, admirals, distinguished and admiring ladies, painters and poets,' while 'he strode up and down, working away with huge brushes and boisterous energy.'[30]

Soon it became clear that Furse was working under the direct influence of his neighbour. 'Sargent's studio has an inspiring light,' he wrote, and 'some of the great man's spirit seems to hang around, though I have not seen much sign of its descent on my pictures.'[31] The influence can be seen in his large oil painting of *R. Allison Esq., Master of the North Hereford*, exhibited at the New English Art Club in 1893, with his free brushstrokes together with lighter colour and strong highlights.

According to critics, however, it was Whistler's spirit, not Sargent's, that resonated most strongly in Furse's pictures. The light and space at No. 33 allowed Furse to work on some equestrian commissions, and he received great praise for his monumental equestrian portrait of the Boer War hero, *Field Marshal Earl Roberts on his Charger 'Vonolel'*, for the Royal Academy exhibition of 1894. Furse 'has entered on a new stage,' wrote the *Magazine of Art*. 'Hitherto he has given us reminiscences of Whistler but never failed to let us feel that he was worthy of something better. This year he has gone to Velazquez . . . the result is a tender harmony of grey-greens, yellows, and flesh pink, with a charming sky and a delicate relief in the red flag carried behind.' 'The hope is encouraged by this year's exhibit,' they continue, 'that in the near future Mr Furse may go further still and from the memories of Whistler, Stubbs and Velazquez he may arise as Mr Furse himself.'[32]

At Furse's Tite Street studio the artists, writers and bohemians of Chelsea gathered as they had done in the days of Whistler's raucous Sunday brunches, and it was there that Rothenstein met the budding poet Laurence Binyon when Furse 'flung' the two together, 'Binyon! Rothenstein! Don't you know one another? Two decadents!'[33] Binyon was a Tite Street poet a decade before he actually moved to the street in May 1904, where he lived in No. 8 above the post office on the corner of Royal Hospital Road. With his 1896 volume, *London Visions*, Binyon synthesises Baudelaire's *Les Fleurs du mal* with the 'art for art's sake' creeds of Whistler and Wilde to encompass a unique vision of the decadent London of the 1890s.

One reviewer called his poems 'Twelve genuine things cut out of the heart of London life,' observing that no other modern poet 'has put so much of actual London into his poetry.'[34] While Rothenstein thought he was 'a true poet,' Bernard Muddiman declared that Binyon had 'rediscovered, through Whistler, London for art.'[35]

By the time his *Second Book of London Visions* appeared in 1899, *Dome* celebrated Binyon as one of the 'high priests' of the 'cult of London', with *London Visions* ranking high among its 'canonical scriptures'[36] for its 'power of making us see pictures.'[37] Binyon shared, along with other New Decadents like Arthur Symons, a 'wonderful spirit of camaraderie' and had, along with the other younger men, created a synergistic energy 'from this meeting together in London.' 'The romance of a great city is so generally tragic, so often merely sordid, that the finding in it of some tender, mysterious beauty has the aspect of deliberate fiction. The wonderful thing is, that the beauty should really be there; that the Thames can be as exquisite as Mr Whistler has made it appear in paint.'[38]

Meanwhile Furse, actively working at No. 33, 'with his high spirits and genial faith in his artistic and social security, behaved like a kind of elder brother' to the charmed circle of Tite Street.[39] Sharing in his 'high spirits' was his young fiancée Eleanor Butcher, who also came to Tite Street. Eleanor was a 'light-hearted and witty' personality who had a *joie de vivre* spirit and would often burst into Jacomb-Hood's house at No. 44 in the evening demanding tea and toast and stay into the late hours. Eleanor's frivolity was, however, tragically cut short when she died of tuberculosis. Furse himself had also begun to suffer failing health and left Tite Street in 1898 to spend his winters in Greece. While travelling in Switzerland, Furse met a young woman named Katherine, daughter of the poet and critic John Addington Symonds. Katherine and Furse married, and she became the model for his most celebrated work, *Diana of the Uplands*. Here, Furse transports the Greek goddess into a contemporary pastoral setting. He 'had the design of the wind-blown figure in his mind and knew exactly what he wished to produce,' recalled Katherine.[40] In 1904, Furse was elected an Associate of the Royal Academy, but later that year he died of tuberculosis. A memorial exhibition was held at the Burlington Fine Arts Club in 1906. Sargent was on the committee for the exhibition and also helped to complete his unfinished work and sell his studio pictures. Katherine Furse would go on to establish the Voluntary Aid Detachment during the First World War.

By the turn of the century the vogue for grandiose history paintings was waning. A new trend in subject painting had taken centre stage, a genre pioneered by the former Tite Street artist, John Collier. The 'problem picture' made its debut in the late 1890s and became a staple of Royal Academy exhibitions well into the twentieth century. Classical mythology, medieval allegories, and the tragedies of Shakespeare were transplanted into the Edwardian drawing-room. Collier's penchant for wild women of Greek myth faded when he left Tite Street. A decade later his fierce femmes fatales were transposed into modern-day Edwardian women.

Perhaps one of the most blatant in the genre of the problem picture was his 1902 painting, *A Confession*, in which a wan, emaciated woman, apparently in the last stage of illness, is

The Doll's House by William Rothenstein, 1899–1900

Group Portrait by William Rothenstein, 1894: D.S. MacColl, Charles Wellington Furse, Max Beerbohm, Philip Wilson Steer and Walter Sickert

telling her story to a saddened man who is sitting with his face in shadow, his head resting on his hand. Collier's problem pictures are essentially illustrative in the sense that they depict a particular moment of high drama or climax in a narrative in minute detail, but ultimately they leave questions unanswered to be considered by viewers.

'Art is surface and symbol,' Wilde once wrote. 'Those who go beneath the surface do so at their own peril.'[41] Collier and his curious public eagerly delved beneath the surface. Debates were opened as a piqued public tried to solve the 'problem pictures'. The details of middle- and-upper-class domestic struggles – addictions, affairs and divorce – were now laid bare on canvas. By the late 1880s and 1890s a small number of artists, including Walter Sickert, Sidney Starr and William Rothenstein, began painting scenes of modern urban life in a manner influenced by Manet, Whistler and Degas.

Sickert delved into the real-world of the music hall and the areas around Camden Town. Rothenstein followed, in 1899, with *The Doll's House*, taken from Ibsen's 1879 play of the same title. The painting depicts the climax of the drama in Act III, during a dance at the Helmers' house, with Augustus John modelled as Krogstad and Alice Rothenstein as Mrs Linde. Augustus John wrote, 'The picture will remain a perpetual enigma, to disturb, fascinate or repel . . . [it points to] Rothenstein's essential romanticism and his *penchant* for the dramatic.'[42]

It was this '*penchant* for the dramatic' that made the genre of problem pictures so appealing to late Victorian audiences. 'I essentially seek out subjects in which the human note is strong,' Collier wrote. He took his subjects, 'from modern life, for, after all, it is our own life which appeals to us more than anything in the dead and gone past.'[43]

The charmed circle of great artists represented a renewed energy in art in the 1890s. Their camaraderie in the studios of Chelsea forged a new direction of forward-thinking, avant-garde aesthetics. Merging the ideas of their French forebears with the decadent maxims of Pater and Wilde, these new bohemians carried the torch of aestheticism into the twentieth century. Rothenstein's portrait of the dark interior of No. 44 Tite Street captured this moment. In *Group Portrait* Rothenstein arranges Philip Wilson Steer, Charles Furse, Walter Sickert, D.S. MacColl and Max Beerbohm in darkness, illuminated by a single light source in a studio once belonging to Frank Miles. From the dim background, faintly recognisable, Godwin's Japanese inglenook emerges, a relic of the not-too-distant past glories of Tite Street and its aesthetes. The portrait, in the same spirit as Fantin-Latour's *Homage to Delacroix* or later *Homage to Manet*, captures the fresh vitality and spirit of the New English Arts Club generation, following in the wake of Whistler.

21.

PLAYS, PANTHERS
& PRISON

...the fall of Wilde killed the age.
– Bernard Muddiman

One afternoon in late June 1891 Oscar Wilde had a young man over for tea in Tite Street, and a few days later at lunch he gave him a book. At the time it was perhaps one of the least significant events in the street's history, and yet it would become one of the most fateful. Within ten years of that June day both Oscar and his wife Constance would be dead, their possessions in Tite Street ransacked and sold, and their two children entrusted to the care of relatives. The book was *The Picture of Dorian Gray*, and the young man was Lord Alfred 'Bosie' Douglas.

An expanded second edition of *Dorian Gray* had been published in book form in 1891. The novel was denigrated as 'immoral'. Wilde struck back, saying that 'It is poisonous if you like, but you cannot deny that it is also perfect, and perfection is what we artists aim at.'[1] Perfect or not, the publication had taken a toll on the social life of No. 34. Constance complained that 'since Oscar wrote *Dorian Gray*, no one will speak to us'.[2] Wilde's mother, however, raved that 'it is the most wonderful piece of writing' and enjoyed it so much that she 'nearly fainted at the last scene'.[3]

Life for the Wildes soon returned to normal. The backlash from *Dorian Gray* was short-lived, and soon their home was alive again with social activity. Constance meanwhile had taken up a few charity projects and was making visits to the poor residents of Paradise Walk. Word of her good deeds spread quickly and it was not long before the residents of Paradise Walk found their way to the white front door of No. 34 Tite Street. 'I see a great deal now of Paradise Walk,' she wrote, 'but I feel hopeless to do anything there ... they all come to me now to help them.'[4]

Wilde was soon engaged in his next venture. Actor turned theatre manager George Alexander had recently taken control of the St James's Theatre on King Street and had approached Wilde for a play. Wilde had done very little work for theatre since his early days, so he offered his previously penned play *The Duchess of Padua*. Alexander turned it down on the basis that it would cost too much for scenery. In July 1890 Alexander had offered Wilde £50 in advance on a new play to be written by January, and Wilde, in need of funds, accepted the offer. As the months passed a new play was not forthcoming, and when Wilde tried to return the advance it was shrewdly declined.

A year after his first social visit, Douglas returned to Tite Street. After a dinner at the Savoy and evening at the theatre, Wilde and Douglas stumbled back at about two o'clock in the morning. With Constance and the children away, Wilde persuaded Douglas to stay the night in the spare bedroom on the second floor, where they did 'what was done among boys at Winchester and Oxford'.[5]

Whatever happened in the spare room in Tite Street, it evidently reinvigorated Wilde's theatrical imagination. That summer an idea came to him for a new play. 'I wonder can I do it in a week, or will it take three?' he mused to Frank Harris. 'It ought not to take long to beat the Pineros and the Joneses.'[6] Wilde escaped to the Lakes to work on the play. *Lady Windermere's Fan* was finished in October. 'Did you like it?' Wilde asked Alexander after he had submitted the play. 'Like is not the word,' Alexander replied, 'it is simply wonderful.'[7] The play opened in February 1892 at the St James's Theatre to a sold-out house.

In the 1880s Wilde had flirted with writing just as he had flirted with Harry Marillier, but by the 1890s it was a full-blown affair. A year after the success of *Lady Windermere's Fan*, Wilde was putting the finishing touches to another play, *A Woman of No Importance*, and by March 1893 it was in rehearsal with leading West End star Herbert Beerbohm Tree. The success of his two plays meant that Wilde was earning an income of over £100 per week, and for once light broke through the dark clouds of unending debt that were hanging over No. 34 Tite Street. For the first time since Wilde left as editor of *The Woman's World*, finances were balanced. But Wilde's literary and financial success was shadowed by a growing intimacy with Douglas. Wilde's adoration for Douglas was blind and absolute. Less than ten years after his marriage vows to Constance, Wilde had altogether abandoned domestic life and had taken to staying at hotels on the pretence that he worked on plays without distractions. And write he did. Within the space of two years he managed to pen three plays, including *Salomé*, which Douglas translated into English from Wilde's French.

But Wilde did more than write. He had cast aside home life for closer intimacy with Douglas. Douglas was young and had an aristocratic confidence and more sexual bravado than Wilde, but more importantly he had connections, connections to many male brothels, including an establishment in Little College Street. There Wilde was enraptured by the beautiful young Sirens luring him towards jagged shoals. A crash was inevitable. 'It was like feasting with panthers,' Wilde later confessed. 'The danger was half the excitement.'[8]

Oscar Wilde and Lord Alfred 'Bosie' Douglas, *c.*1894

In early 1893, Wilde brazenly invited a series of young men to dinner, and in some cases he brought them back to Tite Street for sex. In January, Alfred Taylor visited Tite Street with Wilde, and in March, a clerk at John Lane publishers, a man named Edward Shelley, was also brought to the House Beautiful. There was also an unemployed valet named Charles Parker who would later testify that Wilde had 'committed acts of sodomy' upon him.

Wilde had also begun paying visits to Mrs Robinson, a fashionable fortune teller whom he called 'Sibyl of Mortimer Street'. Her predictions consoled Wilde. In 1894, she told him that he and Bosie would travel on a long voyage together, adding that Bosie's 'lovely life goes always hand in hand with' Wilde's. But her predictions could also take on a more sober note. 'I see a very brilliant life for you,' she told Wilde, 'Then I see a wall. Beyond the wall I see nothing.'[9]

Back in Tite Street dust had begun to settle, and the house sat empty and unused for longer and longer periods of time. Between her charitable ventures in Chelsea and visits to her friends and family in the country, Constance spent a great deal of time away from Tite Street and so did Oscar. The domestic life that No. 34 embodied had now lost its appeal. His new home became the hotels and clubs of the West End with Tite Street there as a safety net. Constance often dined alone at home. When William Rothenstein went to dinner at No. 34 in 1894, he found Constance 'wistful and a little sad'.[10]

With his professional life now based around the West End and St James's, Tite Street became a conveniently inconvenient distance, even though he had travelled much further to work at *The Woman's World*. Oscar later admitted that he had occupied 'rooms at St James's Place, which I took for the purpose of my literary work, it being quite out of the question to secure quiet and mental repose at my own house when my two young sons were at home,'[11] a polite way of saying he had grown tired of family life.

Seeing so little of her husband, Constance travelled across London to the Savoy Hotel where Wilde had taken a room with Douglas. She gave Wilde his post but was not invited into the room. From the corridor, she was forced to ask her husband why he had not been home in so long. The children missed him. Wilde smiled warmly and said he had forgotten the number of his house. In spite of her heartache she just gave a slight laugh as tears streamed down her face. She drove back to Tite Street alone to a cold bed above which hung a star, Wilde's star, which he believed would protect him against malignity.

Both Wilde and Tite Street remained vulnerable. While the Wildes were away in August 1891, No. 34 had been burgled and some valuable items belonging to Constance were stolen. The burglars were later apprehended. Just two years after this incident, during another prolonged absence, Tite Street was burgled for a second time, but this time with more sinister motives. Nothing in the house was reported stolen, but Wilde's association with young male prostitutes had exposed him to blackmail. Wilde was no stranger to blackmail. In 1893 he thwarted the efforts of Alfred Wood, one of many boys he had taken to No. 34 for sex while Constance was away.[12] Being famous made Wilde a more fruitful target. A simple love letter from Wilde to Douglas could be hugely rewarding, and so his home would have seemed like a treasure trove for potential blackmailers.

Through 1893 the Wildes had hardly seen one another, but towards the end of the year the dark clouds lifted momentarily. Douglas, now out of Oxford, and with nothing to show for himself but a translated version of *Salomé* and a seemingly poisonous relationship with Wilde, was being sent by his mother to Cairo. When Constance heard, she returned to Tite Street in a desperate attempt to thaw the marital frost and make a warm nest for Oscar. Wilde returned to his wife and for nearly four months they lived again in peace. Wilde was also thoroughly distracted in writing his next play, *An Ideal Husband*.

Wilde took some time to attend to his friends. He introduced young William Rothenstein to his friends Ricketts and Shannon, and he gatecrashed the Society of Portrait Painters exhibition. Meanwhile, in February 1894 a telegram from Douglas arrived at Tite Street asking Constance to reconcile him with Oscar, who was not answering his letters. Constance assented to the request and asked her husband to meet Douglas in Paris. With the blessing of his wife, Oscar set off for Paris still resolute not to fall back into Douglas's arms.

Wilde returned to Tite Street in late April but he was icy. Events had taken place that would change the course of Wilde's life and the future of Tite Street forever. Back in November 1892 Wilde had been introduced to Douglas's domineering father, the Marquess of Queensberry. The trio shared lunch at the Cafe Royal. Initially the Marquess scowled at his son's 'corrupter' under his brushy eyebrows, but as the evening wore on his Scottish ruggedness was soon smoothed by Wilde's Irish charm. 'I don't wonder you are so fond of him,' he said to Douglas, 'he is a wonderful man.'[13] However, when he was away from Wilde's loquacious wit, he returned to his formidable self. On the journey home he had changed his mind and forbade his son ever to see Wilde again.

For several months things seemed to cool between father, son and lover. At No. 34, Wilde had hired a new valet, a young man named Arthur Fenn, a mere teenager, referred to by Wilde affectionately as 'Ginger'. On the morning of 30 June, a carriage pulled up outside the house. While Wilde was quietly tucked away in his library, there was a knock at the door, and Arthur benignly answered it. The belligerent Marquess stormed into Wilde's library, 'waving his small hands in the air in epileptic fury . . . with his bully, or his friend, between us, had stood uttering every foul word his foul mind could think of, and screaming the loathsome threats he afterwards with such cunning carried out.'[14]

The pressure of a hawkish Marquess, predatory blackmailers, an unhappy wife, and an ever more demanding lover were not enough to deter Wilde from writing. From August to October the Wildes removed to Worthing far from the chaos of London, but they were not alone. Douglas followed. Wilde wrote to Jacomb-Hood from Worthing, 'have you been painting charming things this summer? I have just finished a new play.'[15]

In December Wilde's play, *An Ideal Husband*, had gone into rehearsal and opened at the Haymarket Theatre on 3 January. A few weeks later, on 19 January, the *Pall Mall Gazette* reported that, 'The Prince of Wales, accompanied by Princess Louise, Duchess of Fife, witness the performance of *An Ideal Husband* at the Haymarket Theatre last evening.'[16] Wilde's old acquaintance the Prince of Wales ordered Wilde not to 'alter a single line' of the play, to which Wilde allegedly replied, 'Sire, your wish is my command,' commending Britain for being such a 'splendid country where princes understand poets'.[17]

The success and acclaim of *An Ideal Husband* was soon eclipsed by Wilde's newest play *The Importance of Being Earnest* which went directly into rehearsals at the St James's Theatre. On St Valentine's Day 1895, *Earnest* opened. The Marquess of Queensberry, determined to make a public spectacle and embarrass Wilde and his son, tried to force entry but was barred and left a bouquet of rotten vegetables by the stage door.

Wilde had already received offensive letters from the Marquess at Tite Street, but on the morning of 28 February 1895 he intercepted a card left at his club in Albemarle Street. The porter handed him the card left by Queensberry, with a handwritten note 'To Oscar Wilde posing Somdomite' [sic]. Wilde wrote to his old friend and former lover Robbie Ross, 'Bosie's father has left a card at my club with hideous words on it. I don't see anything now but a criminal prosecution.'[18]

Ross urged Wilde not to take action, but Wilde would not relent. Ross suggested he go to his solicitor, Charles Humphreys. Douglas was thrilled with the result, the Marquess had finally put something down in writing and he looked forward to his father's public humiliation. Ross, however, knew that a criminal prosecution could unearth secrets about Wilde's own criminal life.

With a series of hit plays, and earning an impressive income, Wilde may have felt invincible, and his confidence may have been fuelled by Bosie's demands. Wilde launched a libel trial against Queensberry. The defendant's barrister, Edward Carson, a former student alongside Wilde, sought damning evidence against his former classmate with 'all the bitterness of an old friend'.[19] He did not have to go far to find it. At the 'top flat at 13 Little College Street' he was able to procure more evidence than he required. There he found a register of all the boys with whom Wilde had previously consorted. Wilde's friends meanwhile pleaded with him to drop the case, but Douglas urged his lover to continue.

The trial opened on April 3, 1895 at the Old Bailey, but it quickly turned into a massacre. The defence turned on the prosecution with brute force not only clearing the Marquess of libel, but launching a rebuttal attack on Wilde, supported by shocking 'filth' and incontrovertible evidence. Wilde withdrew from the libel action and the jury were then instructed by the judge to find the defendant, Queensberry, not guilty. Justice Henn Collins wrote to the defence counsel, Carson, 'I never heard a more powerful speech nor a more searching crossXam [sic]. I congratulate you on having escaped the rest of the filth.'[20] Wilde coolly left the courtroom and went immediately to the Cadogan Hotel with Robbie Ross.

Reggie Turner joined them. Fearing the worst, Ross and Turner urged Wilde to flee to Paris, but he remained.

At five o'clock a reporter arrived and told Ross that the warrant for Wilde's arrest had been issued. When Ross relayed the message, 'Wilde went very grey in the face'. But he was defiant, 'I shall stay and do my sentence whatever it is.'[21] It was not long before the police were knocking on the door and Wilde was carted off to Bow Street. His thoughts immediately turned to Tite Street. When Wilde realised he was going to be arrested he sent a letter to No. 34, 'Allow no one to enter my bedroom or sitting room – except servants – today. See no one but your friends.'[22] Robbie Ross went off to break the news to Constance, who was staying with her great aunt Mary Napier in Lower Seymour Street.

With Wilde behind bars the vultures began circling No. 34, now nothing more than a shell of a once-cosy family home. Wilde was already unpopular among the maids and servants of the neighbourhood. When Christabel Macnaughten's nursemaid told her employer 'that dreadful Mr Wilde stopped me again today and talked to Baby and she smiled at him,' her mother replied, 'I'm sure Mr Wilde won't do Baby any *harm*, and in life it is important to smile.'[23] George Percy Jacomb-Hood remembers the maids of Chelsea walking along Tite Street with loot they had stolen from the Wilde's house. Wilde had accrued many debts and suddenly everyone wanted their dues. The landlord who owned the freehold on No. 34 came to Constance demanding that the ground rent be paid. Philip Burne-Jones, son of the painter, came to Constance's aid, 'If the landlord means to distrain for rent,' he advised, 'let him – don't think about the house in Tite Street again – simply leave it.'[24]

An auction at No. 34 was scheduled for 24 April. By that time, the Wilde's home had been thoroughly ransacked by thugs and hoodlums. All of Wilde's first editions, with his personal inscriptions to Constance and the children, had vanished, as had all his letters to Constance. Arthur Fenn, Wilde's valet, helped Ross break into the library to retrieve some books and letters on the day of the arrest, and later, at the auction they tried to salvage as much as possible. Constance also saved what she could, but in the chaos and confusion leading up to the dreaded day, she had no time to salvage or collect any of the children's belongings. 'For months afterwards,' Vyvyan recalls, 'my brother and I kept asking for our soldiers, our trains and our toys, and we could not understand why it upset our mother.'[25] It would be several years before he finally saw in a catalogue of auctioned items that day that lot 237 was 'A very large quantity of toys,' which realised the meagre amount of thirty shillings.[26]

Two days after the humiliating auction of his personal effects, Wilde's first trial began, but the jury could not reach an agreement. Wilde was eventually granted bail. Ross took him to a hotel, but no one would receive him as the Marquess had sent thugs around London to whip up a campaign against him. For once Oscar was truly homeless and alone, but finally he appealed to his brother Willie, living with his mother in Oakley Street, around the corner from Tite Street. Constance, meanwhile, was preparing for a formal separation from her

BY ORDER OF THE SHERIFF.

A.D. 1895.   No. 6907

16, Tite Street, Chelsea.

Catalogue of the Library of

Valuable Books,

Pictures, Portraits of Celebrities, Arundel Society Prints,

HOUSEHOLD FURNITURE

CARLYLE'S WRITING TABLE,

Chippendale and Italian Chairs, Old Persian Carpets
and Rugs, Brass Fenders,

Moorish and Oriental Curiosities,

Embroideries, Silver and Plated Articles,

OLD BLUE AND WHITE CHINA,

Moorish Pottery, Handsome Ormolu Clock,
and numerous Effects :

Which will be Sold by Auction,

By Mr. BULLOCK,

ON THE PREMISES,

On Wednesday, April 24th, 1895,

AT ONE O'CLOCK.

May be Viewed the day prior, and Catalogues had of Messrs. CLARKE & Co.
16, Portugal Street, Lincoln's Inn ; and of the Auctioneer,

211 HIGH HOLBORN, W.C.

Announcement of the sale of the contents of No. 16 (now 34) Tite Street, the
home of Oscar Wilde, April 1895

husband and had plans to take her boys to the Continent and change their names in hope that scandal would not follow them.

A fresh trial was ordered which began on 20 May. The trial was presided over by the Hon. Justice Wills who, ironically, lived in Tite Street. Wilde's past, his early days in Tite Street, his friendships, love affairs, even his own literature was put on trial, and he was forced to defend them. It was revealed that Wilde had welcomed a few 'dear boys' back to his home. One of them, a former valet named Charles Parker confessed that Wilde had taken him to dinner at Kettner's in Soho one evening in early 1893 and then took him back to Tite Street. Around the same time, Wilde had invited a young clerk, Alfred Wood, to a champagne dinner and afterwards he, 'went with Mr Wilde to 16 [now 34] Tite Street . . . Mr Wilde let himself in with a latchkey'. They went up to Wilde's bedroom where the 'grossest indecency occurred'.[27]

The prosecution was ruthless. Wilde was forced into an impassioned defence. 'What is the 'Love that dare not speak its name?' demanded the prosecution, referring to a poem by Alfred Douglas. 'The Love that dare not speak its name,' replied Wilde, 'in this century is such a great affection of an elder for a younger man as there was between David and Jonathan, such as Plato made the very basis of his philosophy, and such as you find in the sonnets of Michelangelo and Shakespeare. It is that deep, spiritual affection that is as pure as it is perfect . . . It is in this century misunderstood, so much misunderstood . . . It is beautiful, it is fine, it is the noblest form of affection. There is nothing unnatural about it. It is intellectual, and it repeatedly exists between an elder and a younger man, when the elder man has intellect, and the younger man has all the joy, hope and glamour of life before him. That it should be so the world does not understand. The world mocks at it and sometimes puts one in the pillory for it.'[28]

'You must not act upon suspicion or prejudice,' Wilde's defence lawyer told the jury, 'but upon an examination of the facts, gentlemen, and on the facts, I respectfully urge that Mr Wilde is entitled to claim from you a verdict of acquittal . . . the brilliant promise which has been clouded by these accusations, and the bright reputation which was so nearly quenched in the torrent of prejudice . . . have been saved by your verdict from absolute ruin . . . a distinguished man of letters and a brilliant Irishman . . . to give in the maturity of his genius gifts to our literature, of which he has given only the promise in his early youth.'[29]

The jury returned its verdict. Justice Wills addressed Wilde. 'It is no use for me to address you,' he said, '[P]eople who can do these things must be dead to all sense of shame, and one cannot hope to produce any effect upon them. It is the worst case I have ever tried . . . . That you, Wilde, have been the centre of a circle of extensive corruption of the most hideous kind among young men, it is equally impossible to doubt.' 'And I?' replied Wilde, aghast. 'May I say nothing, my Lord?'[30]

But there was nothing more to say, or at least, nothing more anyone in the courtroom wished to hear. The great aesthete was finally silenced by the sound of a gavel and cries of 'shame' from a courtroom. The Marquess of Queensberry watched with glib satisfaction as Wilde faltered over the verdict 'Guilty; Two Years' Hard Labour'. Wilde was escorted out of the courtroom and hauled off to prison as the 'harlots in the street outside danced upon the pavement'.[31]

For almost eleven years No. 34 had been a home for the Wildes. Even when Constance was away and Wilde was at the Savoy, it was always there as a safe refuge awaiting their return. But not any more. With the house sold, Constance and her two boys began an unsettled existence relying on the kindness of friends and strangers. England was no longer a suitable place to raise her children, especially as the Wilde name was now a byword for immorality and sin. The plug was finally pulled and even though their closest friends had tried their best to stop the flow, all the wealth, fame and prestige Wilde had achieved simply washed down the drain.

Wilde had left Tite Street twice in his life. The first in 1881, when he had broken an antique table; the second in 1895, when he had broken hearts. On 29 February 29 1896, Constance visited her solicitors and made a new will in which she gave over her whole estate to Adrian Hope, at No. 52 Tite Street, with the wish that in the event of her death he would invest her assets in trust for Cyril and Vyvyan and also that he should be the boys' guardian and have sole control over them. Despite everything, Constance remained loyal to Oscar. She agreed to give him £150 a year as an allowance when he was released from prison, and she even travelled to England in 1896 to tell him in person about his mother's death. By 1898 Constance would be dead and buried in Genoa.

'I don't regret for a single moment having lived for pleasure,' Wilde recalled in *De Profundis*, a letter to Douglas written from Reading Gaol. 'I did it to the full, as one should do everything that one does. There was no pleasure I did not experience. I threw the pearl of my soul into a cup of wine. I went down the primrose path to the sound of flutes. I lived on honeycomb. But to have continued the same life would have been wrong because it would have been limiting. I had to pass on. The other half of the garden had its secrets for me also.'[32]

After two years of hard labour, Wilde was released back into society. 'All trials are trials for one's life,' he wrote from prison, 'just as all sentences are sentences of death; and three times have I been tried. The first time I left the box to be arrested, the second time to be led back to the house of detention, the third time to pass into a prison for two years.'[33] But release from prison was not the end of his woes. Mrs Robinson's prophecy, made years earlier, had come true – Wilde had reached the wall. There was nothing beyond.

22.

ABBEY &
the LODGE

The lamps and the plane-trees, following the line of the
embankment, struck a note of dignity that is rare in English cities.
The seats, almost deserted, were here and there occupied by
gentlefolk in evening dress, who had strolled out from the houses
behind to enjoy fresh air and the whisper of the rising tide. There
is something continental about Chelsea Embankment.
– E.M. Forster, *Howards End*, 1910

After being released from prison, Wilde went into exile, travelling to Italy and finally to Paris, where he would occasionally see his former Tite Street friends and neighbours. Upon entering a restaurant Wilde came face to face with Whistler, commenting under his breath how old the painter now looked. 'My sentence and imprisonment raised Jimmy's opinion of England and the English.'[1] Whistler snidely quipped that his old 'sparring partner' was busy 'working on *The Bugger's Opera*'.[2] William Rothenstein and his wife took Wilde to dinner only to find him flirting with the waiter. When they passed him again on the street, they pretended not to see him.

'Society, as we have constituted it, will have no place for me,' Wilde predicted. 'Nature,' he believed, 'whose sweet rains fall on unjust and just alike, will have clefts in the rocks where I may hide, and secret valleys in whose silence I may weep undisturbed. She will hang the night with stars so that I may walk abroad in the darkness without stumbling, and send the wind over my footprints so that none may track me to my hurt: she will cleanse me in great waters, and with bitter herbs make me whole.'[3]

Nature, however, could not make Wilde whole again. He was now disgraced and destitute. His new home was an old Parisian hotel room. There he died on 30 November 1900. After the jubilant days of Wilde, Constance and their soirées, No. 34 was sold to a genealogist and assistant librarian at the College of Arms named Richard Gordon FitzGerald Uniacke; it later passed to an insurance broker and a barrister, a far cry from the vibrant and vivid life that had once been lived within its walls. The once-famous House Beautiful was quickly disassembled.

In 1898, the year that Wilde was released from prison, Justice Wills, who had presided over the criminal trial, left Chelsea Lodge, his Tite Street home. His house was taken over by American artist Edwin Austin Abbey and his wife Gertrude. To Jacomb-Hood, Abbey was 'a most lovable and delightful man, with a dry, quaint way of saying things, with a roguish look from gleaming, spectacled eyes and a smile which was almost a grin, showing a sparkle of gold in a tooth.'[4] Abbey was born in Philadelphia and had begun his artistic career as an illustrator for *Harper's* magazine, but in 1878 he was lured, like so many other American artists, across the Atlantic to perfect his art in the fashionable manner of the Pre-Raphaelites.

Unlike most of his peers it was to London, not Paris, that the young Abbey was drawn, eagerly embracing an obsession with English literature – particularly Shakespeare – and English history; these would become the predominant subjects of his work. During these early years in London, Abbey busied himself with weekly illustrations for *Harper's*. He supplemented these with larger commissions of books and plays like *Christmas Stories* by Charles Dickens and a new edition of Richard Brinsley Sheridan's eighteenth-century comedy *The School for Scandal*. At an artist's retreat at Broadway in the Cotswolds, Abbey also met and befriended his future neighbour, John Singer Sargent, as well as his future wife, the American artist Mary Gertrude Meade.

In 1889 Abbey won a first-class medal for his drawing at the International Exposition in Paris. Even the French critics were quick to point out the English influences in Abbey's work: 'He continues with the same dignified traditions of famous artists across the Channel: Fred Walker, Pinwell, Millais, and Keene.'[5] Of these artists, Keene, a well-known illustrator for *Punch*, had been the greatest lifelong influence on Abbey. However, more important for young Abbey was the renowned nineteenth-century artist, Frederick Walker. The year after Abbey first arrived in England, he saw Walker's painting *The Harbour of Refuge,* and described it as 'one of the most exquisitely delicate and refined paintings that I know of.'[6]

The qualities of delicacy and refinement that Abbey saw in Walker's painting characterise his own style of the following decade. His illustrations, however, informed his later work in oil both in subject and style. *May Day Morning,* for instance, demonstrates the poetic, rustic nostalgia of Walker's work much in line with Abbey's own neighbour, Robert Walker Macbeth. Macbeth was born in Glasgow, the son of notable portrait painter Norman Macbeth and brother of the artist Henry Raeburn-Macbeth. After studying at the Royal Scottish Academy School and exhibiting at the Royal Scottish Academy in 1867, Macbeth moved to London where he attended classes at the Royal Academy. From the mid-1870s to late 1880s he spent long periods in the fenlands of Lincolnshire, painting scenes of field labourers such as *A Lincolnshire Gang* and *Potato Harvest in the Fens*, which were favourably reviewed.

LEFT The Hon. Justice Alfred Wills around the time of the Oscar Wilde trial
RIGHT Robert Walker Macbeth in his studio by E. H. Mills, *c*.1900

But in an age when modernity and the cosmopolitan were the high pursuits of fine art, Macbeth's 'antique nobility of form'[7] was soon seen as old-fashioned, ruralistic and highly Victorian; Macbeth's work owed little to Whistler, Sargent or the modern aesthetic that was prevalent in Tite Street. Indeed the decline in appeal of Macbeth's work was owed in part to the street in which he lived where 'revolutionaries' like Whistler had weaned the 'fickle public'[8] off a taste for Victorian landscapes and into the modern age.

With low demand for his work, Macbeth was forced to move his family from the countryside and in an attempt to economise they moved into Tite Street just a year before the Abbeys arrived. 'It was pleasant to have Macbeth as a neighbour,' Jacomb-Hood later recalled. 'He was a fine figure of a man – a broad, thick-set Scotsman, with fine eyes, a flowing moustache and pointed beard'[9] while his wife was 'well born and of refined manners' with 'dark red hair and creamy skin of a Titian portrait'.[10] The Macbeths entertained a rather bohemian group of artists and thespians in Tite Street and were welcomed by their neighbours. However, life in Tite Street did not quite match the rural life they had come to love. Their daughter Lydia, homesick for the countryside, wandered up and down the pavements of Tite Street and the Embankment with her little dog.[11]

By the 1890s, Abbey's work moved away from illustrations and towards oil painting. Both Abbey and his neighbour Sargent would retain close connections with America. In 1890 Abbey travelled to Boston with Sargent to meet the Trustees of the new Boston Public Library about the series of murals for the new building designed by the American Beaux-Arts architect Charles McKim. It was agreed that Abbey would decorate the Delivery Room on the second floor, while Sargent would paint murals for the second-floor hall situated at the top of the main stair, leading to the Special Collections Hall. Both artists greeted the project with enthusiasm but the Boston mural commission would demand a great deal more time and energy from Abbey, and would constitute a fundamental redirection of his art – a move away from the delicate, quaint scenes of Walker and Macbeth and into a world of pageantry, theatricality and public display.

From early 1891 until 1895, Abbey set about working on the murals along with Sargent at a specially constructed 64-foot-long studio in Fairford, Gloucestershire, where 'a canvas two metres square looks like a postage stamp.'[12] At first Abbey had toyed with the idea of a Shakespearian theme for the murals but finally settled on *The Quest and Achievement of the Holy Grail*. Eventually his mural series would consist of fifteen paintings, the largest measuring thirty-three feet in width.

Abbey finally exhibited the first five Boston panels in 1895 and could then return to working on oil paintings. Like Macbeth, Abbey's initial transition to painting followed a loyalty to Walker, but, unlike Macbeth, Abbey was captivated not with the quaint countryside but with slightly more highbrow, dramatic Shakespearian scenes which were far more in vogue. In the summer of 1895 he began a painting exhibited at the Royal Academy the following year entitled *Richard, Duke of Gloucester, and the Lady Anne*, followed by *Hamlet* the year after.

With the success of his murals Abbey began to take larger strides away from illustration towards large scale oil painting. Both *Gloucester* and *Hamlet* relied heavily on Abbey's previous work as an illustrator and assumed viewers would understand the narratives to which they referred. Their crisp, clean lines, extraordinary attention to detail, even their rich colour palette – red, black, green and gold – and typically medieval settings drew heavily upon Pre-Raphaelite influences.

In 1898, Abbey was elected to the Royal Academy. Until this point the Abbeys had lived, like the Macbeths, securely in the English countryside, and whenever they came to London would stay with friends or borrow studios – often using Sargent's Tite Street studio when he was away. But with his election to the Royal Academy, Abbey began to feel that a more permanent London residence was needed. With Justice Wills's exit one had recently become available in Tite Street.

As Justice Wills left, Abbey moved in, bringing his materials, canvases, easels and half-completed murals from the countryside. The Chelsea Lodge was perfect for an artist like Abbey. Not only was it in the heart of a flourishing artistic quarter, but the house was well designed for an artist, having one of the largest studios in the street with the entire light-filled

Richard, Duke of Gloucester, and the Lady Anne by Edwin A. Abbey, 1897

top floor devoted to the purpose. The Chelsea Lodge, as its name portends, had a country house feel both inside and out. The original Godwin designs were rustic, more Arts and Crafts than his usual work, with a distinctly country cottage feel. Directly behind the house was a shady partly paved courtyard and garden overlooked by a spacious oak panelled dining room. Downstairs the Abbeys had installed a seventeenth-century chimney over-mantel and had moved most of their belongings from Morgan Hall to London, giving the house a more cluttered, antiquarian feel.

The Abbeys adjusted to life in Tite Street. They entertained twice a week, usually on a Monday and a Thursday; after dinner Abbey and his artist friends would retire to the studio and paint into the late hours of the night. Of the dinner guests, Whistler was an almost permanent fixture. He had returned from Paris in 1896 after the death of his wife Beatrice. He soon found his way back to Tite Street. Whistler would dine at the Chelsea Lodge at least once a week, and it was not uncommon for him to spend all day Sunday in Tite Street as well. The frail artist – a shadow of his once vibrant self – would amble up the stairs in the morning and return to the studio after lunch, where, sitting in a comfortable chair, he would eventually fall asleep, and after a nap, awakened perhaps by the arrival of guests and tea, would linger on until dinner. Afterwards he would amble up and down Tite Street and the Embankment. Perhaps it was nostalgia for his former days of glory that drew Whistler back like a proud father watching his child grow beyond his care.

Before long the ghostly pale figure of Whistler would be seen no more on the pavements of Tite Street. On 17 July 1903 Abbey received a telegram that Whistler had died in his sleep at the home of his sister-in-law in nearby Cheyne Walk. The pioneering artist was gone forever, passing the torch to a new generation of artists who followed in his footsteps. 'Poor dear old Jimmy's death was a great blow to me,'[13] wrote Abbey, who served as pall-bearer at the funeral. 'Few men have made so great a mark upon their time and few men have left their work so complete. He taught men to see something very subtle that *he* saw.'[14]

Abbey was kept busy with work. Queen Victoria's death two years previously heralded the end of an era and the beginning of the Edwardian epoch. Bertie, the Prince of Wales, now King Edward VII, prepared for his coronation. Sargent had initially been appointed to paint the event. He politely declined, recommending Abbey for the job instead. Being asked to paint a coronation of a British monarch was a great honour for the American artist, and Abbey simply could not refuse, but the commission was a momentous undertaking for the already beleaguered artist.

In the weeks leading up to the event, the artist went to Westminster Abbey laden with pencils and sketch pads to make preliminary drawings of the cavernous background. On coronation day, dressed in his Academy robes, Abbey and his wife Gertrude set off at dawn. Traffic delayed their arrival but once inside they were shown to the most exclusive box with the rest of the Royal Family, with prime views of the entire ceremony. Abbey made no sketches, he merely watched history unfold, memorising every minute detail of the scene.

Back in Tite Street, Abbey immediately set to work on the portrait. 'I have got a trench dug in the studio to let part of it down in,' he wrote, 'while I paint the upper-half.'[15] In the studio Abbey worked with the appropriate props and royal paraphernalia, entrusted with the King's Colobium sindonis and Supertunica – a cloth of gold embroidered with rose, shamrock, thistle and gryphon. The new King had been familiar with several Tite Street artists for over twenty years. He had attended a séance at the house of Frank Miles and Oscar Wilde with his mistress Lillie Langtry, who was then being painted by Whistler at his newly built White House. Later the Prince and his wife attended performances at the Shelley Theatre, now demolished. In 1902 he returned to Tite Street, not as Prince of Wales, but as King, to take centre stage in the large portrait of his coronation.

In spite of the immense prestige of painting the coronation, the commission was perhaps Abbey's most difficult. The scope and detail were not a problem. Indeed Abbey had completed far more difficult works in the past with his *The Trial of Queen Katherine* – a busy, crowded scene from the second act of *Henry VIII* – exhibited at the Royal Academy the year before. The real problem for Abbey with the coronation portrait was a discord between painterly imagination and the constraints of a realistic, contemporary portrait. The scene of the coronation was simply too real. Abbey was a master of Pre-Raphaelite romances, mythological scenes and historical dramas. As Henry James aptly noted, Abbey 'spurned the literal': if 'he makes the story familiar, he makes the familiar just strange enough to be distinguished'.[16] For Abbey the coronation lacked the romance and imagination that defined his other work. 'The coronation picture grows,' he mused, 'but I somehow prefer to invent something. This doing just what you saw instead of what you dream is confusing.'[17]

The Coronation of King Edward VII by Edwin A. Abbey, 1902–7

Abbey was never considered a portraitist. Even when he and his neighbour, Sargent, set about on an exercise to paint the same mannequin, each came up with two distinct results. Sargent's was an unmistakeable 'actuality,' the picture of a mannequin adorned with studio props, while Abbey's was the portrait of 'a living troubadour, wearing his cloak and feathered hat with an air and strumming his lute while he lustily sang.'[18] Sargent had made a record of exactly what he saw while Abbey had given free play to his imagination and endowed a senseless thing with life. For Sargent, the art of painting was more straightforward. 'I do not judge,' he said, 'I chronicle.' But the imaginative work that appealed most to Abbey was 'of a quaint and innocent sort, far removed from the tremendous and grandiose.'[19]

Ever since he had moved to London, Abbey found himself encumbered with an increasing workload. The pressures to produce new work mounted. The publicity from the Boston Public Library project along with the royal seal of approval opened the floodgate for new commissions. The Royal Exchange, for instance, had approached him to paint a mural for its newly refurbished main entrance which the artist politely accepted.[20] But as a new Royal Academician, Abbey was also expected to contribute at least one painting every year to the summer exhibition in addition to all his other work.

Abbey decided it was time to enlist the help of an apprentice in Tite Street. He called upon Frank Cadogan Cowper, a promising art student from north London who had studied at St John's Wood College where he and his fellow students were all 'Abbey mad'.[21] Cowper himself had set about collecting his sketches from the pages of *Harper's* and studied Abbey's method in minute detail. In 1897, Cowper applied to the Royal Academy School with his ambitious subject painting, *An Aristocrat answering the Summons to Execution, Paris 1791* which was duly accepted.

The taste for historical subject painting was still alive at the Royal Academy whose presidency had passed from Leighton to Millais and in 1896 to Edward Poynter. Poynter had a penchant for Cowper's allegorical scenes and encouraged his work. Shortly after submitting another Abbeyesque triumph, *Hamlet,* to the Royal Academy – an answer to a painting of the same title by Abbey – Cowper had succeeded in attracting Abbey's attention and was invited to Tite Street to assist with the completion of the coronation picture. Cowper spent roughly six months helping Abbey at his studio, arranging props and tidying up other less important works while Abbey focused on finishing his royal commission.

By the time Cowper left Tite Street, he was fully immersed in every detail of Abbey's life and work. Abbey's influence on Cowper culminated in *St Agnes*, exhibited at the Royal Academy in 1905. Cowper now commanded the attention and support of Abbey, Sargent and Edward Poynter for the painting's acquisition by the Trustees of the Chantrey Bequest. In spite of a trend for younger artists to join the New English Art Club, Cowper remained firmly rooted in the Pre-Raphaelite tradition. 'Certainly I understand the theory of Pre-Raphaelitism perfectly now,' he later wrote to a friend, 'and as far as the method of painting is concerned we understand it better now than all the Pre-Raphaelite Brotherhood (except Millais) did themselves.'[22] Cowper would put this understanding to good use.

After a ruinous fire in 1834, the Houses of Parliament were steadily being rebuilt through until about 1870. A select committee, headed by Lewis Harcourt, was given the task of filling the empty walls of the East Corridor with a series of mural paintings. Harcourt worked with Lord Carlisle, an amateur artist and patron of William Morris and Edward Burne-Jones, and also a good friend of Abbey's, interviewing major figures of the art world – Edward Poynter, Sargent, Abbey and William Holman Hunt. In 1907 they published a report with suggestions for the East Corridor. Instead of having one artist decorate the space, it was decided that Harcourt should accept private donations of paintings from patrons, but Abbey was asked to oversee the project and 'assist the artists in arriving at a general scheme . . . in order that the general treatment shall be harmonious.'[23]

Abbey recommended his former apprentice Frank Cadogan Cowper take up the reins of the project and, alongside five others, create murals for the East Corridor. Cowper eagerly threw himself behind the mural commission along with artists Ernest Board, Frank Salisbury, Denis Eden, Henry Payne and John Byam Shaw. This distinguished group of young artists whom Abbey named 'Primitif',[24] but who were latter dubbed more accurately 'Neo-Pre-Raphaelite' by the German critic Hermann Muthesius,[25] met in Tite Street where they worked on their East Corridor murals.

London, however, was taking a toll on Abbey. By 1910 the rate and scale of work led to Abbey's health quickly deteriorating. He was already overworked and was in the throes of several major mural projects – the Boston Public Library, the Royal Exchange in London and a new commission for the Pennsylvania State Capital building.[26] Under the burden of an increasing work load, in July 1911, the fifty-nine-year-old Abbey collapsed. He was bedridden in Tite Street for almost a week before he died. Sargent, only four years younger than his neighbour, was in Munich when Gertrude Abbey wrote of her husband's sudden illness. Sargent returned immediately. Upon Abbey's wishes, he completed details for the Pennsylvania Capital Building commission and helped to complete his unfinished canvases. Abbey's widow decided to remain in Tite Street where she discussed donating the unused studio-house to the Royal Academy for use as a school. But the project was so mired in bureaucratic weight, the project never materialised.

Abbey's death heralded the twilight of a particular genre of painting. Public taste and artistic trends were changing. In 1910, a year before Abbey's death, Roger Fry had organised the first Post-Impressionist Exhibition. Fry's exhibitions were a nail in the coffin for Abbey's and Cowper's work – a coffin that had been built in part by Whistler in Tite Street. The Abbeyesque Shakespearian painting would struggle to find another outlet in the twentieth century except through the work of Cowper. The public was more interested in looking at itself and its own problems than at some remote narrative of the past. Abbey and Cowper were at the tail-end of a comet that was fading into space, the last of the Pre-Raphaelites.

Lord Ribblesdale by
John Singer Sargent,
1902

23.

The VAN DYCK *of* TITE STREET

The Edwardians knew they were rich but they did not
know how rich until Sargent painted them.
– Osbert Sitwell

The turn of the century was a milestone for Tite Street. The deaths of some of the leading thinkers and artists of the nineteenth century occurred as the new century dawned. Influential critics such as Walter Pater and John Ruskin, towering Royal Academicians such as Sir John Everett Millais and Lord Leighton, and the two greatest Tite Street personalities, Oscar Wilde and James Abbott McNeill Whistler, were all dead.

For Tite Street, the Edwardian years were the culmination of several decades of gradual change that had begun in the late 1870s. 'The forty years from 1870 to 1910 are decades to which one attaches the word transition,' historian Sir Roy Strong has noted. 'On the surface they were years of triumph, optimism and seeming certainty. But beneath the surface pageantry and splendour lurked something rather different, a malignant and eroding cancer containing forces which were irrevocably to change the entire structure of British society.'[1] Bertie, the raffish Prince of Wales now sat on the throne of a vast Empire. Though his reign would be significantly shorter than his mother's, King Edward's decade would have its own distinctive character, a 'surface pageantry and splendour' captured on canvas by a single Tite Street artist, John Singer Sargent.

'Behind the individual he finds the real,' Ellen Terry said about Sargent, and 'behind the real, a whole social order.'[2] While Whistler and Wilde had defined the 1880s and 1890s, Sargent would define the 'social order' of the first decade of the new century. As the golden age of Tite Street was reaching its zenith, Sargent fostered a new character in the Tite Street ensemble – the industrious, dapper, gentleman-bohemian. Gone were the days of the lilies and peacock feathers, Japanese fans and knee-breeches. The *années de combat* of the aesthetes were over. Tite Street was no longer the front line in the crusade against an old-fashioned

Royal Academy. In the battles of attrition during the previous two decades each side had ground the other into a new shape. The Academy was no longer the fiercely orthodox institution it had been in the 1870s, and Tite Street was no longer the hotbed of radical art it had once been.

In the first decade of the twentieth century, Tite Street would instead become a highly respectable factory of faces, and Sargent, a well-tailored, cigar-smoking labourer, manufacturing the Edwardian era – everyone from fellow artists and musicians to nouveau riche industrialists and aristocrats. The scandals that shrouded the street's past melted away, and nearly every name in society clamoured for entrance to the 'sacred centre' of Tite Street. In 1902, the year before Whistler died, Sargent had three portraits of prominent society figures exhibited at the Royal Academy: *The Misses Hunter, The Duchess of Portland* and *Lord Ribblesdale*. When Auguste Rodin saw Sargent's work he declared him to be 'the Van Dyck of our time!'[3] But the three portraits on exhibit were just the first of a much larger catalogue of work that was spilling out of Tite Street year after year.

Sargent had arrived at Tite Street in 1886 where he took over Whistler's old studio at No. 33. A decade later he was elected to full membership of the Royal Academy, which seemed to have rooted the nomadic artist firmly in London. Indeed, the further Sargent ascended in the art world, the deeper his roots in Tite Street grew. Three years after his election to the Royal Academy, in August 1900, he reinforced his commitment to Tite Street, signing a lease for No. 31, creating a small staircase and entry in the connecting wall for access to his studio in No. 33.

No. 31 was a studio-house commissioned by artist Frank Dicey and designed by Colonel Sir Robert Edis in 1881. Shortly after buying the house Sargent hired workmen to make some alterations to the interior, and he set off on a painting expedition to Italy, leaving the workmen to their own devices. He arrived at his destination only to receive 'news of my new house and the workmen doing the wrong thing,' so he rushed back to London where he 'had hoped to find it more or less habitable instead of which hardly anything has been done.'[4]

When he visited Sargent in Tite Street in February 1901, Claude Monet thought it was 'very well arranged' but there was no doubt that it had been one of the many houses that Whistler had inhabited.[5] Sargent had indeed taken great pains to ensure an atmosphere of brightness and light. While Whistler and Wilde had choreographed and carefully composed interiors, Sargent's house lacked any 'deliberate touch of artiness'.[6] From his travels around Europe, North Africa, the Middle East and the United States, the artist had collected an eclectic array of antiques. The house simply overflowed with artistic possessions and pictures – antique frames, rich old textiles, objets d'art and sculptures – including a bronze cast of Rodin's *L'Homme qui Marche* inscribed to the artist. The walls were hung with pictures – a study of Manet's *The Balcony* and Gemit's fountain group. Both the house and studio were full of surprises and mysteries. 'Every dark corner and cupboard in his rooms hid some treasure.'[7] Unlike the fastidious and carefully constructed designs of Whistler and

Interior photographs of Sargent's studio at 31 Tite Street, *c.*1920

John S. Sargent, R.A. by George Percy Jacomb-Hood, *c.*1895

Wilde, Sargent's Tite Street abode was, 'the house of an artist who was very much more. It was the house of a despot and something less. In the majestic values of everything, the sumptuous severity, the absence of any desire to appeal to anyone's taste but the owner's, it stood alone.'[8]

Entering through the front door, visitors were led to the right and immediately up a short flight of stairs to where Sargent had a small office and dining room. Pictures covered almost the entire 'available space in the entrance hall and made the stairways and landings seem narrow.'[9] Going up another flight of stairs led to the spacious studio with enormous floor-to-ceiling windows at both ends. The walls of the studio were hung with 'canvases of Morelli and Mancini, Sargent's studies of his gondolier,' along with pieces of Renaissance furniture and Florentine candelabra.[10]

Scattered around the periphery of the studio were assorted marble busts, a gramophone and, in the corner, a much-used upright piano. Fine oriental rugs and Aubusson carpets covered the floor, while the walls were adorned with pilasters ornamented with swags and garlands. Between these were hung student pictures, copies of Velazquez, and his own portrait of *Madame X*, which followed him from Paris. Light was brought into the studio by two vast windows, one facing onto Tite Street and one on the east wall with a view through the trees of the Royal Hospital in the distance.

Sargent's 'gondolier' was a model-cum-valet, an Italian man named Nicola D'Inverno. Nicola's brother had been working as an artists' model and had been recruited by Abbey for his Boston Library murals. When Sargent expressed a need for a similar model, it was recommended that Nicola call on him in Tite Street. Nicola followed the advice and came to Tite Street where 'a big, burly, bearded six-footed' Sargent greeted him and then directed him to step inside and show his 'figure'. Being a boxer with a well-toned physique, Nicola was the 'very man' Sargent wanted to model for him.[11]

Behind closed doors Sargent's home and professional life were nothing like his more raffish neighbours. He 'kept good company, and he kept regular hours – his life was as orderly as that of a bishop'. Sargent would wake every morning at 'precisely seven o'clock, would have his breakfast on the table at the stroke of eight, and after breakfast would slip into a bath. Between nine and ten he answered letters, and at ten o'clock he was on the way to the studio. Sargent would then work until one o'clock, take an hour for lunch, and go back to his brush again to peg away until precisely five o'clock.'[12]

Amongst his Tite Street neighbours Sargent maintained a good rapport. While the glowing recognition of the past decade was deserved and welcome, entrance into the establishment of the Academy had made Sargent a subject of mystery and jealousy from his more avant-garde contemporaries and neighbours. Whistler had felt a sting of betrayal, 'I wouldn't, for a moment, have anyone think I was saying anything about Sargent, who is a good fellow,' he commented, 'but as for his work it is neither better nor worse than that of the usual Academician.' In an article for the *New Age*, Whistler's former pupil Walter Sickert decried the current trend for 'Sargentolatry'. He mocked contemporary 'flat-belly' critics for their lazy 'prostration before' Sargent's work. 'Some painters are said to have "painted" a picture or "exhibited" a picture,' Sickert wrote, but 'not so Mr Sargent. He "vouchsafes" a picture, a word hitherto confined to the deity.'[13]

Though he was conscious of his talent, success had not gone to Sargent's head, and among his friends and neighbours he was a kind and generous mentor. Like Whistler's studio at No. 33, Sargent's studio at No. 31 was also bustling with young artists. Rothenstein and Jacomb-Hood were frequent visitors. Wilfred de Glehn was one of the most prominent guests. He first met Sargent in the purpose-built studio constructed by Edwin Austin Abbey in the grounds of Morgan Hall, Fairford, in Gloucestershire. Abbey had hired him as his assistant while de Glehn was still a student in Paris, and the two men were working on their ambitious decorative mural panels for the Boston Public Library. De Glehn later accompanied Sargent and Abbey to Boston on a number of occasions to help with installation.

Between 1887 and 1910, the studios of Tite Street were overflowing. In the late 1880s the other studios at No. 33 were occupied by artist Matthew Ridley Corbett and Lawrence Harrison. Corbett was a painter of landscapes who trained first at the Slade and later with Lord Leighton at the Royal Academy Schools. Eventually he found himself in Italy with the landscape painter Giovanni Costa, whose influence would last throughout Corbett's career. Corbett's landscapes combined Romantic poetry with romantic imagery to create ethereal scenes of the Tuscan countryside. In 1889, just two years after he had arrived in Tite Street, he had two landscapes at the Royal Academy: *A golden afternoon* and *On the Tuscan Coast*. But his masterpiece would be a view from the Villa Tolomei over the valley of the Arno just south of Florence. *Val d'Arno: Evening* was exhibited at the Royal Academy in 1901 and later purchased for the Tate by the Trustees of the Chantrey Bequest.

Sargent's rising prestige was responsible for attracting other fresh and talented artists to Tite Street. One day at the Chelsea Arts Club, Jacomb-Hood found himself sitting beside a 'somewhat uncouth, raw young Scotsman'.[14] This 'uncouth' Scotsman turned out to be a Tite Street neighbour Robert Brough. Originally from Aberdeen, Brough had mingled briefly with the Glasgow Boys in the early 1890s before moving to Paris with fellow Scottish artist Samuel Peploe to study painting. There he had universal success with his *Fantaisie en Folie*.

Tall and handsome, Brough had an altogether eccentric flare in his attire and like a dandy wore specially designed top hats made to order. 'His graceful and slim figure, with a well-shaped head and neck set well and high upon his shoulders, combined with a faun-like alertness and boyish enthusiasm,' made him attractive to 'both sexes'.[15] The possibilities of Tite Street were very much open and alive for the twenty-eight-year-old artist who arrived in the year of Whistler's death, taking a studio at No. 33. Sargent befriended the handsome 'raw' Scotsman, who shared an admiration for the art of Velázquez, Manet and Whistler. Over time 'his rough corners' rubbed off 'in intercourse with London Society' and he was taken under Sargent's wing.

Fantaisie en Folie by Robert Brough, 1897

In his work it was noted that Brough sought 'to combine the dash of Sargent and the beautiful refinement of Velazquez.'[16] Sargent attempted to help the young artist where he had failed with Rothenstein. 'When I first met Brough I often criticised his work,' wrote Sargent, 'but though he always agreed and seemed struck by the suggestions he never once changed a detail in response to advice.'[17] 'His brushes are fencing sticks,' wrote the *Art Journal*. 'He dreams his pictures in floating completeness, and confidently fastens it to the canvas. He makes pass after pass with unerring certainty and swift decision, and as the hours move by, the picture takes form. The time lengthens and the passes come more slowly, as of one weaving a subtler spell; finally a touch here – a note of colour there – it is finished – and there it is! The result is astoundingly dexterous, spontaneous, strongly individual, full of vitality and movement, and in its unity absolutely perfect.'[18]

Brough's move to No. 33 was a strategic career advance. Tite Street was now firmly on the radar of wealthy patrons. The street had become fashionable with aristocrats and nouveau riches as well as young bohemians and artists, and Brough had thoroughly charmed his neighbours, patrons and critics alike. 'Should he fulfil the expectations he has excited,' wrote one critic, 'his success is likely to be as phenomenal as his appearance.'[19]

The success, however, was quickly halted. After accompanying his neighbour Jacomb-Hood on a tour of Spain and North Africa, he returned to England. On the night of 20 January 1905 he was returning to London from painting the portrait of the daughter-in-law and grandson of Sir Charles Tennant when his train derailed. The train burst into flames, and Brough was trapped inside his carriage, sustaining fatal burns.

In a letter, Charles Ricketts recalls that Brough's 'hip-bone and seven ribs were crushed by a carriage which fell on him, he became unconscious, and awoke to find two burning holes in the partition (the next carriage was on fire). To save his eyes and face, he put his two hands in the holes and let them burn to stumps. While doing so he knew he would never paint again. He was two hours in the wreckage, two hours in the snow.' Brough was taken to the hospital.

Upon receiving the news, Sargent immediately took the first train to Sheffield to be with his young neighbour in the hospital, before he died. Ricketts reports that Brough only collapsed once in the hospital at the point when Sargent arrived. 'He said, "Oh don't let me live, I could not stand it! I shall never paint again."'[20] Brough died shortly after Sargent's arrival. His death was a tragedy in Tite Street – another aspiring talent brutally cut short in his prime. Jacomb-Hood would later say that Brough was 'one of the few men in my life for whom I have felt a real affection.'[21]

Sargent had very little time for grief. No. 31 Tite Street was not merely a home, it was also a virtual factory for portraits. As early as 1897, Sargent had complained that he was 'having three sittings a day and hardly an interval between'. The names and faces that passed through Sargent's door present a catalogue of all the most distinguished Edwardians: artists and aristocrats, thespians and royalty, politicians and poets. His valet Nicola would later make an inventory of the faces he saw pass into the studio: Queen Alexandra, King George, Anna Pavlova, Sir Charles Beresford, Herbert Beerbohm Tree, Ellen Terry, Mr and Mrs Asquith and Lady Churchill were but a few. The less fortunate seeking to gain entrance to his studio were greeted at the door with the customary, 'I am exceedingly sorry, but Mr Sargent is very busy. Would you care to make an appointment?'[22]

Burgeoning success as a portrait painter to wealthy patrons also meant that Sargent had no trouble affording his new abode. Exaggerated claims of Sargent's wealth abound. Miss Dora Neale, whose father had posed for Sargent, and whose mother was a lady's maid for Anna Lea Merritt at the Cottage across the street, recalled that a basket of money was strung up in the hall of Sargent's house 'so that his friends could help themselves'.[23] While his friend and neighbour Edwin Abbey was painting the Prince of Wales, the future George V, at his studio in Chelsea Lodge, the Prince enquired about Sargent's income, 'Do you suppose it's ten thousand pounds?' Abbey replied that it was probably closer to twenty thousand. 'My God!' exclaimed the heir to the throne, 'I wish I had twenty thousand pounds.'[24]

Sitting for Sargent was an entirely memorable experince. 'It is positively dangerous to sit to Sargent,' said W. Graham Robertson, who had his portrait done at Tite Street in 1894, 'it's taking your face in your hands.'[25] For others it was more pleasant. Sir Frank Swettenham, whose portrait was painted in 1904, 'passed many pleasant hours' in the studio, with Sargent talking while he painted.[26] Henry James had written some words of advice to Mrs Mahlon Sands before she sat in the Tite Street studio for her portrait that same year. He warned her, '[Y]ou cannot "collaborate", "cooperate" or "assist" the painter; it's his affair – yours is only to be as difficult as possible, the more difficult you are the more the artist (worthy of his name) will be condemned to worry over you, repainting, revolutionising, till he, in a rage of ambition and admiration, arrives at the thing that satisfied him and enshrines and perpetuates you.'[27]

Enshrining and perpetuating the growing queues of sitters was exactly what Sargent did. By 1908 Max Beerbohm caricatured Sargent with a host of ladies in furs, jewels and tiaras, interspersed with bored messenger boys filling the pavement of Tite Street and waiting patiently for admission to the green door of No. 31. From the window a pensive Sargent gazes apprehensively upon the cortege. Rodin's estimation of Sargent as the 'Van Dyck' of the times proved apt. Van Dyck's swaggering seventeenth-century nobility and Pompeo Batoni's

31 Tite Street by Max Beerbohm, *c.*1908

Mr Sargent at Work by Max Beerbohm, 1907

gallant grand tourists became Sargent's modern-day *Earl of Dalhousie* or *Charles Stewart, Sixth Marquess of Londonderry*.

From Tite Street the Edwardian image was produced and disseminated, reflecting a society in flux. Like Van Dyck and Reynolds, Sargent's portraits hung on the walls of all the great houses of Britain – Blenheim, Chatsworth and Welbeck Abbey – but, as James

Lomax and Richard Ormond have pointed out, the fact that Sargent's 'greatest patron was a Bond Street art dealer and not a duke is a comment on the nature of Edwardian society.'[28] Sargent's Edwardian subjects were not solely British notables but were 'Jews or Americans, actors or plutocrats, businessmen or professions'.[32] Changes had been taking place throughout the nineteenth century as the Industrial Revolution in Britain reached its peak. In the world-at-large, Britain's power now depended more upon industry and finance than upon military conquest.[29]

'Sargent's art,' writes Richard Ormond, 'was at one with the self-confident spirit of the Edwardian age.'[30] Sargent's powerful plutocrats and portentous patricians stand upright, bold, gazing out of the canvas with confidence and assurance. But it was all an illusion. The sweat and hard work that had created such wealth and power were nowhere to be seen in Tite Street. Sargent's studio was a theatre. Recamier sofas, bergère chairs, chaise longue, Oriental vases, Aubusson rugs and Japanese screens were the props. Polished and glittering, the actors took their places. The performances were highly convincing.

Sittings at Sargent's Tite Street studio were a social event. Friends and visitors would come and watch. Sargent kept them entertained for hours on end. At breaks he might play the piano or sing a duet, afterwards they might share a cigar. 'His studio made me think of one of the transatlantic steamers of the Cunard Line which carried the wealth of two continents,' recalled one French artist, Jacques Emile-Blanche, on a visit to Tite Street. 'Women of decision on the alert, dreaming of Bond Street and the Rue de la Paix, reading magazines, sitting on rocking chairs, weighing up the chances of marrying into a ducal family at Rome.'[31]

Once again the artists of Tite Street mirrored high society while at the same time they defined it. Sargent himself was a model Edwardian – freed from money trouble, socially well-connected and progressive in his ideology. No. 31 became a microcosm of Edwardian society, according to Emile-Blanche: 'The Cunard liner bore within her hull financiers and dealers ennobled by Edward VII, Prime Ministers, actresses and tenors, thinking how their portraits might be reproduced by the million all round the earth. Travelling in the third class there were poor Italians and Catalans, mandolin-players and ballet-girls for whom the captain had a secret weakness. How this gold braid must have weighed on him as he sat at table entertaining his guests!'[32]

The elevated prestige of Tite Street in the early years of the twentieth century was never more evident than on 'Picture Sunday'. The event was a traditional artistic open house held on the first Sunday in April where artists lined up their studios with works selected in advance of the Academy exhibition. It was an opportunity for artists and sitters to view works before they went on public display. Patrons and critics, all the intelligentsia, flocked to the studios of surrounding Chelsea whose pavements were filled with carriages and motor cars delivering fashionable London to its doors.

One of Sargent's patrons, Sir George Sitwell, brought his extended family to show them his portrait before it went to the Academy, but his outspoken mother-in-law, Lady

Conyngham, and her spinster sister, Lady Geraldine Somerset, lumbered into the studio with their ear trumpets to scrutinise the picture. They were not impressed by Sargent's work. 'Why riding things and an evening dress?' they barked. 'Why an evening dress and a hat?' they demanded. 'And why not go to an *ordinary* painter? Why go to an American?'[33] Sargent held his tongue. The entourage were kindly escorted out of the studio and were seen no more in Tite Street.

By 1909 Sargent was tiring of the endless work in Tite Street. His impatience with interfering ladies and bored gentleman became more and more obvious. In response to Lady Radnor's request to paint her second daughter he wrote 'Ask me to paint your gates, your fences, your barns, which I should gladly do, but NOT THE HUMAN FACE.'[34] He later wrote to Richard Curtis, 'No more paughtraits whether refreshed or not. I abhor and abjure them and hope never to do another especially of the Upper Classes.'[35]

A combination of boredom and tiresome sitters led Sargent to refuse more and more commissions. Sargent had pushed portraiture to its limit and was reaching a plateau. By 1910 he was at the pinnacle of success and began to realise that there was nowhere to go but down. Since the 1890s, the Tite Street studio had been filled with three to four sitters per day, including weekends. Perhaps he was also beginning to feel some truth in Wilde's testament that, 'The artist cannot be degraded into the servant of the public.'[36]

The time consumed by portraiture was beginning to weigh on Sargent, who was eager to work on other projects. His Boston murals, for instance, were itching to be finished, and his landscape work was accelerating. Only rarely did he break his vow to give up 'the human face' and only for special friends like Henry James or important figures like President Woodrow Wilson or John D. Rockefeller. Even when the prestigious presidency of the Royal Academy was offered, Sargent turned it down. 'I will do anything for them but that,' he responded.[37]

Sargent's decision to give up 'paughtraits' was timely. The Edwardian age that the Van Dyck of Tite Street had so vividly captured on canvas came to a close with the sudden death of King Edward in May 1910. Royal messengers were immediately dispatched to Tite Street requesting Sargent to come and draw the King's lying in state. Sargent had turned down the coronation portrait but agreed to draw Bertie on his deathbed. His reign marked the beginning of a century in which the torch of world-power would pass from Britain to America. There is irony in the fact that Bertie's reign was bookended by American portraits. It is more than coincidence that both artists lived and worked in Tite Street.

24.

QUEER STREET

The world's not so black as it is painted.
– Radclyffe Hall, *The Well of Loneliness*, 1928

Romaine Brooks arrived in Tite Street in 1904. She left behind a new husband in Capri and began a career as an artist. The two years she spent living in the street formed a significant turning point in her life and her work. She blossomed into a confident and talented artist and celebrated socialite – an Amazon of the drawing room. Brooks was born Beatrice Romaine Goddard to American parents living in Rome. Her father left shortly after her birth and she spent her childhood with a domineering and emotionally manipulative mother in Philadelphia. At the age of nineteen she ran away from home and fled to Paris where she took a job in a cabaret. She eventually made her way back to Italy where she took free classes in painting while her wealthy mother kept her dangling on a pitiful monthly allowance.

She eventually wound up in Capri, a haven for artists, and particularly for homosexuals, many of whom had fled London in the wake of the Wilde trials. There she was introduced to Whistler's work through Charles Freer, a friend and collector of the late artist. But in 1902, with the sudden death of her mother, Goddard's fortunes reversed. Overnight she became rich, inheriting most of the family fortune. 'From possessing almost nothing,' she wrote, 'I now had six flats in Nice alone, another in Monte Carlo, one in Dieppe, an unfurnished one in Paris and a chateau near Mentone.'[1] Her new financial independence allowed her artistic freedom and provided entry to the salons and homes of the European social and intellectual elite.

In Capri, Goddard also met the penniless pianist John Ellingham Brooks who proposed to the newly wealthy artist. She reluctantly accepted on the proviso that she be allowed complete independence. At the time she thought that 'a pleasant unity through isolation might be achieved.'[2] But there was no pleasant unity. Goddard found her husband, who was homosexual, extremely difficult to live with. Moreover, her husband could not accept her disregard for the 'many hateful prerogatives of my sex',[3] which included a tendency to dress in male attire. When the couple took a walking tour in England, she elected to wear men's trousers. John was furious. The lavender marriage barely lasted a year.

Self-portrait by
Romaine Brooks, 1923

One day John returned home to find a note from his wife that she was leaving for London. He had not been invited, nor had he been given an address. When he came to look for his wife, he went to every establishment where he thought she might be. Finally he tracked her down to Tite Street. He gained entrance to the house after persuading the maid that he was her husband. Brooks heard his voice just in time to lock herself inside her studio. 'We were soon talking on either side of the door,' she recalled. 'His intention was to sit where he was until I came out, he said. I replied that my intention was to live in South America or some other out-of-the-way place to deprive him of his income. This clinched the argument and he departed.'[4] Brooks eventually bought off her husband for a sum of £300 a year, which was 'enough for meat,' wrote Somerset Maugham's partner Alan Searle, 'but not enough for pickles'.[5]

The decision to move to London may have been a whim for Brooks, but once there, her choice of Tite Street was intentional. 'I went to live in London,' she wrote, 'at the end of a very interesting period. Whistler, Oscar Wilde and Beardsley were dead, but an afterglow brought into relief such figures as Conder, Sickert, Max Beerbohm and others.'[6] Above all the painters of Tite Street, she 'admired Whistler most'.[7] What better place to start her own artistic career than in the very street that he had helped to fashion.

After Anna Lea Merritt went to live in the 'real country',[8] her studio-house, the Cottage, was occupied by a Quaker-artist, Percy Bigland. In 1904 Brooks secured a temporary lease. With infinite funds at her disposal she proceeded to decorate the house with dark medieval wainscoting and heavy Jacobean furniture.[9] Unlike most artists in Tite Street, Brooks was not formally trained but slowly she revived a weak hope that she could paint. For a few months she set about doing sketches and portraits of friends and maids in Tite Street, but she despaired at her own style believing all her canvases expressed 'uniform melancholy' no better than 'a student's work'.[10] Whistler remained a beacon of inspiration for the otherwise insecure artist. 'I wondered at the magic subtlety of his tones,' she wrote. 'His was a painter's perfect technique expressing delicate visual beauty.'[11] She took Whistler's theories to heart, studying his paintings. In two significant years of trial-and-error she gradually shed her troubled past and evolved her own unique form of expression.

Tite Street had given her a new perspective on life and art. The studio-house was 'none too cheerful'.[12] At the rear of the house there came the sounds of 'doleful hymn-singing' from the chapel at More House next door. Then there were the sounds of the crying sick children brought to the Victoria Hospital across the street. The London fog that Whistler and Wilde had cherished soon invaded Brooks's studio and 'brought its dank note of reality to my ghost-ridden dreams'.[13] In Tite Street the blazing Mediterranean colours of Capri were transformed into a world of 'thick gray fogs' seeping through the windows of her house or over the murky Thames nearby. By the time she left in 1906, Brooks had the beginnings of a unique monochrome palette that would characterise her art for years to come. Many years later the Italian poet Gabriele D'Annunzio would comment that Brooks was 'the most profound and wise orchestrator of greys in modern painting'.[14]

In her work Brooks captured the 'none too cheerful' world of her Tite Street studio. Her portraits of this period show dark-clad women casually seated in front of open windows or posed against monochrome backgrounds. In her restricted palette and subtle tones she owed a debt to Whistler. Paintings such as *Maggie* are strongly reminiscent of Whistler's own *Self-portrait* with a shallow, deeply shadowed space, and a face illuminated with an almost ghostly paleness under a broad-brimmed hat. However, other portraits of the period such as *The Charwoman* and *The Black Bonnet* are closer in feeling to studies by Augustus and Gwen John, Walter Sickert and other painters with roots in the traditions of Whistler and Degas.

While she was living in Tite Street, Brooks immersed herself in a new circle. She met the Anglo-Australian artist Charles Conder living nearby, and later befriended Charles Ricketts and Charles Shannon. She also met Oscar Wilde's former lover Lord Alfred 'Bosie' Douglas, now married to the poet Olive Custance. Almost four years after Wilde's death, Douglas was still making the rounds of polite society. While Brooks had expected to find him prematurely aged and disillusioned with the world after his lover's death, she was astonished instead by his buoyant, youthful optimism. They flirted, and Brooks thought Douglas saw in her, 'a dark edition of his own unquenchable youth, hiding a like rebellion against the world and its censure'.[15] Douglas sent a volume of his poems, *The City of the Soul*, mysteriously inscribed 'We have often spoken of undying things.'[16]

Although her best works, such as *The Weeping Venus* and, eventually, her own iconic *Self-portrait*, were created in Paris, Brooks's years in Tite Street were crucial to her development as an independent artist. Her audacious personality was a mirror of Whistler's, and she would eventually inherit his sense of confidence and subtlety in her later works. 'What we see in her pictorial style,' wrote the *New York Times*, 'is the end of the Whistler inheritance, transmuted and crystallized into a personal vision.'[17]

Brooks moved to Paris where she later met her lifelong partner, a wealthy American named Natalie Barney; their circle in Paris would include Oscar Wilde's niece, Dolly. She returned to London in June 1911 for an exhibition of her work at the Goupil Gallery – the same gallery that hosted Whistler's retrospective exhibition in 1894. In the introduction to the catalogue Claude Roger-Marx remarked that her art was addressed 'to those intelligences and those chosen sensibilities who are fascinated by the exploration of character but who, rejecting obvious effects as offensive, prefer . . . the delicate allusion of implication; they do not ask for light but for gentle shadow; Not colour, nothing but nuance; Not contrasting effects, but a reigning harmony.' It is an art of strong significance and exquisite expression: one believes it made in order to illustrate the aphorism of Edmond de Goncourt, 'The rare is almost always the beautiful.'[18]

Five years after Brooks left Tite Street, another young lesbian followed in her footsteps. With her short hair, slicked to the side, well-cut tuxedos and distinctive Roman nose, 'John' Radclyffe Hall took a flat at the newly constructed Shelley Court flats on the site of the old Shelley Theatre. 'John' was born in 1880 and christened Marguerite. Within weeks of her

*Mrs George Batten
Singing* by John
Singer Sargent, 1897

birth, her older sister Florence died, and her father abandoned his young family in a dim house, ironically called Sunny Lawn in Bournemouth.

Like Romaine Brooks, Hall had a turbulent and troubled relationship with her mother. As a child she had endured both mental and physical abuse, but had inherited a keen interest in music from her. Her mother had moved to London to take singing lessons where John had begun improvising her own lines of verse. 'She has ink in her blood,' wrote Sir Arthur Sullivan, a family friend.[19] Like Brooks, Hall came from a moneyed background. In August 1900, when she came of age, she inherited her grandfather's fortune and purchased a house for herself in Kensington away from the control of her domineering mother.

In the summer of 1906 her first volume of poems was published, *'Twixt Earth and Stars,* containing about eighty love lyrics. The following year Hall's life was changed when she met Mabel Batten at the German spa of Homburg. Batten, whom close friends called 'Ladye', was almost twice Hall's age, married with a grown-up daughter and grandchildren. As a young woman, she had been a noted beauty with a beautiful singing voice and was rumoured to have been a lover of the Prince of Wales. In 1882 she had moved to Tedworth Square at the top of Tite Street, and in 1895 she posed for Sargent at No. 33.

Almost two decades after Sargent's portrait, Batten became a surrogate mother figure for Hall. The two women spent more time together as Hall fell 'head and heart and soul in love'.[20] In her elation Hall published a second volume of poems in the autumn of 1908 entitled, *A Sheaf of Verses,* which she dedicated to 'Sad Days and Glad Days' – 'Believe me, the world is a place full of joy, / And happiness stretches afar.' The following year, in early 1909, Hall moved to Tite Street where she could be closer to Batten, and there she published an anthology of poetry dedicated to 'Mrs George Batten'. One poem, 'The Garden', expressed the unconstrained joy Hall had experienced since becoming Batten's love: 'I knew a region desolate / Unfruitful and without name, / Where all my loving was regret, / Before you came.' But Hall's brief sojourn in Tite Street was marred by tragedy. In October her beloved grandmother died, and shortly afterwards Batten's husband passed away. There was a silver lining in that both were now free to live together, and in May 1911 Hall left Tite Street to live in Cadogan Square with Batten.

* * *

The morning of Tuesday, 21 November 1911 was like any other in Tite Street. Abbey had died just a few months before, and Sargent was away travelling. Any unsuspecting passerby or neighbour would not have noticed anything particularly unusual, except perhaps the steady, stoic cortège of ladies entering two at a time into the front door of No. 48. The women, fizzing with anticipation, anxiety and excitement, had been given detailed directions on how to find their way to Tite Street. They were instructed not to stop and ask directions for fear of arousing suspicion of their planned activities. Once crammed into the studio, the group

The National Union of Women's Suffrage Societies demonstration, 1908

of thirty women were greeted by the organiser of the day's events, the Welsh sculptor, Edith Elizabeth Downing. In a loud, clear voice Downing detailed their battle plan. The women were going to meet their fellow suffragettes at Caxton Hall and then march to the Houses of Parliament. Downing hauled out a bag of stones and distributed them to the ladies to hide under their petticoats.[21]

The women dispersed from Tite Street and headed to their rendezvous location. At first everything went according to plan. The peaceful women led their march with minimal arrests. By seven o'clock, however, a small group of militant suffragettes met at the headquarters of the Women's Press in Charing Cross Road where they armed themselves with heavier artillery, bags of stones and hammers, and then set upon the West End of London with one purpose – windows were smashed at the Home Office, Local Government Board, Treasury, Somerset House and National Liberal Federation. A small riot ensued as police tried to chase suspects through the narrow streets of the West End. Some proudly gave themselves up as a way to register their protest while others easily disappeared among the crowds of London. That night the cells of Bow Street were packed with nearly two hundred and twenty women and three men. Downing had managed to temporarily elude authorities, but two days later the police arrived in Tite Street. She was arrested, charged with throwing stones at the windows of Somerset House and sentenced to seven days in Holloway Prison.

Edith Elizabeth Downing in her studio, *c.*1909–14

Born in Cardiff, Downing moved to London to study art at the Slade School of Fine Art. By the 1890s there was still a narrow empty space next to Godwin's Tower House in Tite Street. A block of studio flats called Dhu House, similar to its neighbour, was built by architect Charles Pawley. Downing moved to Tite Street in 1896 and took a studio at No. 48 with her lover and companion, Ellen Sparks, who specialised in leather embroidery. Throughout the 1890s Downing built her reputation as a sculptor with *Music Sent up to God* and *There is a Silence that Says, Ah Me*, exhibited at the Royal Academy.

In 1903 Downing had joined the Central Society for Women's Suffrage, but 'learning the futility of quiet work',[22] she joined the Chelsea branch of the Women's Social & Political

Union (WSPU) in 1908. The following year she began selling pieces of art in aid of the suffrage campaign. She made small portraits of Christabel Pankhurst and Annie Kenney which were priced at five guineas and two guineas respectively and sold to support the WSPU.

Downing joined forces with her Chelsea neighbour Marion Wallace-Dunlop to organise a series of spectacular WSPU processions through London. Wallace-Dunlop, herself an artist, had joined the suffrage movement in 1909 and was arrested after putting her art to use stamping pro-suffrage emblems on the stone walls of the House of Commons. For this offence she was imprisoned in Holloway Prison for a month where she had demanded, like other suffragist prisoners, to be kept in the 'First Division' and treated as a political prisoner, but her request was denied. As a result, she became one of the first hunger strikers in the movement. 'What will you have today?' asked the doctors. 'My determination,' she answered.[23]

Despite their relentless efforts, political change for women's suffrage had been unbearably slow. During the 1910 General Election, the National Union of Women's Suffrage Societies (NUWSS) organised petitions in 290 constituencies across the country. They managed to obtain 280,000 signatures which they presented to the House of Commons in March 1910. With the support of thirty-six MPs, a new suffrage bill was discussed in Parliament. For a moment there was a glimmer of hope and the WSPU suspended all militant activities. When Parliament refused to pass the new bill, the WSPU protested with a peaceful demonstration but were brutally attacked by police, an event which became known as 'Black Friday'. By 21 November 1911, the WSPU ended its truce, thus igniting the night of demolition that lead to Downing's arrest.

Women artists had been experiencing 'difficulties and contradictions in their situation' for centuries.[24] The American artist Anna Lea Merritt had spoken out about the difficulties she faced as a female artist and by the time Downing came to Tite Street very little had changed. 'They needed citizenship as women,' explains historian Lisa Tickner. 'They were well aware of the outside pressures that shaped their private time in the studio, and of the remaining restrictions on their careers.'[25] In 1907 the Artists' Suffrage League was established (followed by the Suffrage Atelier in 1909) which gave women an opportunity to organise and contribute their professional skills to the suffrage. There was a great deal of work to be done – posters, invitations, flags, banners and placards, not to mention the various publications which needed illustrations and caricatures, most notably *Votes for Women*.

As suffrage processions and marches became more and more frequent, the importance for each to seem different and new was greater than ever. Downing lent her skills as an artist to several impressive displays of the suffrage movement. For the joint WSPU and WFL 'From Prison to Citizenship' procession on 18 June 1910 Downing and Wallace-Dunlop designed a 'Prisoners Tableau'. 'One tableau' reported *Votes for Women*, 'was supplied by the girls' contingent, and was very striking. Clad in pure white and wearing caps of green and violet, the girls, ranging from thirteen to twenty years, typified the devotion and thanks of the younger generation to those who had suffered in the cause of women'.[26]

Downing helped design the East Procession and the Prisoners' Pageant, the Historical Pageant and the Pageant of Empire for the 17 June 1911 Women's Coronation Procession. For the 'Citizenship' march, authorities had agreed that there could be two processions as the organisers had confidently expected 20,000 women to take part. The West Procession would form up on the north side of Holland Park, proceeding along Bayswater Road and into Hyde Park at Marble Arch. The East Procession, formed up on the Embankment between Westminster Bridge and Blackfriars, would march up Northumberland Avenue to Pall Mall and Piccadilly, and enter the park at Hyde Park Corner.

Elaborate schemes were drawn up for the East Procession by Edith Craig[27] and Laurence Housman (co-founder of the Suffrage Atelier), and for the West by Marion Wallace-Dunlop and Edith Elizabeth Downing. The East Procession was intended to demonstrate an 'Oriental' theme that would complement the Roman legions of the West Procession. There were few large banners but 'innumerable standards, prison gates, sails and pennons' and the tinkling of hundreds of tiny silver wind-bells in the breeze. The prisoners led the procession, and behind them came the 'actresses, representatives from the colonies, nurses, the Kensington and Chelsea artists with silver palettes gleaming in the sun, women gardeners with garlands of smilax and heather, chemists, teachers, civil servants, typists, and the green, white and gold pennons of the Women's Freedom League (WFL) with coaches, cars and carriages bringing up the rear.'[28] To pull off the spectacle, legions of volunteers were recruited for 'nailing, painting, pasting, sewing, machining'.[28] Throughout the spring of 1911 Downing's own Tite Street studio became a hotbed of activity for volunteers labouring day and night to finish the decorations and costumes.

Despite the increase in public presence, legal progress for the suffrage was slow. Christabel Pankhurst decided that the WSPU needed to intensify its militant campaign. On 1 March 1912, a group of suffragettes volunteered to take action in the West End of London. *The Daily Graphic* reported the following day, 'The West End of London last night was the scene of an unexampled outrage on the part of militant suffragists . . . Bands of women paraded Regent Street, Piccadilly, the Strand, Oxford Street and Bond Street, smashing windows with stones and hammers.'[30]

The disruptions were celebrated by some, but denounced by many, including Radclyffe Hall. 'Have the Suffragettes no spark of patriotism left,' she wrote in a high-handed tone, 'that they can spread revolt and hamper the Government in this moment of grave national danger? According to Mrs Pankhurst, they are resorting to the methods of the miners! Since when have English ladies regulated their conduct by that of the working classes? But, indeed, up to the present, the miners have set an example of orderly behaviour which the Suffragettes might do well to follow! I was formerly a sympathiser with the cause of female suffrage, as also were many women who, like myself, are unrepresented, although tax payers. Women who are capable of setting a revolutionary example at such a time as this could only bring disgrace and destruction on any Constitution in which they played an active part.' The letter was signed 'A Former Suffragist'.[31]

Gluck by Gluck (Hannah Gluckstein), 1942

* * *

When he visited Romaine Brooks's studio in Paris in the late 1940s and saw her vast collection of portraits, the American writer Truman Capote called it the 'ultimate gallery of all the famous dykes from 1880 to 1935 or thereabouts'.[32] One of those 'dykes' was a cross-dressing artist called Gluck. In 1926, Brooks returned to Tite Street, not to live, but to have her own portrait painted by Gluck. Hannah Gluckstein was a wealthy Jewish woman, heiress to coffee and catering empire J. Lyons & Co. At the age of sixteen the rebellious aspiring artist had run off to Cornwall where she shortened her name to Gluck and mixed with the Newlyn Group at Lamorna, where Alfred Munnings painted her portrait. But the long-haired, feminine girl painted by Munnings was a far cry from the trouser-wearing woman with cropped hair Gluck was to become.

In Cornwall, Gluck met her lover and lifelong friend, Effie Craig, a woman known simply as Craig. Together the two women took to wearing pleated trousers and smoking pipes. Although she returned to London, she remained at a distance from her family, kept afloat by a doting brother and the trickle of income from sales of her artwork. In 1924, Gluck exhibited fifty-seven pictures at the Dorien Leigh Gallery in Kensington. 'The new and much-discussed artist, Gluck,' wrote *The Sketch*, 'wears her hair brushed back from her forehead just like a boy and when in Cornwall goes about in shorts. At her show at the Dorien Leigh Galleries she had a long black cloak covering a masculine attire.'[33] With the proceeds from exhibition sales, Gluck had enough money to purchase a larger studio, and she chose one in the Tower House, a studio once occupied by Whistler.

In 1926 she staged her second exhibition, *Stage and Country*, at The Fine Art Society. Critics and commentators had drawn attention to her unusual style of dress – Eton crop, breeches and pipe. An 'onlooker' in the *Daily Graphic* wrote, 'I addressed him naturally as Mr Gluck. It was with a considerable shock that I found myself being answered in a soft voice, essentially feminine. I do not know that I should altogether like my own wife or my own daughters to adopt Miss Gluck's style of dressing her hair or clothing her limbs, but I do know that I should be proud of them if they could paint as well as Miss Gluck paints.'[34] Gluck's art proved as androgynous as her appearance. The *Art News* thought her paintings were 'a curious compound of the masculine and the feminine point of view in art. There is the fine delicacy of the woman artist and the humour and clear-cut vision of the man.'[35]

In 1910 Brooks had hosted her first solo exhibition in Paris. She painted Jean Cocteau, the elegant Russian dancer Ida Rubinstein, and the American writer Natalie Clifford Barney. In 1915, Barney became the central figure in Brooks's life and the two women embarked on a love affair that would last for the next fifty years.

Brooks visited Gluck in London and they agreed to paint each other's portraits. Brooks's portrait of Gluck, entitled *Peter, A Young English Girl*, was exhibited in 1925 and became quite a success. *Peter* depicts a fine-looking young person of indeterminate gender who sports a handsome suit, smart cravat, crisp white collar.

In exchange for her portrait Gluck agreed to do a reciprocal portrait of Brooks. 'The elephant has come to the temple,'[36] Gluck remarked of Brooks's visit to Tite Street. Secretly she thought Brooks's work was technically and psychologically inferior to her own. Even more, she scorned the pretentious 'lesbian haute-monde',[37] as she called Brooks's social circle. And when it came time to paint the portrait, Brooks 'wasted so much sitting time in making

Peter, A Young English Girl by Romaine Brooks, 1923–4

a row that at last I was only left an hour in which to do what I did – but my rage and tension gave me almost superhuman powers. She insisted I should do one of my "little pictures". I refused so she left me with the unfinished portrait. However, I had to give many photographs of it to her friends.'[38]

Gluck's Tite Street days were short. By 1926 she was flying high, and much to her parents' delight she split with Craig, although they would remain friends. Gluck's capital was increased by her father to £20,000, and he bought her the home of her choice: Bolton House in Hampstead. Gluck would go on to become one of the most notable artists of her time in Britain, designing her own unique aesthetic and frame, simply called 'Gluck frame'.

Meanwhile, in 1928, just two years after Gluck's departure from Tite Street, Radclyffe Hall would publish one of the most controversial works of literature of the twentieth century. *The Well of Loneliness* is an autobiographical novel that deals explicitly with 'sexual inversion', cross-dressing and lesbian love. The novel's protagonist, Stephen Gordon, an upper-class English woman, resembles Hall, who, by this point was calling herself 'John'. Gordon falls in love with Mary Llewellyn, whom she meets while serving as an ambulance driver in the First World War. Their relationship encounters criticism from society, friends, family and eventually even from themselves.

This highly autobiographical account features many of Hall's lesbian friends like Brooks, and her lover Natalie Barney. This is not to say that Brooks approved of the book, which she dismissed as 'trite, superficial' and labelling Hall as 'a digger-up of worms with the pretention of a distinguished archaeologist'.[39]

Apart from its 'fine qualities as a novel by a writer of accomplished art,' writes Havelock Ellis, 'it possesses a notable psychological and sociological significance.' Ellis goes on to say that, 'the relation of certain people – who, while different from their fellow human beings, are sometimes of the highest character and the finest aptitudes – to the often hostile society in which they move, presents difficult and still unsolved problems.'[40] Hall felt herself a martyr, drawing attention to the forbidden love 'that dare not speak its name' in a way that had not been attempted since the days of Oscar Wilde. Indeed, while awaiting the crucial reply from her American publisher on whether or not to publish, she had Una, Lady Troubridge read her selections from Wilde's *De Profundis*.

'All trials are trials for one's life,' Wilde had written in *De Profundis*, and soon Hall would realise the true meaning of these words. After a gruelling campaign to get the novel published, the glowing critical reception of the novel was quickly overshadowed by a campaign launched by James Douglas, editor of the *Sunday Express*. 'Let me warn our novelists and our men of letters that literature as well as morality is in peril,' he argued. 'Fiction of this type is an injury to good literature. It makes the profession of literature fall into disrepute. Literature has not yet recovered from the harm done to it by the Oscar Wilde scandal. It should keep its house in order.'[41] On 18 August 1928 a poster advertised *The Well of Loneliness* as 'A Book That Should Be Suppressed'.

Medallion (YouWe) by Gluck (Hannah Gluckstein), 1936

The situation quickly got out of hand. Virginia and Leonard Woolf both fought against the censorship and suppression, along with writers E.M. Forster and T.S. Eliot. By November 1928 a full-scale obscenity trial was launched. Arguments for both sides were presented, but Hall inevitably lost. The book was ordered to be destroyed and the defendant ordered to pay the court costs. For Hall the conviction was a devastating blow, but at the same time the struggle had given a voice to a silent minority. 'In the heart of every woman is the desire for protection,' she said in an interview. 'In the heart of every man is the desire to give protection to the woman he loves. The invert knows she will never enjoy this and because of her affliction will face social ostracism.'[42] The novel would not be reprinted until several years after Hall's death.[43]

25.

TWILIGHT *in* TITE STREET

He laughed bitterly. The mordant witticisms of Lancelot
Mulliner at the expense of the Royal Academy were quoted
from Tite Street in the south to Holland Park in the north
and eastward as far as Bloomsbury.
– P.G. Wodehouse, *Mulliner Nights*, 1933

On 28 July 1914, war was declared in Europe and Sargent found himself trapped in the
Austrian Alps far from the comforts of Tite Street. Despite repeated warnings about the
increasing tensions on the Continent, he had set off from London. On the declaration of war
Austria's borders were closed. Sargent and the small party travelling with him attempted to
leave but found trains were packed full of people trying desperately to escape the maelstrom
that was engulfing Europe. To make matters worse, neither Sargent nor anyone in his party
had passports. They decided to stay put and Sargent continued painting, but by October they
had received notice that Major Armstrong, who had travelled with them but departed upon
the declaration of war, was being held prisoner on suspicion of being a spy. Suddenly alarmed,
Sargent scrambled to get a passport and, after a testing journey, was finally allowed back into
England.

Life in London had already changed dramatically by the time Sargent returned. The
gilded, bejewelled Edwardians were now marching around in khaki Red Cross uniforms,
leading troops off to France and Belgium. Increasingly agitated by newspaper accounts of
German brutality in the Low Countries, the seventy-two-year-old Henry James launched
a diatribe against all things German. Unlike James, who had renounced his American
citizenship in protest against American neutrality, Sargent remained aloof from the chaos
around him. 'The spirit of isolation belonged markedly to Sargent,' wrote his friend, Evan
Charteris, 'he read no newspapers; he had the sketchiest knowledge of current movements
outside art.'[1]

He would not be allowed to bury his head in the sand for long. Artists were soon drawn into the conflict. With fundraising in full swing, the American Red Cross in London asked leading portraitists to contribute empty frames to an auction held at Christie's, whereby the highest bidders would sit for their portraits. Sargent had agreed to paint two three-quarter length oils for the benefit of the American Red Cross in London. However one of the buyers, Sir Hugh Lane, died when the Lusitania was sunk. The estate executors took a vote and it was agreed that President Woodrow Wilson would be selected to sit for the empty canvas.

Sargent spent most of the War in the United States. There he painted President Wilson and took an opportunity to travel to the Rocky Mountains. He arrived back in London in 1917. After only a month back in London the artist received a letter from the Prime Minister, David Lloyd George, stating that the British War Memorials Committee had suggested Sargent paint a mural to commemorate the war. The subject had already been selected – they wanted him to depict 'British and American troops engaged in unison'. The painting would form the centrepiece of a proposed Hall of Remembrance.

The British Government were sending war artists to the front to capture the grim realities of horror and heroism for posterity. Henry Tonks had been making sketches of the horrific injuries inflicted upon the mutilated soldiers returning from the trenches. Sargent greeted the commission with trepidation. At the age of sixty-two he was being taken into the heart of a war zone. 'But would I have the nerve to look,' he asked Evan Charteris, 'not to speak of painting? I have never seen anything in the least horrible – outside of my studio.'[2]

Eventually Sargent did look. The horror beyond his studio was immense. He travelled to the war zone with Henry Tonks as his companion. By August they had been through the badly bombed town of Arras where he painted *Ruined Cathedral*. As they moved through the devastated towns and villages Sargent documented what he saw in a series of sketches, but never once found any evidence of 'British and American troops engaged in unison'. He wrote to Charteris: 'How can there be anything flagrant enough for a picture when Mars and Venus are miles apart whether in camps or front trenches?'[3] 'I have wasted lots of time going to the front trenches,' he wrote. 'There is nothing to paint there – it is ugly and meagre and cramped, and one only sees one or two men. In this Somme country I have seen what I wanted, roads crammed with troops on the march. It is the finest spectacle the war affords.'[4]

Towards the end of his tour, Sargent began to despair. The stress of the situation had eventually taken its toll and the artist came down with flu. He was sent out to a casualty clearing station to recover 'in a hospital tent with the accompaniment of groans of the wounded and the choking and coughing of gassed men, which was a nightmare. It always seemed strange on opening one's eyes to see the level cots and the dimly lit long tent looking so calm, when one was dozing in pandemonium.'[5] Later that month, however, Sargent witnessed a gruesome scene that burned into his memory. On a sunny afternoon in August, he travelled to a casualty clearing station on the Arras-Doullens road. At dusk they came upon 'a harrowing sight, a field full of gassed and blindfolded men'.[6] Sargent immediately sat down and began to draw in his sketchbook.

By the end of the ordeal Sargent asked to be sent back to Tite Street where he could recover. He had seen enough of the war. The commission had been to find British and American troops working in unison, but the memory of the clearing station was something he could not get out of his head. Casting the brief aside Sargent faced his blank canvas and began to sketch. In his Tite Street studio he immediately set out to work on the commission while the harrowing images were still fresh in his memory.

With the Armistice of 11 November 1918 the Great War ended, but Sargent battled on with his epic. Finally, in March 1919 he presented the British War Memorials Committee with a twenty by seven-foot painting featuring a row of gassed and blindfolded soldiers being led to a medical tent. The men in the room gasped. Lord Beaverbrook complained that the picture altogether failed to meet the requirements, but he was soon silenced. Everyone else knew it may not have been what they asked for, but it was exactly what they needed. Sargent chose the 'matter of fact' and anonymous title *Gassed*.

With *Gassed* complete there was still very little rest for Sargent. There was an end in sight for the Boston mural project which he had been working on for twenty-five years. But soon after the Armistice Sir Abe Bailey offered to pay for three pictures for the National Portrait Gallery which would include the major political, naval and military figures involved in the Great War. Sargent was again approached to do a group portrait of the Generals of the Great War, but he declined. In January 1919 he relented but with great reluctance. He had asked for a 'great liberty of time'[7] in finishing the portrait, and it would have to be fitted around his Boston work. 'The Generals loom before me like a nightmare,'[8] he complained to Charteris. Although he claimed that he had firmly given up portraiture, for some reason he felt impelled to undertake the commission. *The Generals* was a mammoth portrait, unlike any he had done before, though it lacked the finesse and character of his earlier work.

Sargent was not the only war artist in Tite Street. Like Sargent, Glyn Philpot was an ardent hispanophile, and whenever he got the chance, travelled to Spain to study the work of Velazquez. In February 1910 he exhibited his acclaimed *Manuelito* at the Modern Society of Portrait Painters. The painting was hailed a success. *The Times* commented that it was 'quite the most striking modern picture now exhibiting in London',[9] and the *Westminster Gazette* said '[T]he pose is original and difficult, but characteristic and brilliantly drawn. The colour is daring and luminous, the brushwork able in the extreme.'[10]

With strong influences of Velazquez, but also reminiscent of Sargent's *Carmencita* or *El Jaleo*, *Manuelito* put Philpot on the artistic map. While Romaine Brooks had loathed the bright colours of the Mediterranean, Philpot could not get enough. He started *La Zarzarosa*, translated as 'the wild rose', at Glebe Place nearby in Chelsea, but the project required more space so he took a more spacious studio at the Tower House in Tite Street, where Whistler had lived with his wife Beatrice from 1888 to 1890.

General Officers of World War I by John Singer Sargent, 1922

Philpot arrived in Tite Street in 1910. It was clear that he was working under the influence of Sargent with his portrait of *Mrs Emile Mond*, which combines elements of *Madame X* and even Whistler's *Arrangement in Grey and Black, No. 1*. Shortly after moving into the Tower House, he began work on his unfinished *La Zarzarosa*. With the success of *Manuelito*, society sensed the possibility of another Sargent-in-the-making and rushed to Tite Street.

The year Philpot exhibited *Manuelito* was a significant one for the London art world. Roger Fry's landmark *Manet and the Post-Impressionists* exhibition was held at the Grafton Galleries in 1910 and was followed by a second, more ambitious exhibition two years later, which showed, for the first time in England, the range and depth of work of late Impressionist and of Post-Impressionist artists. 'The battle is won,' declared Clive Bell at the Second Post-Impressionist Exhibition in 1912. 'We have ceased to ask, "What does this picture represent?" and ask instead, "What does it make us feel?"'[11]

The 'old guard' of the New English Art Club now felt themselves isolated and were fiercely critical. Augustus John, who had been regarded as the heir apparent of the New English generation, had reservations about Fry's exhibition and chose to refrain from submitting any work. By 1912 John found himself in the rearguard of British art. At the Slade School Henry Tonks advised his students to stay away from Fry's exhibition for fear of ideological contamination. Philip Wilson Steer developed a loathing for Cezanne, his 'toppling jugs, botched-bashed apples, bodiless clothes, muddled perspectives and the rest, thought to illustrate the cubical nature of the sphere, the generosity of colour and other brown profundities.'[12]

In response to this flexing of muscle by Fry and the Post-Impressionists, and the seeming lack of progression in the New English Art Club, another clique splintered from the already vibrant group of artists living in Fitzroy Street. The group was spearheaded by Walter Sickert, once a devout pupil of Whistler's Tite Street circle. Sickert pioneered an all-male exhibiting group, called the Camden Town Group, whose work went on show in 1911. The avant-garde hotbed had moved, and the spotlight was ranging brightly over Bloomsbury, Fitzrovia and Camden.

The rise in Philpot's career as a portraitist had been momentarily interrupted with the outbreak of war when he joined the Royal Fusiliers and was sent to Winchester for training. His sister Daisy took over his Tite Street studio and volunteered at the Victoria Hospital for Sick Children nearby. Philpot, however, was never sent away to battle, and when the war ended he returned to Tite Street and took a studio at No. 33. During his time in the service he met his lifelong lover Vivian Forbes, a handsome young man who had begun a career in Egypt as a businessman. Forbes was encouraged, and taught, by Philpot to become an artist.

Philpot had studied at Lambeth School and at the tender age of twenty had already exhibited at the Royal Academy. One of Philpot's earliest successes was the 'problem picture' *Death Contemplating a Dandy*, a provocative glimpse of the fascination with the conflict of morality and sensuality that was to inform his later work. Philpot was keen to work on a war project similar to Sargent's *Gassed* and asked to paint the subject of 'A Bathing Parade' which was rejected by the British War Memorials Committee hinting at the latent homoeroticism in his work. 'I cannot say whether this is a really significant incident in the life of soldiers,' wrote one of the organisers, 'but I will bet anything that Philpot suggested it because it gave him the opportunity of painting the nude.'[13] Instead Philpot was commissioned to paint portraits of the senior Admirals, produced under the aegis of the Admiralty subcommittee of the newly founded Imperial War Museum.

In Chelsea, Philpot became acquainted with the artists Ricketts and Shannon. Another visitor to Philpot's studio, Robbie Ross, was all too familiar with Tite Street. Ross had been a devoted friend of Oscar Wilde and had spent a summer with the Wildes in Tite Street. His endeavours to dissuade his friend not to pursue his libel case failed, and he later had the harrowing task of informing Constance about her husband's fate after his trial. In Tite Street he came to collect valuable manuscripts before the contents of the house were auctioned and after Wilde's death he became the executor of his estate.

Ross was now running the Carfax Gallery which hosted three solo exhibitions of Sargent's works in 1903, 1905 and 1908. He was now back in Tite Street but this time with a more cheerful purpose – to introduce Philpot to the poet Siegfried Sassoon. Sassoon had been in battle during the war and was about to publish a new volume of poetry for whom Philpot's portrait would serve as the frontispiece. Originally Philpot arranged to do a drawing, but as Ross was such a 'great friend' and Sassoon such a 'good subject', he

La Zarzarosa by Glyn Philpot, 1910

Siegfried Sassoon by Glyn Philpot, 1917

insisted on doing an oil for an agreed fee of £50, a tenth of his usual charge. The two men met in May 1917, when Sassoon gave Philpot an inscribed copy of his book of poems *The Old Huntsman*. Over two weeks in early June, Sassoon spent several afternoons sitting for his portrait at Philpot's Tite Street studio. Sassoon found him a 'delightfully modest and likeable companion'.[14] The studio was 'a perfect place in which to forget.' Sassoon recalled:

Philpot's own existence was one that consisted largely in an ultra-refined appreciation of beautiful objects. He had what might be called a still-life temperament; his eyes delighted not so much in the living realities of nature as in the richness and elegance of things contrived by human handiwork. This was shown in his painting of silks, velvets and brocades, and in anything which evoked his sensuous joy in surface qualities and harmonious arrangements of colour. Too subtle and fine to be accused of precocity, his taste was superbly artificial. The interior environment he had devised for himself was a deliberately fastidious denial of war-time conditions, a delicate defence against the violence and ugly destruction which dominated the outside world. All this made sitting for my portrait a most tranquillizing occupation, slowing down my thoughts and soothing my sensibilities…when I spoke my thoughts aloud he replied from only half his attention, and this created a sort of absent-minded atmosphere which made the place seem more peaceful than ever.[15]

At the end of one sitting, Philpot quietly observed that the portrait, which Sassoon had 'conscientiously avoided looking at', was now completed. Examining it for the first time, Sassoon remarked that it was 'rather Byronic'. 'You *are* rather, aren't you?' Philpot replied.

Over tea Sassoon could not help glancing at his own portrait 'occasionally with a pleasant feeling that I had acquired a romantic, illustrative personality to preside over my published work.'[16] Sassoon found the face on the portrait 'almost scornfully severe and unspeculative, giving no indication of the conflict that was being enacted behind the mask of physical prosperity.'[17] And the idea that he was 'rather Byronic' helped 'to sustain [Sasson's] belief that [he] was about to do something spectacular and heroic.'[18] To Ross, Sassoon remarked that, 'Philpot has undoubtedly made a good job' of the portrait but to Lady Ottoline Morrell, who disliked it, he wrote 'it is a little popular. No doubt it will help to sell my posthumous works.'[19]

Philpot continued to paint portraits but later branched off into more allegorical subject matter, often explicitly homosexual. In 1919, at the height of his popularity, he painted *Melampus and the Centaur*, one of his most successful subject paintings set in a desertscape. The painting depicts a youthful Melampus, the first physician, being instructed by Chiron, the centaur, in the rudiments of botany. Yet the painting speaks of homosexual desire with its nude male subject barely covered.

As the war in Europe drew to a close Philpot left Tite Street, eventually moving to Paris where his work shifted from the influence of Sargent to a style more reminiscent of Gauguin

Melampus and the Centaur by Glyn Philpot, 1919

and Cezanne. Forbes would remain with Philpot until the latter's unexpected death in 1937. Then, stricken with grief, Forbes would take his own life with an overdose of pills.

Meanwhile Sargent's health had remained robust. The 'big, burly man'[20] he had been in his twenties had now become 'cut out of beef'[21] in his sixties. He finished his Boston murals, and in April 1925 he was planning to return to Boston to see them installed. 'Now the American things are done,' he joked, 'I suppose, I may die when I like.'[22] He did just that. On the evening of 14 April his sister Emily held a dinner for him at 10 Carlyle Mansions, just around the corner from Tite Street. Some of Sargent's closest friends were in attendance, including Wilson Steer and Henry Tonks. Later that night Sargent waved off his friends and headed off along Cheyne Walk in the direction of Tite Street. As it started to rain, Nelson Ward, passing in a taxi, pulled aside, asked Sargent to step in, and dropped him off a few minutes later outside No. 31. Inside Sargent sat down at his desk and scribbled out a note he had forgotten to write earlier and went back up to the top of the street to post it. Back at No. 31 he went to his library and plucked Voltaire's *Dictionnaire Philosophique* off the shelf and retired to his bedroom. The rain continued, but by the next morning Sargent would be dead and an important chapter of Tite Street's history would be closed.

26.

LAST *of the* TITANS

Our late Victory has left us with a headache, and the Peace we are
enjoying is too much like the morning after a debauch.
– Augustus John, 1945

Sargent died in his sleep on 14 April 1925 and was discovered the following morning in bed by his parlour maid, who noted that 'he looked peaceful, just like a little child sleeping.'[1] At noon that day Sir Philip Sassoon, a Trustee of the National Gallery, arrived and placed a floral wreath outside the famous green door of No. 31 Tite Street. The figure of the burly, cigar-smoking Sargent would be no more than ghostly memory, and with his passing the golden age of Tite Street came to a close.

As the 1930s approached, the great titans of Tite Street – Whistler, Wilde and Sargent – were all dead and Chelsea had changed beyond recognition. In the 1870s the quiet and rural village of artists and artisans stood on the fringes of the capital, but in just fifty years it had been engulfed into the folds of the bustling metropolis as the edges of the capital stretched further westward. The art world had changed too. The seeds that Whistler and his followers had planted in the 1870s had now come to full bloom, and by the 1930s modern art was flourishing in London. The Royal Academy had evolved, and the once avant-garde and progressive New English Art Club had been sidelined by Roger Fry and Samuel Courtauld's Post-Impressionists. In this fray Tite Street seemed somehow lost. It was no longer centre stage. The torch was passed to new groups and areas like Bloomsbury and Camden, with their own unique sets of characters and their own aesthetics and intellectual communities.

Sargent was one of the last of a dying generation of great artists trained in the nineteenth century. The world was growing faster and art moved at the same pace. Despite the rapid progress of early twentieth-century London, some artists remained uncomfortably straddling a transitional period in British art punctuated by Pre-Raphaelites at one end and the abstract modernism of the Vorticists at the other. Contemporary taste had little time or consideration for meticulously painted literary and historical scenes. The work of John Collier, Edwin Abbey and Frank Cadogan Cowper no longer held the same aesthetic or commercial interest.

Once an apprentice to Edwin Abbey at the Chelsea Lodge, Frank Cadogan Cowper, now a mature artist, returned to Tite Street in 1932 and took a studio at No. 33. Cowper's early successes at the Royal Academy with paintings like *An Aristocrat answering the Summons to Execution, Paris 1791* or *Lucretia Borgia Reigns in the Vatican in the Absence of Pope Alexander VI* earned him little regard in the modern art world of the 1930s. Nevertheless he had continued to submit portraits regularly, predominantly of young society ladies, to the Royal Academy summer exhibitions. Fortunately for Cowper there were still patrons like the writer Evelyn Waugh and the Wills family of Miserden Park, who ensured that his subject pictures found their way to appreciative homes. Yet it was clear that artists like Cowper were a dying species, 'the Last Pre-Raphaelite'.[2]

Four years after Sargent's death, in September 1930, a young musician, Peter Warlock, wrote to his mother that 'by great good fortune' he had been able to 'find a cheap and very comfortable flat in Chelsea'.[3] The 'comfortable flat' he found was in the basement of No. 30 Tite Street. For Warlock the physical environment was 'a matter of the greatest importance,' and he found Tite Street a 'quiet and secluded spot' where he was 'full of hope' for the future of his work and compelled to 'go steadily ahead without any difficulty'. But all this hinged on the 'testimony of various friends,' upon whom he relied to convince the landlord that he could in fact pay the £2 a week rent.[4]

Tite Street was the last of nearly a dozen Chelsea addresses that housed Peter Warlock. Warlock was born Philip Heseltine at the Savoy Hotel, where his parents 'lived lavishly'.[5] After studying at Eton, and two unsuccessful spells at Christ Church, Oxford, and University College London, Warlock eventually found a job as a music critic on the *Daily Mail* in 1915, but this lasted only four months. As a conscientious objector, he spent the years of the First World War researching and editing early music in the British Museum, dividing his time between Cornwall and bohemian Battersea, and, to avoid conscription, lived briefly in Dublin. While he was still at Oxford, Warlock had been introduced to the novels of D. H. Lawrence, and he later wrote that Lawrence's poems were some of the most 'wonderful love poems in the world'.[6] The feeling of admiration was reciprocal. Lawrence wrote that Warlock would be 'one of the men who will count, in the future'.[7] With that in mind Warlock orchestrated a meeting with the writer at a dinner party in November 1915. He soon found himself swept up in the intellectual and artistic circles of aristocratic bohemians like Augustus John and Minnie 'Puma' Channing.

Warlock became Lawrence's devoted disciple, but after a very intense 'friendship' with the writer came a sudden and inexplicable split. 'The truth is', wrote Warlock, 'that Lawrence was always inclined to treat his friends and acquaintances as if they were characters in one of his novels, and sought accordingly to mould their characters and direct their actions as he desired.'[8] Lawrence was in fact moulding Warlock into one of his characters. He would later make a literary debut as Julius Halliday, a raffish bohemian of the Cafe Royal featured in *Women in Love*.

Hasan Shahid Suhrawardy, Philip Heseltine (later Peter Warlock) and D.H. Lawrence, 1915

The Cafe Royal had been at the centre of bohemian social life in London since the 1890s. It was there that Bosie, Oscar and the Marquess of Queensberry had their fateful meeting and it was there, nearly thirty years later, that Warlock met another painter, named Augustus John. The 'tall blond young man,' as Augustus John later recalled, 'usually accompanied by two or three young females bearing portfolios and scrolls,'[9] had indeed become a regular patron at the Cafe Royal. For John, however, Warlock's 'pale handsome face always wore a smile and made one feel rather uncomfortable'.[10]

As a young man Warlock drew inspiration from a number of musical influences. He had come under the influence of composer Frederick Delius while still a student at Eton. He later befriended leading composers such as Bernard van Dieren and Béla Bartók. During the 1920s, Warlock supported himself with sporadic journalistic work. In this time he also composed *The Curlew* song cycle, inspired by the poetry of W. B. Yeats. Later, while living in the village of Eynsford in Kent with his girlfriend Barbara Peache, he composed a suite called 'Capriol' inspired by tunes from a treatise on dancing by Thoinot Arbeau. At Eynsford, Warlock and Peache indulged in a lifestyle fuelled by alcohol and uninhibited sex, complete with wild, drunken parties that at least once brought police intervention.[11] In November 1928, Warlock returned to London during a slump in his career when he was offered a job as editor of the magazine of the new Imperial League of Opera by Sir Thomas Beecham. Warlock had also taken up the opportunity to help organise a festival to honour his favourite composer Frederick Delius. But the final summer of Warlock's life was marked by gloom, depression, and inactivity. Warlock became obsessed with imminent death.[12]

In September 1930 Warlock moved with Peache into a basement flat at 30 Tite Street. The street suited Warlock's bohemian sensibilities and he thought he would be 'able to do good work' here.[13] Tite Street may not have been the same bohemian environment that it once was, but the name and reputation still carried certain associations.

Warlock also had tenuous links to both Sargent and Whistler. Of his expansive family, there were two uncles in particular who held great interest and affection in Warlock's life. Arthur Joseph Heseltine, whom Warlock called Uncle Joe, was one of a nest of 'English Bohemians' that Sargent met in Grez.[14] Another uncle, John Postle Heseltine, was an etcher and an avid collector who had sympathised with Whistler's plight in his trial against Ruskin. In 1877 when Whistler pursued his libel case and later faced bankruptcy, John had put up twenty-five guineas to start a subscription to benefit the artist. The money was intended 'as a mark of my sympathy with you and as a protest against what seems an illogical verdict,' he wrote to Whistler. 'If for the plaintiff then the damage done seems to me more than one farthing.'[15] Whistler gratefully accepted the money as a 'warm expression of sympathy for my cause and strong assertion of regard for the works over which the battle has been fought.'[16]

Though he lived in Tite Street only a few short months, Warlock, like Whistler, would leave his imprint on the street's history. Just a week before Christmas 1930, on Tuesday, 16 December, Warlock met his friends, the composer Bernard and his wife Frida van Dieren, at the Duke of Wellington pub near Sloane Square. After a few drinks Warlock invited the couple back to Tite Street where they stayed until shortly after midnight.

The landlady of No. 30, Mary Venn, who lived above Warlock's flat, later recounted how, at about 6.40 the next morning, she had heard a noise like the shutting of doors and windows: 'There was a lot of noise. I really wondered what was happening.' When she got out of bed and looked out of the window, 'the place downstairs was all lit up'.[17] Another Tite Street neighbour added that they 'heard the piano being played early this morning and the playing continued until about seven o'clock when it stopped.'[18]

When Venn woke again later that morning, she was suddenly aware of a strong smell of gas and began to inspect the flat for any leaks. At about 10.45 that morning Barbara Peache arrived home. 'Mrs Warlock, as we knew her, came along, and I sent my woman down to see her. She was in the area downstairs, and said she could not get in. She said to my maid, "Send for the police."'[19] The police broke the window and found Warlock 'fully dressed except for his shoes.' When the body arrived at St. Luke's Hospital, it was determined that Warlock had been dead for about three or four hours as a result of coal-gas poisoning.

An inquest was held on 22 December; the jury could not determine whether the death was an accident or suicide. An open verdict was returned. Warlock's death would remain shrouded in mystery. Most commentators have considered suicide the more likely cause; Warlock's close friend Lionel Jellinek and Peache both recalled that he had previously threatened to take his life by gas, and the outline of a new will was found among the papers in the flat. However, there is also much conjecture that it was a loose gas tap that caused Warlock's death. Years later, Warlock's son Nigel Heseltine introduced a new theory – that his father had been murdered in cold blood by rival composer Bernard van Dieren, the sole beneficiary of Warlock's 1920 will, which stood to be revoked by the new one, though it had never been signed or witnessed.

Whether suicide, murder or accident, the mystery of Warlock's death has loomed over Tite Street ever since. 'My memories of this extraordinary being will always be charged', Augustus John later wrote, 'with the bitter and futile reflection that, had we but set out in time on a tour into Wales we had projected, that fatal hour might have been perhaps averted when he put the cat out, locked the door, and turned on the gas.'[20] John himself was the last remnant of the golden age of Tite Street having lived in the heyday of Whistler, Wilde and Sargent, and would be the last of the 'smart bohemians'[21] to inhabit the street in the mid-twentieth century.

An entire decade separated Warlock's tragic death and John's arrival in Tite Street. The 1930s had been a 'disastrous decade',[22] and even John himself admitted it was 'the worst spell of my bloody life'.[23] Britain was teetering on the brink of economic stagnation, and National Socialism was on the rise across Europe. In art, Whistler's greys and Godwin's whites were eclipsed by the abstraction of the Vorticists and the stark buildings of Le Corbusier and the Bauhaus movement in Germany. John struggled to define his role in the brave new world.

John was a Welshman and had come to London, along with his highly talented sister Gwen, to study art at the Slade School. Here he became a star pupil under Sargent's friend Henry Tonks. Along with the other young artists of his generation, John had gone to Paris and there had spent time with the 'distinguished reprobate' Oscar Wilde. Though 'appreciative of him as a great man,' and as 'a big and good-natured fellow with an enormous sense of fun, impeccable bad taste, and a deeply religious apprehension of the Devil,'[24] John felt embarrassed by Wilde's elaborate performances of wit, not knowing how to respond. 'I could think of nothing whatever to say. Even my laughter sounded hollow.' Wilde, however, seemed to be quite taken with the 'charming Celtish poet in colour,'[25] as he described the young artist. When Alice Rothenstein took the dishevelled John for a haircut, Wilde was aghast. 'You should have consulted me', he said, laying a hand on John's shoulder, 'before taking this important step.'[26]

In the years before the First World War, John spent a considerable time in the south of France with his wife, Ida, and for a time formed a *ménage a trois* with Dorothy McNeill, one of many mistresses in John's long and active sexual life. During the war, John was attached to the Canadian forces as a war artist and made a number of memorable portraits of Canadian infantrymen. John had painted *Canadians Opposite Lens,* which Sargent called 'a hideous Post-Impressionist picture' done in 'his free and script style, but without beauty of composition'.[27]

As a portrait artist John picked up where Sargent left off, albeit with less acclaim. He painted some of the most famous faces of the early twentieth century. Both W. B. Yeats and fellow Irishman James Joyce sat for John. A decade later, John painted the highly unusual, and rather unflattering, portrait of *Lady Ottoline Morrell*, along with the iconic portrait of *T. E. Lawrence* in his Arabian robes, and the ageing author, *Thomas Hardy,* who remarked about his finished portrait, 'I don't know whether that is how I look or not, but that is how I feel.'[28]

By the 1930s John's art was already in steady decline. One night, fellow artist and writer, Michael Ayrton, almost ran over John in his taxi as it passed through Chelsea. When he pulled John inside he found his friend in tears. 'It's not good enough,' he sobbed. 'What girl is that, Augustus?' asked Ayrton. But when he took John home, and put him to bed, John just mumbled repeatedly, 'My work's not good enough.'[29]

John had moved into Whistler's and Sargent's old studio at No. 33 in 1940, after bombs had destroyed his former studio. There was a new war now, far more destructive than the last, and Chelsea would not escape unharmed. Most artists fled to the countryside to escape the Blitz of 1941, but John remained. 'London is being badly bombed,' he wrote to his sister, Gwen. 'Still people are sticking it out wonderfully. Life goes on as usual – in the day time, and the streets are full of people and all very cheerful in spite of loss of sleep. The row at night is hellish.'[30] For respite, John would visit friends at the Pier Hotel across the river in Battersea, where the 'drink supply had generously expanded – to steady the clients' nerves'.[31] After an evening drinking, either at the Pier Hotel or in a nearby Chelsea pub, John would usually invite his drinking companions for a last drink in Tite Street, and from the enormous studio window they would watch the fires raging in the rubble beyond the Royal Hospital.

Despite this, John was determined to carry on as usual. In the 1870s, Whistler had watched rockets exploding over Chelsea from the Cremorne Pleasure Gardens. In the 1940s, John watched as German 'doodlebugs' or 'buzz-bombs' fell and twice 'buggered up'[32] his Tite Street studio. One sitter, Constance Graham, remembers posing for him when an air-raid broke out. John 'was utterly unperturbed, and we were seated by the enormous studio window while the bombs buzzed overhead. They might have been blue bottles for all he cared so of course I felt obliged to remain equally unmoved.'[33]

After weeks and months of refuge, 'from contact with a depressing epoch', in his studio spent painting 'huge decorations as remote as possible from the world we precariously live in,'[34] the desire to paint portraiture had returned. John had already made enough of a reputation for himself as a rakish bohemian to the extent that the more conservative artist, Anna Lea Merritt, who lived in Tite Street in the 1880s, called him 'Disgustus John'.[35]

John was 'usually asleep when I arrived at Tite Street,' Lord Portal remembered, 'and loud knocks were required to rouse him. When roused he came noisily to the door, greeted me gruffly and started clearing the space for my chair by kicking away any pieces of furniture that were in the way.'[36] Shortly before the Normandy landings, another sitter came to John's Tite Street studio – Field Marshal Lord Montgomery. The stoic and reserved Montgomery would arrive every day in his Rolls Royce, and sit 'as tense as a hunting dog on a shoot'[37] upon the dais in the studio where John had positioned him. 'Monty has been sitting like a brick,' John reported, 'and the picture progresses,'[38] but Monty was suspicious of the whole Tite Street scene around him. 'Who is this chap?' he exclaimed. 'He drinks, he's dirty, and I know there are women in the background!'[39] He was not the only one uncomfortable with the arrangement. 'It is rather unfortunate the Colonel has to be in the room,' John lamented, 'as I feel his presence through the back of my head, which interferes with concentration.'[40]

To alleviate the tension, John's friend, and renowned playwright, George Bernard Shaw, was brought in for distraction. For an hour he 'talked all over the shop to amuse your sitter and keep his mind off the worries of the present actual fighting.'[41] While John had no interest in Monty, Shaw had a 'wild admiration,' but when the picture was finally completed, the sitter was not impressed, dismissing it as not the 'sort of likeness he would want to leave his son'.[42]

During the destructive war, Chelsea had become a village again. People stopped each other in the street to share stories and even look in on neighbours. But the war was the death-blow to an already faltering artistic milieu in Tite Street. The great names were all gone, and the other minor artists had fled the bombing, never to return. Tite Street had been abandoned at the outbreak of war and almost completely deserted during the Blitz. The only people to remain in Tite Street were Augustus John and the Hope-Nicholsons at More House.

'More House was no ordinary home,' recalled Sir Peregrine Worsthorne, a frequent visitor. 'It was a period piece as was its owner – pure fin de siècle, Wildean, *Yellow Book* decadence with an extra touch of Catholic exoticism thrown in for good measure. Vast and dark, it contained many rooms filled with undusted treasures and people to match.'[43] Laura and Adrian Hope, who had bought the house in 1894, had died, and the house was passed to their daughter Jacqueline and son-in-law Hedley Nicholson. The Hope-Nicholsons shared an intense interest in the Stuart dynasty and Anglo-Catholicism. Jacqueline's love of seventeenth-century costume and interiors led her to redecorate the house with seventeenth- and eighteenth-century antiquarian furniture, with her bedroom based on Maurice Leloir's depiction of Louis XIII's bed, which she found in a biography of Richelieu.

The family created a private chapel in the first-floor conservatory, where regular services were held, and the Hope-Nicholsons' son Felix was an altar boy. The chapel was soon filled with relics and memorabilia which ranged from a red leather slipper of Pius IX to the gift from Oscar Wilde's son, Cyril, of a piece of Charles I's coffin. Meanwhile, the rest of the house was a menagerie of oddities, relics and historic artefacts that the family had been collecting over the past century.[44]

Felix eventually inherited the Tite Street house. 'Although Felix was homosexual himself,' continued Worsthorne, 'he loved the company of beautiful girls who were no less fond of him'. At More House he 'spent most of the war pretending it did not exist and while you were under his roof the pretence was so complete that even a bomb falling next door was somehow transformed into an escape for "madder music and for stronger wine".'[45] More House became a place of sanctuary and refuge for the 'Beautiful Young Things' of London. When Worsthorne visited he found a host of bohemians, 'lying around on *Recamier* sofas'.[46] Along with the 'other unmentionables'[47] there was the artist Brian Howard, purportedly Evelyn Waugh's model for Anthony Blanche in *Brideshead Revisited*. At the More House retreat congregated actresses, writers and artists, including their Tite Street neighbour Augustus John.

In 1940 the National Gallery held an exhibition including works by Whistler, Sargent and John. 'It is an astonishing record,' wrote Herbert Read of John's work, 'and it is doubtful if any other contemporary artist in Europe could display such virtuosity and skill.'[48] But while John and his neighbours were 'lying around on *Recamier* sofas' at More House, the rubble-strewn streets beyond had changed.

For John, post-War Britain had grown 'more and more to resemble a mixture of a concentration and a Butlin camp'.[49] The world of individuality and personality that Tite Street had embodied would be swept away. In the wake of war came crippling austerity. All across Britain localism and personality were crushed into identical, pre-fabricated tower blocks. The free-spirited world of bohemia that had prevailed before was now homeless. 'The sense of futility and boredom,' wrote John, 'which, together with general restlessness and unease, marks the end of an epoch.'[50]

There was little room for characters like Augustus John in the post-war years. 'Look at Augustus John,' proclaimed Norman Douglas. 'Take away his beard, close-crop his hair and Augustus would be as impressive as before. Him I admire not only as a fine man but for his way of thinking about life.'[51] In many ways John embodied the story of Tite Street, and his story is a fitting close to the street's tapestry of artists and bohemians. His career bridged the world of Whistler and Sargent, and stretched into the new realms of abstraction. In personality, he was like one of those 'intense, vague duffers'[52] from the days of Miles and Wilde. But the artists of Tite Street had all gone. Only John remained and the street no longer held any promise for him. 'Alas!' lamented Douglas, 'I fear he's the last of the Titans.'[53] And so he was. In 1950, Augustus John finally left Tite Street and its wonderful possibilities receeded.

Field Marshall Lord Montgomery by Augustus John, 1944

TITE STREET MAP

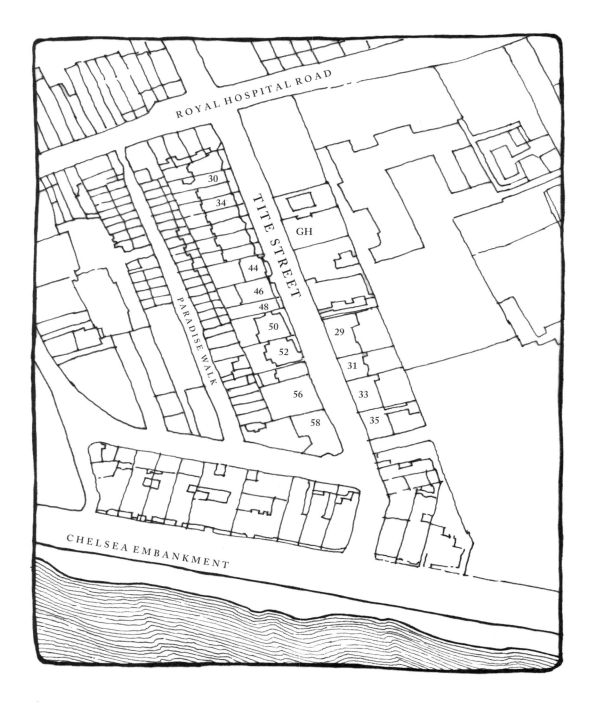

TITE STREET CHRONOLOGY
1875–1950

1875   Chelsea Embankment opened by the Duke and Duchess of Edinburgh

Tite Street created by Metropolitan Board of Works (MBW)

1877   May: Opening of Grosvenor Gallery in New Bond Street – Whistler's *Nocturne in Black and Gold: The Falling Rocket* attracts John Ruskin's criticism

September: Whistler commissions White House in Tite Street by E.W. Godwin

A new farce, *The Grasshopper*, opens in the West End, mocking the budding aesthetic movement

1878   Godwin and Whistler battle against the MBW / White House completed

June: Whistler and Godwin exhibit at Paris Exposition Universelle

25 June: Whistler moves into Tite Street

Godwin designs Chelsea Lodge for portrait painter Archibald Stuart-Wortley and cartoonist Carlo 'Ape' Pellegrini

Sir Percy Shelley builds house on Chelsea Embankment

Whistler finishes portrait of Rosa Corder called *Arrangement in Brown and Black*, works on an unfinished portrait of Lillie Langtry

November: Whistler wins trial against Ruskin then publishes *Whistler v Ruskin*

1879   Archibald Stuart-Wortley and Pellegrini split; Chelsea Lodge sold to the Hon. Slingsby Bethell

Society portrait painter Frank Miles commissions a Godwin house in Tite Street

7 May: Auction of Whistler's paintings and belongings at the White House

Frank Waller builds No. 50, the Cottage, for American artist Anna Lea Merritt

Shelley Theatre built in Tite Street by Sir Percy Shelley

1880   Frank Waller builds No. 52, More House, for newlywed painters John and Marian Collier

August: Frank Miles and Oscar Wilde move into No. 44 – Wilde christens it Keats House

1881   Colonel Sir Robert William Edis designs studio-house at No. 31 for Frank Dicey

Prince of Wales and his mistress Lillie Langtry attend spiritualist séances at No. 44, Keats House, with Miles and Wilde; Sally Higgs, a flower girl at Victoria Station, is brought to live in as model for Miles; police come to No. 44 searching for Miles on suspicion of paedophilia

22 March: Whistler returns to Tite Street at No. 33 where he intends to 'paint all the fashionables'

Wilde and Whistler reconnect and become 'inseparable'

Stuart-Wortley has a second studio-house built by Godwin at No. 29 called Canwell House; Pellegrini briefly takes a studio above Whistler's at No. 33

A new comedy, *The Colonel*, caricatures the aesthetic movement and opens at Prince of Wales Theatre – later receives a command performance for Queen Victoria

Wilde publishes controversial volume *Poems*; storms out of No. 44 after altercation with Miles

John Collier begins to receive significant portrait commissions including one from the
    Linnean Society to paint the ageing Charles Darwin

1882   Whistler works on portraits of Lady Archibald Campbell and Lady Meux

Walter Sickert leaves Slade and becomes Whistler's pupil

Carlo 'Ape' Pellegrini leaves Tite Street impoverished

1883   Sir Percy Shelley taken to court by neighbour the Hon. Slingsby Bethell and Shelley Theatre
    is forced to close

Whistler paints Theodore Duret, Lois Cassatt and actress Milly Finch

1884   Whistler moves to Fulham Road studio

May: Oscar Wilde and Constance Lloyd marry

Oscar and Constance Wilde move into No. 34, commission Godwin to design interior

Marian Collier has first baby and begins to show signs of severe post-natal depression

1885   February: Whistler delivers ten o'clock lecture which strikes directly at Wilde

Stuart-Wortley sells lease of No. 29, Canwell House, to Scottish artist Mary Grant

Godwin's Tower House built

1886   Whistler elected President of Society of British Artists

E.W. Godwin dies – Whistler, Beatrice and Lady Archibald Campbell have lunch on his coffin

John Singer Sargent moves to London after *Madame X* scandal in Paris and takes lease of
    studio at No. 33

1887   Frank Miles admitted to Brislington House asylum

Sargent leaves for America where he is given an enthusiastic reception

Robbie Ross spends summer with Wildes in Tite Street

Marian Collier dies in Paris

1888   John Collier sells No. 52 to Admiral Sir Alfred and Lady Jephson who calls it More House

Wilde publishes *A Happy Prince and Other Stories* illustrated by George Percy Jacomb-Hood

Sir Melville MacNaughten purchases No. 9 Tite Street – later appointed to write the first
    official report on the Jack the Ripper murders

Whistler marries Beatrice Philip Godwin, wife of his recently deceased best friend – the
    couple move to Tower House

William Butler Yeats spends Christmas with the Wildes at No. 34

1889   January: Sargent paints Ellen Terry as *Lady Macbeth,* and George Henschel

March: Sargent becomes Chevalier of the Légion d'honneur in France

Wilde publishes *The Decay of Lying, Pen, Pencil and Poison, The Birthday of the Infanta* and
    The Portrait of Mr W. H. – gives up editorship of *The Woman's World*

1890   Merritt paints *Love Locked Out* purchased by Chantrey Bequest for Tate Gallery

Welsh sculptress Edith Elizabeth Downing moves into No. 48 with lover Ellen Sparks

Whistler made Chevalier of the Legion d'honneur – leaves Tite Street for the last time

Wilde publishes *The Picture of Dorian Gray* in *Lippincott's Monthly Magazine*

Charles Augustus Howell dies

1891	Frank Miles dies in Brislington House asylum – Keats House remains empty
	Wilde publishes *The Soul of Man under Socialism*; *Intentions* and *A House of Pomegranates*
	Wilde meets Lord Alfred Douglas (Bosie) in Tite Street; writes *Salomé*
	The Hon. Slingsby Bethell leaves Chelsea Lodge – Justice Wills takes over lease
	Society of Portrait Painters established – of the sixteen founding members, almost half were Tite Street artists
	Chelsea Arts Club established
1892	Adrian and Laura Hope buy More House from Admiral Jephson
	Wilde's newest play *Lady Windermere's Fan* opens at the St James's Theatre
	Sargent paints *Lady Agnew* and *Mrs Hammersley*
1893	*A Woman of No Importance* opens at the Haymarket Theatre
	Lady Agnew and *Mrs Hammersley* exhibited – Sargent has 'London at his feet'
	Wilde and Bosie begin to pursue a dangerous affair – Bosie takes Wilde to numerous male brothels – Wilde later recalls it was like 'dining with panthers'
1894	January: Sargent elected as an Associate of the Royal Academy
	George Percy Jacob-Hood moves into No. 44 (previously owned by Frank Miles)
	Marquess of Queensberry confronts Wilde at his house in Tite Street
	Sargent paints *W. Graham Robertson*, *Coventry Patmore* and *Ada Rehan*
1895	January: *An Ideal Husband* produced at the Haymarket Theatre
	February: *The Importance of Being Earnest* produced at the St James's Theatre; Queensberry leaves card at Wilde's club The Albemarle calling him a 'posing somdomite' [sic]
	3 April: Queensberry libel trial begins
	6 April: Wilde arrested at Cadogan Hotel
	24 April: Contents of No. 34 Tite Street auctioned off
	26 April: Wilde's first trial for gross indecency begins
	25 May: Wilde convicted of gross indecency; sentenced to two years' hard labour by Justice Wills who is living at Chelsea Lodge in Tite Street
1896	Adrian and Laura Hope become guardians of Cyril and Vyvyan Wilde
	Sargent paints *Mrs Meyer and her Children*
	Anna Lea Merritt leaves the Cottage; the studio-house is purchased by artist Percy Bigland
	William Rothenstein spends several months in Tite Street – studies with Sargent
1897	Sargent elected full member of Royal Academy – sketches William Rothenstein
	Oscar Wilde released from prison
1898	Asher Wertheimer commissions Sargent portrait, also paints *Octavia Hill*
	Justice Wills leaves Tite Street
	Constance Wilde dies in Genoa
1899	American artist Edwin Abbey elected to Royal Academy and buys the Chelsea Lodge
	Shelley Theatre demolished and block of flats built called Shelley Court
1900	Sargent purchases lease on No. 31 and knocks a passage to No. 33 – paints the Sitwell family,

hosts Claude Monet, paints *Earl of Dalhousie* and *Robert Brough;* receives
Medal of Honour at Paris Exhibition.

30 November: Wilde dies in exile in Paris

1901 Sargent approached to paint coronation portrait but declines; Edwin Abbey commissioned
to paint coronation of Edward VII

Scottish artist Robert Brough moves to No. 33 – becomes close with Sargent and Jacomb-Hood

Sargent paints *Ena and Betty, Daughters of Asher and Mrs Wertheimer*

1902 Frank Cadogan Cowper apprenticed to help Abbey complete coronation portrait

Auguste Rodin declares Sargent the 'Van Dyck of our time' – Sargent has two to three
sittings per day

1903 Whistler dies at 74 Cheyne Walk – Edwin Abbey is pallbearer at his funeral

1904 American artist Romaine Brooks moves to No. 50 for two years

1905 Sargent begins to complain about the drudgery of portrait painting

1906 Robert Brough involved in train accident – Sargent travels by train to see Brough in hospital
before he dies

1907 Sargent offered Knighthood but declines

1908 Sargent sketches *William Butler Yeats*

1910 Edith Elizabeth Downing organises 'Prisoners' Tableau'

May: Sargent summoned to sketch King Edward laying-in-state

1911 Edwin Abbey dies

Edith Elizabeth Downing organises suffragette protest from Tite Street – studio becomes
a workshop for banners and suffragette art

1912 Edith Elizabeth Downing arrested, spends twelve nights at Holloway Prison

Glyn Philpot moves to Tower House

1913 Sargent paints Henry James as a special favour – portrait later slashed by a militant suffragette

1914 Britain declares war on Germany – Sargent briefly trapped in Austria on holiday

1918 Sargent paints *Gassed* and offered Presidency of the Royal Academy but declines

Philpot moves across the street to No. 33; paints Admirals

1919 Philpot leaves Tite Street

1920 Sargent begins *General Officers of World War I*

1925 Sargent dies

1926 Gluck takes a studio at No. 46; Romaine Brooks visits and Gluck paints her portrait

1930 Peter Warlock moves in to No. 30 and dies of coal gas poisoning – suicide is suspected

1937 Chelsea Lodge demolished; block of flats built on the site

1940 Augustus John moves into No. 33

1941 German bomb hits Tite Street during the Blitz; bohemian crowd assembles in the home of
Felix Hope-Nicholson during the war

1945 After the war Tite Street nearly completely vacant

1950 Augustus John leaves No. 33

NOTES

Introduction

1. W. Graham Robertson, *Time Was* (London: Hamish Hamilton, 1945), 233.

2. See Stanley Weintraub *The London Yankees: Portraits of American Writers and Artists in England, 1894–1914* (London: W. H. Allen, 1979).

3. Letter from Whistler to the Duke of Marlborough [25/31 January 1892] GUL / MS Whistler B36b / 13544.

Chapter 1. Visionary & Unreal

1. For references to the funeral by Charles Lang Freer see Louisine W. Havemeyer, *Sixteen to Sixty: Memoirs of a Collector* (New York: Ursus Press, 1993), 212–13.

2. For more on the Paris art world and its influence on English decadence see Matthew Sturgis, *Passionate Attitudes: English Decadence of the 1890s* (London: Macmillan, 1995).

3. William Gaunt, *The Aesthetic Adventure* (London: Jonathan Cape, 1945), 33.

4. Daphne du Maurier (ed.), *The Young George du Maurier: A Selection of his Letters, 1860–67* (London: Peter Davies, 1951), 4.

5. Ibid.

6. Quoted in Linda Merrill, *The Peacock Room: A Cultural Biography* (Washington D.C.: Smithsonian American Art Museum, 1998), 97.

7. Tim Barringer, Jason Rosenfeld, & Alison Smith, *Pre-Raphaelites: Victorian Avant-Garde* (London: Tate Publishing, 2012).

8. Ibid., 162.

9. Algernon Swinburne to William Bell Scott, 16 December 1859, quoted in Cecil Y. Lang (ed.), *The Swinburne Letters* (New Haven: Yale University Press, 1959–62).

10. William Holman Hunt to Thomas Combe, 12 February 1860, quoted in Virginia Surtees, *The Paintings and Drawings of Dante Gabriel Rossetti: 1828–82* (Oxford: Clarendon Press, 1971), 69.

11. Whistler to James Nicol Dunn, 3 August 1902. James McNeill Whistler, 'Latest Bulletin From Mr Whistler', *Morning Post*, 6 August 1902; GM B.95.

12. Robert Buchanan in the *Athenaeum*, 4 August 1866.

13. Anna Whistler to James Gamble, 10-11 February 1864, GUL W516; GUW 06522.

14. Anna Lea Merritt recalled: 'In Chelsea, Whistler was much talked of. I first heard from Mr and Mrs De La Rue that, having greatly admired his work in the Academy Exhibition when first shown about 1869, they were invited to his studio at … Mrs De La Rue, being a thoroughly discreet early Victorian, was startled, shocked, to be shown only one picture, which represented some six ladies lying flat on their tummies on the balcony looking over the river – over their heads they held elaborate and brilliant Japanese sunshades – their only garments! From the shadow of the sunshades emerged twelve bare legs and more besides, all bare, which so horrified my dear friends that they ran away and never wished to see Whistler again.' (Merritt, *Memoirs*, 1982, 125.)

15. Anna Whistler to James Gamble, 10-11 February 1864, GUL W516; GUW 06522.

Chapter 2. Paradise Lost

1. Thea Holme, *Chelsea* (London: Hamilton, 1972), 162.

2. Stephen Inwood, *City of Cities: The Birth of Modern London* (London: Macmillan, 2005).

3. Anna Whistler, the artist's mother, in a letter to Julia and Kate Palmer, 3 November 1871, quoted in Richard Dorment & Margaret MacDonald (eds.), *James McNeill Whistler* (London: Tate Gallery Publications, 1994), 122.

4. Margaret MacDonald & Patricia De Montfort, *An American in London: Whistler and the Thames* (London: Philip Wilson, 2013), 11.

5. Thomas Carlyle to Jane Welsh Carlyle (21 May 1834). *The Carlyle Letters* [CLO]. Ed. Brent Kinser (Duke University Press, 2007). DOI: 10.1215/lt-18340521-TC-JWC-01; *CL* 7:167-78.

6. See Lesley Bairstow, *Paradise Walk, Chelsea: The History of a Chelsea Street 1796–1994*, limited publication, copy held at the Kensington Central Library.

7. Later renamed Royal Hospital Road.

8. Charles Dickens Jr., 'Old Chelsea' in *All the Year Round* (2 June 1888), 523.

9. Metropolitan Board of Works, *Chelsea Embankment, opened*

by their Royal Highnesses the Duke and Duchess of Edinburgh on May 9th, 1874: An Account of the Works, with a Plan (London: Judd & Co., 1874)

10. Chelsea Vestry Minutes, 1885–7, Kensington Central Library, London.

11. Ibid.

Chapter 3. The Wicked Earl & the Butterfly

1. Oscar Wilde, *The Picture of Dorian Gray* (London: *Lippincott's Monthly Magazine*, 1890).

2. Wilde's first published piece of journalistic writing was a review of the opening in *Dublin University Magazine*.

3. Quoted in Dudley Harbron, *The Conscious Stone: The Life of Edward William Godwin* (London: Latimer House Ltd, 1949), xiii.

4. Oscar Wilde, 'Truth of Masks' (1930), 238.

5. According to Godwin, eighty designs were submitted for the project. Sir William Tite was called in to adjudicate. Tite initially voted against Godwin's designs but later changed his mind.

6. Walter Crane, *Of the Decorative Illustration of Books* (London, 1896), 132.

7. E.W. Godwin, 'Ex-Classic Style Called Queen Anne' in *Building News* (1875), 442.

8. Beatrice's decorative brick panels for a Godwin house on the Tite Street corner of Chelsea Embankment were published in *British Architect*, 9 May 1879.

9. Virginia Surtees, editor, *The Diaries of George Price Boyce* (Norwich: Real World, 1980), 39.

10. The term 'chinamania' was coined by George du Maurier, a friend of Whistler's, and regular contributor to *Punch* magazine, which lambasted the 'Chelsea set' for their love of everything Japanese.

11. Quoted in Elizabeth and Joseph Pennell, *The Whistler Journal* (Philadelphia: Lippincott, 1921), 7.

12. Whistler to F.R. Leyland, 20/31 August 1876, Library of Congress, PWC 2/16/11.

13. Thomas Sutherland to F.R. Leyland quoted in Elizabeth and Joseph Pennell, *The Whistler Journal* (Philadelphia: Lippincott, 1921).

14. Joseph Comyns Carr, 'Mr Whistler's Decorative Painting', *Pall Mall Gazette* (15 February 1874).

Chapter 4. The White House

1. Whistler to Lewis Strange Wingfield, May 1877, GUL / MS Whistler W1075.

2. Anna Whistler to James Anderson Rose, 28 July 1870, Library of Congress, PWC 21.

3. Building agreement quoted in letter from W. Wykes Smith to George and William Webb (27 February 1878). Glasgow University Library, MS Whistler M321 / 04050.

4. Metropolitan Board of Works Minutes, Mark Girouard, 'Chelsea's Bohemian Studio Houses: The Victorian Artist at Home II', *Country Life* (23 November 1972), 1371.

5. Ibid.

6. Ibid.

7. Ibid.

8. Lillie Langtry, *The Days I Knew* (London: Hutchinson, 1925), 65.

9. Edward Verrall Lucas, *Edwin Austin Abbey: The Record of his Life and Work* (London: Methuen, 1921), 80.

10. Susan Webber Soros (ed.), *E. W. Godwin: Aesthetic Movement Architect and Designer* (New Haven: Yale University Press, 1999).

11. E.W. Godwin, 'To Our Readers', *British Architect* (4 January 1878), 1.

12. Susan Webber Soros (ed.), *E. W. Godwin: Aesthetic Movement Architect and Designer* (New Haven: Yale University Press, 1999).

13. Mortimer Menpes, *Whistler As I Knew Him* (London: Adam & Charles Black, 1904), 128.

14. Pennington's comments were originally published in *McClure's Magazine* (8), 374; cited in Arthur Jerome Eddy, *Recollections and Impressions of James A. McNeill Whistler* (London: 1903), 112.

15. Whistler to George and William Webb, 1 March 1878, Library of Congress, PWC 3/28/10.

Chapter 5. Archie & Ape

1. A small boat.

2. Lady Tweedsmuir, *The Lilac and the Rose* (London: Gerald Duckworth, 1952).

3. Paula Gillett, *The Victorian Painter's World* (Stroud: Sutton Publishing, 1990).

4. John Everett Millais, *The Life and Letters of John Everett Millais: Volume II* (London: Methuen, 1899), 61.

5. Ibid.

6. See Chapter 20 for information on the Royal Society of Portrait Painters. Archibald Stuart-Wortley was the Society's first president in 1891.

7. John Ruskin, 'Academy Note 1875' retrieved from *John Ruskin: The Complete Works*, Volume 14.

8. Louise Jopling, *Twenty Years of My Life* (London: 1925), 251.

9. Ibid.

10. See Joseph Lamb, 'The Way We Live Now: Late Victorian Studios and the Popular Press', *Visual Resources: An International Journal of Documentation*, Volume 9, Issue 2, 1993.

11. Quoted by E.W. Godwin, 'Architectural Association. Studios and Mouldings', *Building News* (7 March 1879), 261.

12. 'Chelsea Embankment', *Building News* (11 April 1879), 373.

Chapter 6. Aesthetes and Dandies

1. William M. Rossetti, edited, *The Works of Dante Gabriel Rossetti* (London: Ellis, 1911).

2. 'Notes on current events', *British Architect* (18 July 1879), 25.

3. Elizabeth & Joseph Pennell, *The Life of James McNeill Whistler* (London: William Heinemann, 1925).

4. George Boughton, 'A Few of the Various Whistlers I have Known', *Studio*, vol. 30 (December 1903).

5. Ibid.

6. She appeared in *Arrangement in Black and White*. See *Whistler, Women and Fashion* for a more detailed account of Maud Franklin.

7. John Alexander quoted in Elizabeth & Joseph Pennell, *The Whistler Journal* (Philadelphia: Lippincott, 1921), 164.

8. Lillie Langtry, *The Days I Knew* (London: Hutchinson, 1925), 67.

9. Elizabeth & Joseph Pennell, *The Life of James McNeill Whistler* (London: William Heinemann, 1925), 89.

10. Quoted in Helen Maria Madox Rossetti, *Pre-Raphaelite Twilight: The Story of Charles Augustus Howell* (London: Richards Press, 1954), 15.

11. Ellen Terry, *The Story of My Life* (London: Victor Gollancz, 1933).

12. Stanley Weintraub, *Whistler: A Biography* (London: Collins, 1974), 165.

13. Helen Rossetti Angeli, *Pre-Raphaelite Twilight: The Story of Charles Augustus Howell* (London: Richards Press, 1954), 234.

14. W. Graham Robertson, *Time Was* (London: Hamish Hamilton, 1945), 190.

15. Ibid.

16. Whistler to Miss Rosa Corder, 1 September 1878, Harry Ransom Humanities Research Center, University of Texas at Austin, Texas.

17. *Echo de la Semaine* (24 May 1891).

18. *The World* (1 May 1879).

Chapter 7. Between the Brush and the Pen

1. John Ruskin, 'Letter the Seventy-ninth', *Fors Clavigera* (2 July 1877), 181–213.

2. George Boughton, 'Reminiscences of Whistler,' volume 30, 1904, 212.

3. See E.W. Godwin's article 'Is Mr Ruskin Living too Long?' in 'Notes on Current Events', *British Architect* (15 February 1878), 75.

4. James McNeill Whistler, 'Whistler v. Ruskin', *The Gentle Art of Making Enemies* (London 1890), 25.

5. James McNeill Whistler, *The Gentle Art of Making Enemies* (London 1890), 6.

6. Francis Mewburn to friend, 11 December 1878.

7. James McNeill Whistler, *The World* (11 December 1878).

8. Whistler quoted in Elizabeth & Joseph Pennell, *The Life of James McNeill Whistler* (London: William Heinemann, 1925), 182.

9. W. Graham Robertson, *Time Was* (London: Hamish Hamilton, 1945), 188.

10. Ironically Venice was Ruskin's favourite city. He called it the 'Paradise of cities' and his love is evidenced in his study *The Stones of Venice* (1852). For more on Whistler in Venice see Margaret MacDonald's *Palaces in the Night* (Aldershot: Lund Humphries, 2001).

11. Alan Summerley Cole's diary, 7 September 1879, GUL / MS Whistler LB 6/244-226.

12. Anna Lea Merritt records an entertaining anecdote of Whistler bypassing bailiffs: 'He and his confidant ordered pleasant wine and cakes and fruit that very warm afternoon, invited the bailiffs to sit with them around the fountain in the garden. Whistler told many stories and cheered them with many glasses of good wine, also a specially recommended American cocktail, carefully mixed by the great artist. The bailiffs fell asleep! Whistler and his friend slipped away, carrying a particularly good piece of antique

furniture, enjoyed a pleasant evening, returned late, without the cabinet, and went to bed. On awaking in the morning, with some alarm they beheld the bailiffs still sleeping heavily on the wet grass. The man of brilliant resources immediately joined them, ordered coffee out-of-doors and sat there again with coffee and cigars, keeping up a perpetual sound of amusing anecdotes until by afternoon the bailiffs awake and never discovered that it was not yesterday. How much cleverer to invent these unusual manoeuvres than to build a railway in Russia!' (Merritt, *Memoirs*, 125.)

Chapter 8. Frank Miles, Oscar Wilde & Keats House

1. Oscar Wilde to Mrs Alfred Hunt, 25 August 1880, Merlin Holland & Rupert Hart-Davis (eds.), *The Complete Letters of Oscar Wilde* (London: Fourth Estate, 2000).
2. E.W. Godwin, 'Architectural Association: Studios and Mouldings', *Building News* (7 March 1879), 261.
3. Ibid.
4. E.W. Godwin, 'Architects and Their Judges', *British Architect* (14 March 1879), 111.
5. E.W. Godwin, diary entry for 20 June 1879, V&A Godwin Collection.
6. E.W. Godwin 'Architectural Association: Studios and mouldings', *Building News* (7 March 1879), 261.
7. E.W. Godwin letter to Frank Miles dated 22 May 1879, V&A AAD, 4/159-1988.
8. Lillie Langtry, *The Days I Knew* (London: Hutchinson, 1925), 60.
9. Edwin Ward, *The Recollections of a Savage* (London: Herbert Jenkins, 1923), 108.
10. Quoted from Richard Ellman, *Oscar Wilde* (London: First Vintage Books, 1988), 116.
11. Lillie Langtry, *The Days I Knew* (London: Hutchinson, 1925), 68.
12. Not to be confused with *Life* magazine in America.
13. Heinrich Felberman, *The Memoirs of a Cosmopolitan* (London: Chapman Hall, 1936), 117.
14. *Life* [November 1880], quoted in Thomas Toughill, *The Ripper Code* (Stroud: Sutton Publishing, 2008), 167.
15. Jacqueline Hope-Nicholson, *Life Amongst the Troubridges: Journals of a Young Victorian 1873–1884*, (London: Tite Street Press, 1999, revised edition), 152.
16. Ibid.
17. Lady Augusta Fane, *Chit-Chat* (London: Thornton Butterworth, 1926), 103.
18. Edwin Ward, *Recollections of a Savage* (London: Herbert Jenkins, 1923), 305.
19. Ibid.
20. Ibid.
21. Lady Augusta Fane, *Chit-Chat* (London: Thornton Butterworth, 1926), 103.
22. Hesketh Pearson, *Oscar Wilde: His Life and Wit* (London: Harpers, 1946), 50.
23. Ibid.

Chapter 9. Paradise in Tite Street

1. Louise Jopling, *Twenty Years of My Life* (London: John Lane, 1925), 252.
2. Elizabeth & Joseph Pennell, *The Life of James McNeill Whistler* (London: William Heinemann, 1925).
3. Joseph Comyns Carr, *Some Eminent Victorians* (London: Duckworth, 1908), 125.
4. A theatre manager and impresario who later produced Gilbert and Sulivan's *Patience*. He would later sponsor Wilde's North American lecture tour in 1882.
5. Walter Pater, *The Renaissance: Studies in Art and Poetry* (London: 1873), 239.
6. James McNeill Whistler, *Ten O'Clock Lecture*, 20 February 1885, GUL.
7. Harry Quilter, 'The Apologia of Art' (1879), reprinted in Mary Quilter, *Opinions on Men, Women and Things by Harry Quilter* (London: Swan Sonnenschein & Co., 1909), 181.
8. *Furniture Gazette*, 1876.
9. Harry Quilter, 'The Gospel of Intesity', *Contemporary Review*, 1895, reprinted in Mary Quilter, *Opinions on Men, Women and Things by Harry Quilter* (London: Swan Sonnenschein and Co., 1909), 339–40.
10. See Anne Anderson, 'Oscar's Enemy … and neighbour: 'Arry Quilter and the Gospel of Intensity', *The Wildean*, 27 (July 2005), 17.
11. Walter Hamilton, *The Aesthetic Movement in England* (London: Reeves & Turner, 1882), vii.
12. Harry Quilter, 'The New Renaissance or, The Gospel of Intensity', *Macmillan's Magazine*, September 1880, XLII (New York), 391–400.
13. George du Maurier to Thomas Armstrong, October 1863, printed in Daphne du Maurier (ed.), *The Young George du*

Maurier: A Selection of His Letters, 1860–67 (London: Peter Davis, 1951), 216.

14. Harry Quilter, 'The New Renaissance or, The Gospel of Intensity', *Macmillan's Magazine*, September 1880, XLII (New York), 391-400.

15. Whistler to Henry Labouchère , October 1886, GUL / MS Whistler L4.

16. Col Sir Robert Edis, *Healthy Furniture and Decoration* (London: International Health Exhibition, 1884).

17. Letter to 'Atlas' [Edmund Yates], dated October 14, written from Tite Street, printed in 'What the World Says', *The World: A Journal for Men and Women*, no. 485, vol. 19, 17 October 1883, 13; reprinted in Whistler, James McNeill, *The Gentle Art of Making Enemies* (London and New York: 1890), 124–125 under the title 'Sacrilege', and in Whistler, James McNeill, *The Gentle Art of Making Enemies*, ed. Sheridan Ford (Paris: 1890), 94–5.

18. Hesketh Pearson, *The Man Whistler* (London: Macdonald & Jane's, 1978), 91.

Chapter 10. All the Fashionables

1. Alan Summerley Cole's diary, 26 May 1881, GUL / MS Whistler LB 6/244-226.

2. Charles Augustus Howell quoted in Elizabeth & Joseph Pennell, *The Life of James McNeill Whistler* (London: William Heinemann, 1925), 300.

3. Thomas Way, *Memories of James McNeill Whistler: The Artist* (London: John Lane, 1912), 62.

4. Ibid., 63.

5. *The Weekly Register*, 24 February 1883, GUL / PC6/49.

6. Jacques-Emile Blanche, *Portraits of a Lifetime* (London: J.M. Dent & Sons, 1937), 224.

7. Ibid., 75.

8. Paula Gillett, *The Victorian Painter's World* (Gloucester: Sutton, 1990), 17.

9. Harper Pennington, 'Artist Life in Venice,' *Century*, 64 (October 1902), 836–7.

10. Jacques Emile-Blanche, *Propos de Peintre*, vol I (1919), 19.

11. Whistler to Helen Whistler, September 1881, GUL / MS Whistler W688.

12. Mortimer Menpes, *Whistler As I Knew Him* (London: Adam & Charles Black, 1904), 89.

13. Anna Gruetzner Robins (ed.), *Walter Sickert: Complete Writings on Art* (Oxford: Oxford University Press, 2000), 150–55.

14. Whistler and Legros were friends many years earlier but had a nasty falling out in 1867.

15. Walter Sickert to Alfred Pollard, ALS, 19 May 1879, quoted in Matthew Sturgis, *Walter Sickert: A Life* (London: Harper Perennial, 2005), 67.

16. Maggie Cobden to Dorothy Richmond, 11 December 1881, quoted in Matthew Sturgis, *Walter Sickert: A Life* (London: Harper Perennial, 2005), 92.

17. Eric Newton, 'As I Knew Him: A Personal Portrait of Walter Sickert' quoted in Matthew Sturgis, *Walter Sickert: A Life* (London: Harper Perennial, 2005), 100.

18. Mortimer Menpes, *Whistler As I Knew Him* (London: Adam & Charles Black, 1904).

19. Ibid.

20. Ibid., 15.

21. Ibid.

22. Ibid.

23. Walter Sickert to John Collier published in *Fortnightly Review* (1892); Anna Gruetzner Robins (ed.), *Walter Sickert: Complete Writings on Art* (Oxford: Oxford University Press, 2000), 93.

24. Walter Sickert to John Collier quoted in Matthew Sturgis, *Walter Sickert: A Life* (London: Harper Perennial, 2005), 96.

25. Whistler to Wilde, May 1883, Library of Congress, PWC 19/1871/7.

26. Mortimer Menpes, *Whistler As I Knew Him* (London: Adam & Charles Black, 1904).

27. Paula Gillett, *The Victorian Painter's World* (Stroud: Sutton Publishing, 1990).

Chapter 11. Masquerading

1. Reported in *Sunday Herald* (January 1886), Boston, Massachusetts: 'Whistler had been notably witty during the evening and finally made a bon mot more than usually pointed and happy that convulsed his listeners...Wilde, who was present, approved Mr Whistler's brightness, and wondered why he had not thought of the witticism himself. 'You will,' promptly replied Whistler, 'you will.' This lightning comment on Mr Wilde's wonderful ability to think of other people's bright things and to repeat them as his own had, you may imagine, an immediate and most discomforting effect on Mr Wilde.'

2. Between April 1881 (Whistler's return from Venice) and November (Wilde's departure).

3. Ellen Terry, *The Story of My Life* (London: Victor Gollancz, 1933), 101.

4. Oscar Wilde, 'The Grosvenor Gallery, 1877', *Dublin University Magazine*, July 1877.

5. Elizabeth & Joseph Pennell, *The Life of James McNeill Whistler* (London: William Heinemann, 1925), 226.

6. Ibid., 227.

7. Ibid., 226.

8. Jane Stedman, *W.S. Gilbert: A Classic Victorian and His Theatre* (Oxford: Oxford University Press, 1996), 181.

9. George du Maurier, *Pall Mall Gazette*, 19 May 1894.

10. In the late 1880s Beerbohm Tree (half-brother of Max Beerbohm) would rise in the London theatre world to become an actor-manager of the prestigious Haymarket Theatre. Wilde's *A Woman of No Importance* (1893) was produced at the Haymarket with Tree in the role of Lord Illingworth.

11. *New York Daily Tribune* (6 February 1881).

12. Carolyn Williams, *Gilbert and Sullivan: Gender, Genre, Parody* (New York: Columbia University Press, 2011).

13. *Illustrated London News* (18 June 1881), 598.

14. E.W. Godwin, 'Theatrical Notes', *British Architect* (29 July 1881), 379.

15. Wilde to George Grossmith, April 1881, Merlin Holland & Rupert Hart-Davis (eds), *The Complete Letters of Oscar Wilde* (London: Fourth Estate, 2000), 109.

16. William Powell Frith, *My Autobiography and Reminiscences* (London: Richard Bentley & Son, 1888), 441.

17. Quoted in Richard Ellman, *Oscar Wilde* (London: First Vintage Books, 1988), 144.

18. Neil McKenna, *The Secret Life of Oscar Wilde* (London: Arrow Books, 2004), 26.

19. Edwin Ward, *The Recollections of a Savage* (London: Herbert Jenkins, 1923), 109.

20. Ibid.

21. Ed Cohen, 'Posing the Question: Wilde, Wit and the Ways of Man', Elin Diamond (ed.), *Performance and Cultural Politics* (London: Routledge, 1996), 42.

22. Taken from an interview in the *Philadelphia Press* (17 January 1882).

23. Keeper of Prints and Drawings at the British Museum.

24. Whistler to Wilde, 4 February 1882, Library of Congress / PWC 19/1871/6.

25. Wilde to Whistler, February 1882, GUL / MS Whistler W1042.

26. Whistler to Wilde, February 1882, GUL / MS Whistler W1043.

27. Quoted in Elizabeth & Joseph Pennell, *The Life of James McNeill Whistler* (London: William Heinemann, 1925), 328.

28. Ibid.

29. Whistler to Mr Currie, between 1885–8, GUL Special Collections, MS Whistler C268.

30. Whistler to Wilde, published in *The Gentle Art of Making Enemies* (London: William Heinemann, 1890), 243. The original letter may have read 'how dare you! – What means this unseemly carnival in my Chelsea', see Library of Congress, PWC 19/1871/5. Nathan's was a theatrical costumier in the West End. Lajos Kossuth was a Hungarian revolutionary who lived in England from 1851 to 1859 and wore a Polish cap. Mr Mantalini was the husband of a milliner in Dickens's *Nicholas Nickleby* and wore a flamboyant morning gown.

31. Whistler to Henry Labouchère, 2 January 1890, GUL / MS Whistler T206.

32. Conversation published in *The World*, 14 November 1883, also published in James McNeill Whistler, *The Gentle Art of Making Enemies* (London: William Heinemann, 1890).

Chapter 12. Two Ladies

1. See Harry Quilter, 'The New Renaissance; or, The Gospel of Intensity' in *Appletons' Journal: A Magazine of General Literature* (Volume 9, Issue: 53, November 1880), 453–60.

2. Theodore Duret, *Whistler* (London: Grant Richards, 1917), 65.

3. *Truth*, Volume 4, No. 98 (14 November 1878), 545.

4. Quoted in Richard Dorment & Margaret Macdonald, *Whistler* (London: Tate Gallery, 1994), 203.

5. Elizabeth Bradburn, *Margaret McMillan: Portrait of a Pioneer* (London: Routledge, 1989), 29.

6. Theodore Duret, *Whistler* (London: Grant Richards, 1917), 66.

7. Valerie Meux to Whistler, 13 Jan. 1892, GUL / MS Whistler M341.

8. Mrs Julian Hawthorne, 'A Champion of Art', *Independent*, 52 (2 November 1899), 2957–8.

9. 'Something mysterious and fantastic'. Duret (1904), 94.

10. Thomas Way, *Memories of James McNeill Whistler: The Artist* (London: John Lane, 1912), 71.

11. '*Un Whistler etonnant, raffine a l'eces, mais d'une trempe!*' Marcel Guerin, (ed.), *Lettres de Degas*, (Paris, 1945), 62.

12. Bruscambille, 'Chez John Bull', *Chronique de Paris* (18 Aug. 1888), 1.

13. Theodore Duret, *Whistler* (London: Grant Richards, 1917), 66.

14. Wilde to Whistler, June 1882, Merlin Holland & Rupert Hart-Davis (eds), *The Complete Letters of Oscar Wilde* (London: Fourth Estate, 2000), 173–4.

15. Letter dated 9 February 1937, quoted in Kerrison Preston (ed.), *Letters of W. Graham Robertson* (London: Hamish Hamilton, 1953).

16. Theodore Duret, *Whistler* (London: Grant Richards, 1917), 67.

17. Whistler to Valerie Meux (30 July 1886), GUL 04068; M338a.

18. Whistler to Valerie Meux, 30 July 1886, GUL / MS Whistler M338a.

19. Quoted Elizabeth & Joseph Pennell, *The Life of James McNeill Whistler* (London: William Heinemann, 1925), 210.

20. Eleanor Calhoun refused to marry William Randolph Hearst. He later formed the basis for Charles Foster Kane in Orson Welles's film *Citizen Kane*.

21. Eleanor Calhoun, *Pleasures and Palaces; The Memoirs of Princess Lazarovich-Hrebelianovich*, New York: The Century Co. (1915), 88.

22. A copy exists in the Enthoven Collection along with correspondence.

23. Eleanor Calhoun, *Pleasures and Palaces; The Memoirs of Princess Lazarovich-Hrebelianovich*, New York: The Century Co. (1915), 75.

24. Ibid., 87.

25. Ibid., 81.

26. Max Beerbohm, *The Yellow Book*, Volume IV (1880), 280.

27. Oscar Wilde, 'The Truth of Masks: A Note on Illusions' in *Intentions* (London: Methuen, 1891).

28. 'The Pastoral Players', *The Era*, 4 July 1885, 12.

Chapter 13. Shelley Theatre

1. Metropolitan Board of Works archive; quoted in Jacob 'Chelsea's Forgotten Theatre' in the *Chelsea Report*, 47.

2. Quoted in Jacob 'Chelsea's Forgotten Theatre' in The Chelsea Society *Annual Report* (1983), issue 38, 47–51.

3. Ibid.

4. *Morning Post*, Issue 34507 (29 January 1883), 2.

5. Ibid.

6. *The Era*, Issue 2315 (3 February 1883).

7. Horace Wigan, 'Sir Percy Shelley's Theatre', *The Era*, Issue 2319 (3 March 1883).

8. The Hon. Slingsby Bethell, *The Era*, Issue 2319 (3 March 1883).

9. Sir Percy Shelley, *The Era*, Issue 2319 (3 March 1883).

Chapter 14. John Collier and the Wild Women

1. See Neil McKenna, *Fanny and Stella: The Young Men Who Shocked Victorian England* (London: Faber & Faber, 2013).

2. Metropolitan Board of Works, *Chelsea Embankment, opened by their Royal Highnesses the Duke and Duchess of Edinburgh on May 9th, 1874: An Account of the Works, with a Plan* (London: Judd & Co., 1874)

3. The influence registered on a personal level and Collier's first son would be named Lawrence after the great artist.

4. Lady Monkswell, *A Victorian Diarist* (London: John Murray, 1944), 115.

5. George Roames to Charles Darwin, 25 May 1881, Ethel Romanes (ed.), *The Life and Letters of George John Romanes* (London: Longmans Green, 1896), 118.

6. Charles Darwin to George Romanes, 27 June 1881. The original is at the American Philosophical Society, Philadelphia, PA, USA. Letter 312, Cambridge University.

7. Charles Darwin to John Collier, 16 February 1882, Ethel Romanes (ed.), *The Life and Letters of George John Romanes* (London: Longmans Green, 1896).

8. Lady Monkswell, *A Victorian Diarist* (London: John Murray, 1944).

9. Elizabeth Linton, 'The Wild Women as Social Insurgents' *Nineteenth Century* 30 (October 1891), 596.

10. Thomas Huxley quoted in Ronald Clark, The Huxleys (London: Heinemann, 1968), 109.

11. With Thomas Huxley's approval, Collier went on to marry Marian's younger sister Ethel, although not everyone was as accepting of the union.

Chapter 15. Love Locked Out

1. Sir Wyke Bayliss, *Olives: The Reminiscences of a President* (London: George Allen, 1906), 48–52.

2. Anna Lea Merritt, *Love Locked Out: The Memoirs of*

Anna Lea Merritt with a checklist of her works, ed. Galina Gorokhoff (Boston: Boston Museum of Fine Art, 1982).

3. Ibid., 116.

4. Ibid.

5. Ibid.

6. Ibid., 136.

7. Ibid.

8. Ibid., 116.

9. See Stanley Weintraub, *London Yankees: Portraits of American Writers and Artists in England: 1894–1914* (London: W. H. Allen, 1978).

10. 'The International Exhibition, XI – American Art – II', *Nation*, Volume 23 (3 August 1876), 7.

11. 'Memorial Hall', *Frank Leslie's Illustrated Historical Register of the Centennial Exposition* (New York, 1876), 185.

12. Anna Lea Merritt, *Love Locked Out: The Memoirs of Anna Lea Merritt with a checklist of her works*, ed. Galina Gorokhoff (Boston: Boston Museum of Fine Art, 1982), 125.

13. Ibid., 126.

14. Ibid., 87.

15. Ibid., 136.

16. Ibid., 129.

17. Ibid., 164.

18. *Standard* (London, England), 9 June 1890, Issue 20567, 5.

19. '*Quid quid erit, superanda omnis fortuna fer endo est.*' Virgil, *Aeneid*, 5.710.

20. Lady Butler (aka Elizabeth Thompson), Clara Montabla and Henrietta Rae all prominent female artists of the mid- to late nineteenth century.

21. Anna Lea Merritt, 'The Royal Academy', *Standard* (London, England), 6 November 1886, 3.

22. M.H. Spielmann, *British Sculpture and Sculptors of Today* (London: Cassell, 1901), 161.

23. George Percy Jacomb-Hood, *With Brush and Pencil* (London: John Murray, 1925), 122.

24. Grant's former tutor John Henry Foley would have several of his own sculptures destroyed following the creation of the Irish Free State in 1922.

25. Anna Lea Merritt, 'A Letter to Artists: Especially Women Artists', *Lippincott's Monthly Magazine*, 1900, vol. 65, 467–8.

26. Anna Lea Merritt, *Love Locked Out: The Memoirs of Anna Lea Merritt with a checklist of her works*, ed. Galina Gorokhoff (Boston: Boston Museum of Fine Art, 1982), 166.

Chapter 16. Wilde's Closet

1. Quoted in Franny Moyle, *Constance: the Tragic and Scandalous Life of Mrs Oscar Wilde* (London: John Murray, 2011), 86.

2. Oscar Wilde to Waldo Story, 22 January 1884 in Merlin Holland & Rupert Hart-Davis (eds.), *The Complete Letters of Oscar Wilde* (London: Fourth Estate, 2000), 225.

3. James McNeill Whistler, *The Gentle Art of Making Enemies* (London: William Heinemann, 1890), 252.

4. V&A Picture Library, London (Ref. E.557-1963).

5. Oscar Wilde 'House Decoration', *Essays and Lectures by Oscar Wilde*, London 1908.

6. Oscar Wilde quoted in Geoff Dibbs, *Oscar Wilde: A Vagabond with a Mission: The Story of Oscar Wilde's Lecture Tours of Britain and Ireland* (London: The Oscar Wilde Society, 2013), 26.

7. Johnston Forbes-Robertson, *A Player Under Three Reigns* (London, 1925), 109–10.

8. Wilde's tenure in Tite Street was bookended by legal actions.

9. See H. Montgomery Hyde's article 'Oscar Wilde and His Architect', *Architectural Review* (March 1951).

10. Letter from Wilde to W.A.S. Benson (16 May 1885), Merlin Holland & Rupert Hart-Davis (eds), *The Complete Letters of Oscar Wilde* (London: Fourth Estate, 2000), 258.

11. Letter from Wilde to E.W. Godwin (March 1885), Merlin Holland & Rupert Hart-Davis (eds), *The Complete Letters of Oscar Wilde* (London: Fourth Estate, 2000), 252.

12. For more on Oscar Wilde's book collection and library see Thomas Wright's, *Oscar's Books: A Journey Around the Library of Oscar Wilde* (London: Vintage, 2009).

13. Laura Troughbridge to Adrian Hope in *Letters of Engagement: 1884–1888*, ed. Marie-Jacqueline Lancaster (London: Tite Street Press, 2002), 102–3.

14. Vyvyan Holland, *Son of Oscar Wilde* (London: Penguin Books, 1957), 35.

15. Anna, Comtesse de Brémont, *Oscar Wilde and His Mother* (London: Everett & Co., 1914), 87–8.

16. Oscar Wilde quoted in Rupert Hart-Davis, *The Letters of Oscar Wilde* (1962), 135.

17. Letter from James Whistler to Ralph Waldo Story, 20/25 May 1884, Library of Congress, PWC 2/61/8.

18. *The Bat* (23 March 1886).

19. Vyvyan Holland, *Son of Oscar Wilde* (London: Penguin Books, 1957), 41.

20. Ibid., 43.
21. *Funny Folks*, 14 April 1888.
22. Vyvyan Holland, *Son of Oscar Wilde* (London: Penguin Books, 1957), 42.
23. The Wildes asked Mortimer Menpes to be Vyvyan's godfather after Ruskin declined on grounds of age.
24. Love is winged for two, / In the worst he weathers, / When their hearts are tied; / But if they divide, / O too true! / Cracks a globe, and feathers, feathers, / Feathers all the ground bestrew. / I was breast of morning sea, / Rosy plume on forest dun, / I the laugh in rainy fleeces, / While with me / She made one. / Now must we pick up our pieces, / For that then so winged were we.
25. Constance's visitors' book, Eccles Collection, BL Add. MS. 81755A.
26. See Michael Field journal, BL, Add, MSS, 46779: 541. 54v (1891); Correspondence of Katharine Bradley and Edith Cooper.
27. Anna, Comtesse de Brémont, *Oscar Wilde and His Mother* (London: Everett & Co., 1914), 89.
28. Oscar Wilde to Harry Marillier, 27 November 1885, published in *The Complete Letters of Oscar Wilde* (London: Fourth Estate, 2000), 269.
29. Oscar Wilde to Harry Marillier, 11 June 1886, published in *The Complete Letters of Oscar Wilde* (London: Fourth Estate, 2000), 282.
30. Oscar Wilde to Harry Marillier, 1 January 1886, published in *The Complete Letters of Oscar Wilde* (London: Fourth Estate, 2000), 274.
31. Franny Moyle, *Constance: the Tragic and Scandalous Life of Mrs Oscar Wilde* (London: John Murray, 2011), 59.
32. Oscar Wilde to Douglas Ainslie, May-June 1886, in *The Complete Letters of Oscar Wilde* (London: Fourth Estate, 2000), 281.
33. Elizabeth & Joseph Pennell, *The Whistler Journal* (Philadelphia: Lippincott, 1921), 183.
34. Oscar Wilde quoted in Neil McKenna, *The Secret Life of Oscar Wilde* (London: Arrow Books, 2004), 105.
35. Henry Labouchère, *Truth* (18 July 1883).
36. Section 11 of Criminal Law Amendment Act.
37. Hesketh Pearson, *Oscar Wilde: His Life and Wit* (London: Harpers, 1946), 319.
38. Lord Alfred Douglas, *The Autobiography of Lord Alfred Douglas* (London: Martin Secker, 1931), 70.
39. Franny Moyle, *Constance: the Tragic and Scandalous Life of Mrs Oscar Wilde* (London: John Murray, 2011), 121.
40. Oscar Wilde to Wemyss Reid, 5 Sept. 1887, in *The Complete Letters of Oscar Wilde* (London: Fourth Estate, 2000), 317.
41. See Neil McKenna, *The Secret Life of Oscar Wilde* (London: Arrow Books, 2004), 121.
42. Ibid., 123.
43. Mary Lago, editor, *Men and Memories: Recollections, 1872–1938 of William Rothenstein* (London: Chatto & Windus, 1978), 75 (quoting letter from William Rothenstein to Charles Conder, 19 January 1891, Boston Public Library).

Chapter 17. A Prince in Piccadilly

1. W. Graham Robertson, *Time Was* (London: Hamish Hamilton, 1945), 233.
2. The uncle of C. R. Cammell (poet and close friend of Aleister Crowley) and great uncle of Donald Cammell (film director and artist) including co-directing (with Nicolas Roeg) Mick Jagger in *Performance* – who lived in Flood Street for a while.
3. 'Ma fille est perdue. Tout Paris se moque d'elle. Mon genre sera force de se battre. Elle mourir de chagrin.' Ralph Curtis quoted in Evan Charteris, *John Sargent* (London: William Heinemann, 1927), 61.
4. John Singer Sargent to Edward Russell, 10 September 1885, Tate Archives.
5. Henry James, 'John Singer Sargent', *Harper's Magazine* (Oct. 1887), 683–91.
6. Henry James, *Letters*, Volume 3, ed. Leon Edel (London, 1980), 42–3.
7. John Singer Sargent to Edward Russell, 10 September 1885, Tate Archives.
8. Quoted in Stanley Olson, *John Singer Sargent: His Portrait* (London: Macmillan, 1989), 128.
9. Lucia Millet to her family, 15 and 28 November 1886, American Art Archives, Washington D.C..
10. Jacques-Emile Blanche, *Portraits of a Lifetime* (London: J.M. Dent & Sons, 1937), 158.
11. Ibid.
12. Nicola D'Inverno, 'The Real John Singer Sargent' in *Boston Sunday Advertiser* (1926).
13. Osbert Sitwell, *Left Hand, Right Hand* (London: Macmillan, 1945), 222.

14. Ronald Gray, Memoirs (unpublished MSS in Tate Archives), 80.

15. Henry James, 'John Singer Sargent', *Harper's Magazine* (October 1887), 683–91.

16. Fitzwilliam Sargent to Tom Sargent, 13 May 1886, quoted in Stanley Olson, *John Singer Sargent: His Portrait* (London: Macmillan, 1989), 128.

17. Fitzwilliam Sargent to Tom Sargent, 13 May 1886, American Art Archives, roll D 317, frame 486.

18. While in Paris in 1883, Wilde gave Sargent a volume of Rennell Rodd's poetry that he inscribed 'To my friend, John S. Sargent with deep admiration of his work'. Richard Ormond collection.

19. Elizabeth & Joseph Pennell, *The Whistler Journal* (Philadelphia: Lippincott, 1921), 39.

20. Nicola D'Inverno, 'The Real John Singer Sargent', *Boston Sunday Advertiser* (1926).

21. Charles Merrill-Mount, *John Singer Sargent: A Biography* (London: Cresset Press, 1957), 124.

22. Ibid.

23. Harry Quilter in *The Spectator* (1 May 1886).

24. William Ernest Henley, *Magazine of Art* (1885), 470.

25. Kenneth McConkey, *Edwardian Portraits: Images of an Age of Opulence* (Woodbridge: Antique Collectors' Club, 1987), 15.

26. Henry James, 'John Singer Sargent', *Harper's Magazine* (October 1887), 683–91.

27. William Howe Downes, *John Singer Sargent: His Life and Work* (London: Thornton Butterworth, 1925), 26.

28. Charles Merrill-Mount, *John Singer Sargent: A Biography* (London: Cresset Press, 1957), 118.

29. Oscar Wilde, 'Portia': (To Ellen Terry. Written at the Lyceum Theatre) / I marvel not Bassanio was so bold / To peril all he had upon the lead, / Or that proud Aragon bent low his head / Or that Morocco's fiery heart grew cold: / For in that gorgeous dress of beaten gold / Which is more golden than the golden sun / No woman Veronese looked upon / Was half so fair as thou whom I behold. / Yet fairer when with wisdom as your shield / The sober-suited lawyer's gown you donned, / And would not let the laws of / Venice yield / Antonio's heart to that accursed Jew – / O Portia! take my heart: it is thy due: / I think I will not quarrel with the Bond.

30. Joseph Comyns Carr, *Some Eminent Victorians* (London: Duckworth, 1908).

31. Letter to Eva Gardner quoted in Evan Charteris, *John Sargent* (London: William Heinemann, 1927), 100–1.

32. Alice Comyns Carr was the wife of Joseph Comyns Carr, Director of the New Gallery. Sargent also painted her portrait that same year.

33. Ellen Terry, *The Story of My Life* (London: Victor Gollancz, 1933), 234.

34. Percy Grainger, 'Sargent's Contributions to Music' (6 May 1926), quoted in Evan Charteris, *John Sargent* (London: William Heinemann, 1927), 149.

35. Nicola D'Inverno, 'The Real John Singer Sargent', *Boston Sunday Advertiser* (1926).

36. Jacques-Emile Blanche, *Portraits of a Lifetime* (London: J.M. Dent & Sons, 1937), 157.

37. Evan Charteris, *John Sargent* (London: William Heinemann, 1927), 158.

38. W. Graham Robertson, *Time Was* (London: Hamish Hamilton, 1945), 244–5.

39. *Art Journal* (1893), 242.

40. Letter from Clementia Anstruther-Thomson to Vernon Lee, 1893.

41. Lewis Hind, *Black and White – a Handbook to the RA and New Gallery Pictures* (1893), 8.

42. Elaine Kilmurray & Richard Ormond (eds), John Singer Sargent: Portraits of the 1890s; Complete Paintings: Volume II (New Haven: Yale University Press, 2002), 15.

43. *New York Times* (21 January 1894).

44. James Whistler to John Singer Sargent, 20 January 1894, GUL MS Whistler LB 1/141.

Chapter 18. Aesthetic Rivalries

1. Eleanor Bagot was married to Vice-Admiral Henry Bagot who died in 1877 before they had a chance to realise their Tite Street venture. Eleanor Bagot died in 1886.

2. Beatrice's sister Frances would remain a spinster and live at 36 Tite Street until she was ninety.

3. E.W. Godwin to William Webb, V&A Theatre Archive, Godwin collection, box 7.1.

4. Margaret MacDonald, *Beatrice Whistler: Artist and Designer* (Hunterian Art Gallery, Glasgow, 1997), 8.

5. Whistler to Helen Whistler, [1887/8], GUL MS Whistler W706.

6. Beatrice Whistler to Whistler, [1895], MS Whistler W639 / AN2491.

7. Henry Labouchère, *Truth* (23 July 1903).

8. Richard Caton Woodville, *Random Recollections* (London, 1914), 137.

9. See Margaret Macdonald, *Whistler, Women and Fashion* (New Haven & London: Yale University Press, 2003).

10. Oscar Wilde in *Lecture to Art Students*. For further information on Oscar Wilde's lectures see Geoff Dibb, *Oscar Wilde: A Vagabond with a Mission: The Story of Oscar Wilde's Lecture Tours of Britain and Ireland* (The Oscar Wilde Society, 2013).

11. Whistler's theories, however, were not entirely original but were instead a synthesis of work already posited by Théophile Gautier and Algernon Swinburne several decades before.

12. Mortimer Menpes, *Whistler As I Knew Him* (London: Adam & Charles Black, 1904).

13. Elizabeth & Joseph Pennell, *The Life of James McNeill Whistler* (London: William Heinemann, 1925), 243.

14. Ibid.

15. James McNeill Whistler, 'Mr Whistler's Ten O'Clock', *The Gentle Art of Making Enemies* (London: William Heinemann, 1890), 134–59.

16. Oscar Wilde, *Pall Mall Gazette* (21 February 1885); published in Whistler, *The Gentle Art of Making Enemies* (London: William Heinemann, 1890).

17. James McNeill Whistler, 'Mr Whistler's Ten O'Clock', *The Gentle Art of Making Enemies* (London: William Heinemann, 1890), 134–59.

18. Ibid.

19. Wilde had already posited this ideal in his *Lecture to Art Students* in June 1883. According to Robbie Ross, Wilde had asked Whistler to help him prepare the lecture.

20. James McNeill Whistler, 'Mr Whistler's Ten O'Clock' in *The Gentle Art of Making Enemies* (London: William Heinemann, 1890), 134–59.

21. Lady Archibald Campbell was writing a book called *Rainbow-Music* at this same time.

22. James McNeill Whistler, 'Mr Whistler's Ten O'Clock' in *The Gentle Art of Making Enemies* (London: William Heinemann, 1890), 134–59.

23. Oscar Wilde, 'The Decay of Lying' in *Intentions* (London 1891).

24. Originally published in *Pall Mall Gazette* (21 February 1885), Whistler, *The Gentle Art of Making Enemies* (London: William Heinemann, 1890) and again privately printed in *Wilde v Whistler: Being an Acrimonious Correspondence on Art between Oscar Wilde and James A McNeill Whistler* (London: 1906).

25. Ibid.

26. Wilde to Whistler, 23 February 1885 in *The Complete Letters of Oscar Wilde*, eds Merlin Holland & Rupert Hart-Davis (London: Fourth Estate, 2000), 250.

27. 'Art Notes and Reviews', *Art Journal* (December 1886), 381.

28. James McNaiell Whistler, 'To the Committee of the 'National Art Exhibition' in *The World* (17 November 1886) Comparing Wilde to Harry Quilter was a deep insult. Wilde had attacked his neighbour Quilter's book *Sententiae Artis* which sparked a rather bitter string of editorial letters between the two neighbours. Quote from James Whistler, *The World* (17 November 1886).

29. Conversation published in *World* (24 November 1886).

30. Ibid.

31. 'The New President', *Pall Mall Gazette* (26 January 1889).

32. Mortimer Menpes, *Whistler As I Knew Him* (London: Adam & Charles Black, 1904), 22.

33. Conversation published in *World* (14 November 1883).

34. William Butler Yeats, *Autobiographies* (London, Macmillan, 1980), pp. 134-5.

35. Ibid.

36. Later collated into a volume of essays called *Intentions* (London, 1891).

37. Oscar Wilde, 'The Decay of Lying' in *Intentions* (London 1891).

38. Ibid.

39. Ibid.

40. Ibid.

Chapter 19. Dorian Gray & Tite Street

1. Oscar Wilde to Joseph Stoddart, 17 Dec. 1889 in *The Complete Letters of Oscar Wilde*, eds Merlin Holland & Rupert Hart-Davis (London: Fourth Estate, 2000).

2. Kenneth McConkey, *Edwardian Portraits: Images of an Age of Opulence* (Woodbridge: Antique Collectors' Club, 1987).

3. Archibald Stuart-Wortley, George Percy Jacomb-Hood, Charles Wellington Furse, Percy Bigland, John Singer Sargent, James Whistler, John Collier, and Anna Lea Merritt (joined later).

4. Vyvyan Holland, *Son of Oscar Wilde* (Harmondsworth: Penguin Books,1957), 43.

5. E.W. Godwin, 'Architectural Association: Studios and Mouldings', *Building News* (7 March 1879), 261.

6. George Percy Jacomb-Hood, *With Brush and Pencil* (London: John Murray, 1925), 114.

7. E.W. Godwin, 'Architectural Association: Studios and Mouldings', *Building News* (7 March 1879), 261.

8. Vyvyan Holland, *Son of Oscar Wilde* (Harmondsworth: Penguin Books,1957), 34.

9. Ibid.

10. Elizabeth & Joseph Pennell, *The Life of James McNeill Whistler* (London: William Heinemann, 1925), 227.

11. In *Palace and Hovel: Phases of London Life* (London, 1878) Daniel Joseph Kirwan describes the Casino de Venise: 'The street was lined with cabs, and policemen were thick in the vicinity of the entrance, ordering the men and women just coming out to pass on, and keep the street clear, a duty which gained for them a great deal of abuse from the intoxicated women, who did not want to pass on by any means. The entrance to this place is through a gaudy, gilded vestibule and down a descent of four or five steps to a spacious marble floor, which was covered with dancers. The whole interior was gilded, gold leaf and white predominating above all other colors.' Another amusing anecdote concerns Gabriel Rossetti and Alfred, Lord Tennyson in the autumn of 1855: after a reading of his poems, the forty-six-year-old Tennyson recklessly allowed himself to be escorted home by the twenty-seven-year-old Rossetti. When they crossed High Holborn, Tennyson remarked on the abundance of cabs crowded round the Casino de Venice and innocently wondered what was going on inside at which point his young companion Rossetti thoroughly enlightened him. Social commentator William Acton observed disapprovingly that most of the female dancers at the Casino were prostitutes or *grisettes* (aspirational shopgirls, seamstresses and artists' models). Still, he had to admit that the Casino's 'athletic amusements' and 'prevalent sobriety' were an improvement on 'the grosser haunts of prostitution formerly in fashion'. According to Rossetti, when he told Tennyson of the character and goings-on at the Casino, the poet was intrigued. 'I'd rather like to go in there', he said. But at the last minute he backed out, worried that he might be spotted by a newspaper man.

12. Kenneth McConkey, *Edwardian Portraits: Images of an Age of Opulence* (Woodbridge: Antique Collectors' Club, 1987), 9.

13. 'je travaille tous les jours jusqu'a la nuit au portrait.' GUL AM 1962/30.

14. W. Graham Robertson, *Time Was* (London: Hamish Hamilton, 1945), 236.

15. George Moore, *Criticisms, with caricatures by Harry Furniss* (London: Royal Academy of Art, 1895), 19.

Chapter 20. The Charmed Circle

1. William Rothenstein, *Men and Memories: 1872–1900* (London: Faber & Faber, 1931), 167.

2. Benjamin Martin Ellis, *Old Chelsea* (London: T. Fisher & Unwin, 1889), 17.

3. Frank Miles, 'The Reform of the Royal Academy' in *Pall Mall Gazette* (1 September 1886).

4. Ibid.

5. The painting was voted 'Worst Picture of the Year' by *Pall Mall Gazette* visitors poll. See James Hamilton, *The Misses Vickers: The Centenary of the Painting by John Singer Sargent* (Sheffield: Sheffield Arts Dept., 1984).

6. Frank Miles, 'The Reform of the Royal Academy' in *Pall Mall Gazette* (1 September 1886).

7. Tom Cross, *Artists and Bohemians: 100 Years with the Chelsea Arts Club* (London: Quiller Press, 1992), 7.

8. John Birnie Philips had a studio here where his daughter Beatrice Whistler worked for a time.

9. Philip Macer-Wright, *Brangwyn: A Study at Close Quarters* (London: Hutchinson, 1940), 7.

10. Whistler was a natural clubman, but he also had an uneasy membership of the Arts Club in Dover Street. On one occasion, following his bankruptcy, he had been suspended for non-payment of dues. Pleading poverty he had offered a painting instead, but the Secretary of the club, with heavy-handed humour replied 'It is not a Nocturne in Purple or a Symphony in Blue and Green that we are after, but an Arrangement in Gold and Silver'.

11. Tom Cross, *Artists and Bohemians: 100 Years with the Chelsea Arts Club* (London: Quiller Press, 1992), 9.

12. George Percy Jacomb-Hood, *With Brush and Pencil* (London: John Murray, 1925).

13. Ibid.

14. Elizabeth & Joseph Pennell, *The Life of James McNeill*

Whistler (London: William Heinemann, 1925), 296.

15. Ibid.

16. Frank Miles to Mrs George Boughton, Williams Andrews Clark Memorial Library, University of California, Los Angeles; quoted in full, Molly Whittington-Egan, *Frank Miles and Oscar Wilde: 'Such White Lilies'* (High Wycombe: Rivendale Press, 2008), 84–5.

17. George Percy Jacomb-Hood, *With Brush and Pencil* (London: John Murray, 1925), 114.

18. Ibid., 113.

19. According to Jacomb-Hood, the concealed staircase inspired Miss 'Frankie' Forbes-Robertson to write a novel entitled *The Hidden Model*. The studio-house in the novel is identical to 44 Tite Street.

20. George Percy Jacomb-Hood, *With Brush and Pencil* (London: John Murray, 1925), 115.

21. Ibid.

22. Michael Field, *Works and Days* (London: John Murray, 1933).

23. Ibid.

24. William Rothenstein, *Men and Memories 1872–1900* (London: Faber & Faber, 1931), 167.

25. Walter Pater, *The Renaissance: Studies in Art and Poetry* (London, 1873).

26. William Rothenstein, *Men and Memories 1872–1900* (London: Faber & Faber, 1931), 190.

27. George Percy Jacomb-Hood, *With Brush and Pencil* (London: John Murray, 1925), 118.

28. William Rothenstein, *Men and Memories 1872–1900* (London: Faber & Faber, 1931), 192.

29. Ibid., 190.

30. Ibid., 172.

31. Charles Wellington Furse letter to his mother (18 January 1903) quoted in *Illustrated Memoir of Charles Wellington Furse A.R.A.* (London: Burlington Fine Arts Club, 1908), 35–6.

32. 'Royal Academy Pictures' in *Magazine of Art* (1894), 292.

33. William Rothenstein, *Men and Memories 1872–1900* (London: Faber & Faber, 1931), 172.

34. *The Sketch* (5 February 1896), 53.

35. Bernard Muddiman, *The Men of the Nineties* (London: Henry Danielson, 1920), 6.

36. *Dome* (2 January 1899), 89.

37. *Bookman* (9 March 1896), 189.

38. Charles Holmes, 'Nature and Landscape', *Dome,* (2/5 February 1899), 146.

39. William Rothenstein, *Men and Memories 1872–1900* (London: Faber & Faber, 1931), 172.

40. Katherine Furse, *Hearts and Pomegranates: The Story of Forty-five Years, 1875 to 1920* (London: Peter Davies, 1940), 251.

41. Oscar Wilde, *The Picture of Dorian Gray*.

42. *William Rothenstein Memorial Exhibition* exhibition catalogue (London: Tate Gallery, 1950), 5.

43. Rudolph De Cordova, 'The Dramatic Expression of Emotion in Art: An Interview with the Hon. John Collier', *Great Thoughts* (April 1908), 72.

Chapter 21. Plays, Panthers & Prison

1. Wilde's letter published in the *Daily Chronicle* (2 July 1890).

2. Richard Ellman, *Oscar Wilde* (London: First Vintage Books, 1988), 302.

3. Ibid.

4. Letter from Constance Wilde to Lady Mount-Temple, 23 Oct. 1892, BR 57/48/13.

5. Letter from Bosie to Frank Harris in 1925 quoted in Sturgis, *Passionate Attitudes* (1995), 131. The full quote reads: 'I did with him and allowed him to do just what was done among boys at Winchester and Oxford . . . Sodomy never took place between us; nor was it thought or dreamt of. Wilde treated me as an older boy treats a younger one at school, and he added what was new to me and was not (as far as I knew) known or practised among my contemporaries: he "sucked" me.'

6. Frank Harris, *Oscar Wilde: His Life and Confessions* (New York: printed and published by the author, 1916).

7. George Alexander, quoted in *Evening Standard* (29 November 1913).

8. Oscar Wilde, *De Profundis*.

9. Count Louis Hamon, *Cheiro's Memoirs: The Reminiscences of a Society Palmist* (Philadelphia, 1913), 152–3.

10. William Rothenstein, *Men and Memories 1872–1900* (London: Faber & Faber, 1931), 133.

11. H. Montgomery Hyde, *The Trials of Oscar Wilde* (London, William Hodge, 1948), 233.

12. Alfred Wood was introduced to Wilde through Douglas. He acquired some explicit letters between Wilde and Douglas and intended to exploit them to fund a passage to

America. Wood sent one letter to Herbert Beerbohm Tree to extract the necessary funds. When Tree alerted Wilde he refused to give him any money saying that if he could get £60 for them by a blackmailer he should accept the offer as it was an 'unusual price for a prose piece this length'. See Richard Ellman, *Oscar Wilde* (London: First Vintage Books, 1988), 390.

13. Richard Ellman, *Oscar Wilde* (London: First Vintage Books, 1988), 417.

14. Oscar Wilde, *De Profundis*.

15. Merlin Holland & Rupert Hart-Davis (eds), *The Complete Letters of Oscar Wilde* (London: Fourth Estate, 2000), 601.

16. *Pall Mall Gazette* (19 January 1895).

17. See Michael Seeney, 'An Ideal Husband: The First Night', *The Wildean*, No. 44 (January 2014).

18. Oscar Wilde to Robbie Ross, 28 February 1895 in Merlin Holland & Rupert Hart-Davis (eds), *The Complete Letters of Oscar Wilde* (London: Fourth Estate, 2000), 634.

19. Sir Travers Humphries in Foreword to H. Montgomery Hyde, *The Trials of Oscar Wilde* (London, William Hodge, 1948), 8.

20. Note passed by Mr Justice Henn Collins to Carson at the end of the Queensberry libel trial; Merlin Holland, *The Irish Peacock and the Scarlet Marquess* (London: Fourth Estate, 2002), xxx.

21. Frank Harris, *Oscar Wilde: His Life and Confessions* (New York: printed and published by the author, 1916), 240.

22. Oscar to Constance, [5] April 1895 in Merlin Holland & Rupert Hart-Davis (eds), *The Complete Letters of Oscar Wilde* (London: Fourth Estate, 2000), 637.

23. Christabel Aberconway, *A Wiser Woman? A Book of Memories* (London: Hutchinson, 1966), 19.

24. Philip Burne-Jones to Constance, 11 April 1895, MSS collection of John Holland.

25. Vyvyan Holland, *Son of Oscar Wilde* (Harmondsworth: Penguin Books, 1957), 52.

26. Whistler purchased several of his own drawings and sketches from No. 34 including a Drawing of Maud Franklin (M.0693).

27. H. Montgomery Hyde, *The Trials of Oscar Wilde* (London, William Hodge, 1948), 201–2.

28. Ibid., 236.

29. Ibid., 323.

30. Ibid., 339.

31. William Butler Yeats, *Autobiographies* (London: Macmillan, 1980), 291.

32. Oscar Wilde, *De Profundis*.

33. Ibid.

Chapter 22. Abbey & the Lodge

1. Richard Ellman, *Oscar Wilde* (London: First Vintage Books, 1988), 575.

2. Frank Harris, *My Life and Loves* (New York: Grove Press, reprint 1991), 814.

3. Oscar Wilde, *De Profundis*.

4. George Percy Jacomb-Hood, *With Brush and Pencil* (London: John Murray, 1925), 119.

5. [Il continue ainsi dignement les traditions des fameux dessinateurs d'outre Manche: des Fred Walker, des Pinwell, des Millais, et des Keene]; Frederick Walker; George John Pinwell; John Everett Millais; and Charles Keene; see Edward Lucas, *Edwin Austin Abbey: The Record of his Life and Work* (London: Methuen & Co., 1921), 35.

6. Edward Lucas, *Edwin Austin Abbey: The Record of his Life and Work* (London: Methuen & Co., 1921), 82.

7. *The Times* (27 June 1881).

8. Edwin Ward, *Recollections of a Savage* (New York 1923), 112.

9. George Percy Jacomb-Hood, *With Brush and Pencil* (London: John Murray, 1925), 121.

10. Ibid., 120.

11. That young red-haired girl that Hood saw wandering in Tite Street would grow up to become the actress and comedian Lydia Bilbrook and in later years she would play Mrs Vane in the 1945 film version of her neighbour's novel, *The Picture of Dorian Gray*.

12. [où une toile de deux metres a l'air d'un timbre poste] JSS/Helleu, Collection Mme Paulette Howard-Johnston, quoted in Stanley Olson, *John Singer Sargent: His Portrait* (London: Barry Jenkins, 1988), 174.

13. Edward Lucas, *Edwin Austin Abbey: The Record of his Life and Work*, volume I, (London: Methuen & Co., 1921), 592.

14. Ibid., 395.

15. Ibid., volume II, 344.

16. Ibid., volume I, 149.

17. Ibid., volume II, 367.

18. Quoted from *Paintings, Drawings and Pastels by Edwin*

Austin Abbey (New Haven: Gallery of Fine Arts, Yale University, 1939), 3.

19. Edward Lucas, *Edwin Austin Abbey: The Record of his Life and Work*, volume I (London: Methuen & Co., 1921), 199.

20. The Royal Exchange was designed and built by Sir William Tite whose name was given to the street upon which Abbey lived.

21. Edward Lucas, *Edwin Austin Abbey: The Record of his Life and Work*, volume II (London: Methuen & Co., 1921), 369.

22. Frank Cadogan Cowper. Letters to his mother, Edith Cowper. 1899. 1906. Cow 1/ 2, Royal Academy Archives, London.

23. Letter from Harcourt to Solomon, 24 July 1908, Harcourt Archive, Bodleian Library, Oxford.

24. Letter from Abbey to Carlisle, 17 July 1908, Castle Howard Archive, J22/84.

25. Muthesius 'Kunst and Leben in England', *Zeitschrift fur bildende Kunst*, 13 (1902), 69.

26. Abbey had been asked to paint the coronation of George V, but he declined.

Chapter 23. The Van Dyck of Tite Street.

1. Roy Strong, *The Spirit of Britain: A Narrative History of the Arts* (London: Hutchinson, 1999), 561.

2. Ellen Terry, *The Story of My Life* (New York, 1908), 314–15.

3. 'le Van Dyck de l'époque'; 'M. Rodin in London', *Daily Chronicle* (16 May 1902), 6.

4. JSS/Curtis [October 1900], Archives of the Boston Athenaeum.

5. Letter from Claude Monet to Alice Monet, London, Saturday, 2 February 1901, in Wildenstein *Claude Monet: Biographie et catalogue raisonne: Tome IV: 1899–1926*; No. 1592; Paris: La Bibliotheque des Art, 1985, 35.

6. Jacques Emile-Blanche, *Portraits of a Lifetime* (London: J.M. Dent and Sons, 1937).

7. Martin Birnbaum, *John Singer Sargent: A Conversation Piece*, New York, William E. Rudge's Sons, 1941, 16.

8. William Downes, *John S. Sargent: His Life and Work* (London, 1926), 17.

9. Martin Birnbaum, *John Singer Sargent: A Conversation Piece* (New York: E. Rudge's Sons, 1941), 16.

10. Jacques Emile-Blanche, *Portraits of a Lifetime* (London: J.M. Dent & Sons, 1937), 156.

11. Nicola D'Inverno, 'The Real John Singer Sargent', *Boston Sunday Advertiser*, 1926.

12. Ibid.

13. Walter Sickert 'Sargentolary', *New Age* (19 May 1910).

14. George Percy Jacomb-Hood, *With Brush and Pencil* (London: John Murray, 1925), 61–2.

15. Ibid.

16. Obituary, W.G. Robb, 1905.

17. Quoted in Evan Charteris, John Sargent (London: William Heinemann, 1927), 222.

18. Edward Pinnington, 'Robert Brough, Painter', *Art Journal* (1898), 149.

19. Ibid., 147.

20. Charles Ricketts, 4 February 1905, 117 Charles Ricketts, *Self-portrait, Taken from the Letters and Journals of Charles Ricketts, RA*, collected and compiled by T. Sturge Moore, edited by Cecil Lewis (London: Peter Davies, 1939).

21. George Percy Jacomb-Hood, *With Brush and Pencil* (London: John Murray, 1925), 61–2.

22. Nicola D'Inverno, 'The Real John Singer Sargent', *Boston Sunday Advertiser* (1926).

23. Quoted in Thea Holme, *Chelsea*, p. 210.

24. Stanley Weintraub, *The London Yankees: Portraits of American Writers and Artists in England, 1894-1914* (Harcourt Brace Jovanovich, 1979), 198.

25. W. Graham Robertson, *Time Was* (London: Hamish Hamilton, 1945), 233.

26. Sir Frank Swettenham, *Footprints in Malaya* (1942), 141.

27. Leon Edel (ed.), *Henry James, Letters*: Volume 3 (Cambridge, Mass.: Harvard University Press, 1980), 156.

28. James Lomax & Richard Ormond, *John Singer Sargent and the Edwardian Age* (Leeds Art Gallery, 1979), 8.

29. David Cannadine, 'The British Aristocracy in the Age of Sargent', *Portrait of a Lady: Sargent and Lady Agnew* (Edinburgh: National Gallery of Scotland), 47.

30. Kenneth McConkey, *Edwardian Portraits: Images of an Age of Opulence* (Woodbridge: Antique Collectors' Club, 1987), 14.

31. Elaine Kilmurray & Richard Ormond (eds), *John Singer Sargent* (London: Tate Gallery, 1998), 38.

32. Jacques Emile-Blanche, *Portraits of a Lifetime* (London: J.M. Dent & Sons, 1937), 155.

33. Ibid.

34. Quoted in Stanley Olson, *John Singer Sargent: His Portrait* (London: Barry Jenkins, 1988), 228.

35. Ibid.

36. JSS to Curtis in Evan Charteris, *John Sargent* (London: William Heinemann, 1927), 155.

37. Robbie Ross interview with Oscar Wilde, *St James's Gazette* (18 January 1895).

Chapter 24. Queer Street.

1. Romaine Brooks, 'No Pleasant Memories' [unpublished memoir] American Art Archives, Smithsonian, Washington D.C.

2. Ibid.

3. Ibid.

4. Ibid.

5. Meryle Secrest, *Between Me and Life* (London: Macdonald & Jane's, 1976), 173–4.

6. Romaine Brooks, 'No Pleasant Memories' [unpublished memoir] American Art Archives, Smithsonian, Washington D.C., 201.

7. Ibid.

8. Anna Lea Merritt, *Love Locked Out: The Memoirs of Anna Lea Merritt with a checklist of her works*, ed. Galina Gorokhoff (Boston: Boston Museum of Fine Art, 1982).

9. Romaine Brooks, 'No Pleasant Memories' [unpublished memoir] American Art Archives, Smithsonian, Washington D.C., 209.

10. Ibid., 203.

11. Ibid., 205.

12. Ibid., 209.

13. Ibid.

14. Meryle Secrest, *Between Me and Life* (London: Macdonald and Jane's, 1976), 419.

15. Romaine Brooks, 'No Pleasant Memories' [unpublished memoir] American Art Archives, Smithsonian, Washington D.C., 205.

16. '*Nous avons souvent dit d'imperissables choses*' from Charles Baudelaire poem 'Le balcon' in *Les Fleurs du mal*. Quoted in Romaine Brooks, 'No Pleasant Memories' [unpublished memoir] American Art Archives, Smithsonian, Washington D.C., 206.

17. Hilton Kramer, 'Romaine Brooks: Revelation in Art' in *New York Times* (14 April 1971).

18. Claude Roger-Marx, Groupil Gallery exhibition catalogue, June 1911.

19. Michael Baker, *Our Three Selves: A Life of Radclyffe Hall* (London: Hamish, 1985), 18.

20. Una Troubridge, *The Life and Death of Radclyffe Hall* (London: Hammond & Hammond, 1961), 30.

21. See Elizabeth Crawford (ed), *The Women's Suffrage Movement: A Reference Guide 1866–1928* (Routledge, 2000), 172, and the Edith Downing files at National Museum Wales, Cardiff (uncatalogued).

22. Edith Elizabeth Downing in *Votes for Women* (25 November 1910).

23. Belinda Hollyer, *Votes for Women* (London: Scholastic, 2003), 81.

24. Lisa Tickner, *The Spectacle of Women: Imagery of the Suffrage Campaign 1907–1914* (London: Chatto & Windus, 1987), 15.

25. Ibid.

26. *Votes for Women*, 24 June 1910, 628.

27. Daughter of Ellen Terry and E.W. Godwin. Craig was a principle member of the Suffrage Atelier founded in February 1909 'with the special object of training in the arts and crafts of effective picture propaganda for the Suffrage'. The Common Cause (24 June 1909) cited in Lisa Tickner, *The Spectacle of Women: Imagery of the Suffrage Campaign 1907–1914* (London: Chatto & Windus, 1987), 20.

28. See Lisa Tickner, *The Spectacle of Women: Imagery of the Suffrage Campaign 1907–1914* (London: Chatto & Windus, 1987), 119.

29. Votes for Women (15 and 22 July 1910) cited in Lisa Tickner, *The Spectacle of Women: Imagery of the Suffrage Campaign 1907–1914* (London: Chatto & Windus, 1987), 116.

30. *The Daily Graphic* (2 March 1912).

31. Radclyffe Hall, *Pall Mall Gazette* (5 March 1912).

32. George Wickes (ed.), *The Amazon of Letters: The Life and Loves of Natalie Barney* (London: W.H. Allen, 1977), 257.

33. *The Sketch* as quoted in Diana Souhami, *Gluck: Her Biography* (London: Pandora, 1989), 62.

34. *Daily Graphic* (9 April 1926).

35. *Art News* (4 April 1926).

36. Quoted in Diana Souhami, *Gluck: Her Biography* (London: Pandora, 1989), 63.

37. Diana Souhami, *Gluck: Her Biography* (London: Pandora, 1989), 63.

38. Gluck, Notes on the back of a photograph of her painting of Romaine Brooks. Quoted in Diana Souhami, *Gluck: Her Biography* (London: Pandora, 1989), 63.

39. Meryle Secrest, *Between Me and Life* (London: Macdonald and Jane's, 1976), 291.

40. Havelock Ellis in Michael Baker, *Our Three Selves: A Life of Radclyffe Hall* (London: Hamish Hamilton, 1985), 205.

41. James Douglas, 'A Book That Must Be Suppressed', *Sunday Express* (19 August 1928).

42. *The Nation* (8 April 1928).

43. An edition of the book published in 1982 by Virago Press featured Gluck's *YouWe* portrait on the cover.

Chapter 25. Twilight in Tite Street.

1. Evan Charteris, *John Sargent* (London: William Heinemann, 1927), 202.

2. 19 October 1916; Evan Charteris, *John Sargent* (London: William Heinemann, 1927), 207.

3. Ibid., 214.

4. 18 October 1918, JSS to Mrs Hunter, AAA.

5. Letter to Eva Gardner quoted in Evan Charteris, *John Sargent* (London: William Heinemann, 1927), 216.

6. John Singer Sargent to Evan Charteris, 11 September 1918 in Evan Charteris, *John Sargent* (London: William Heinemann, 1927), 214.

7. Letters to Evan Charteris of January 1919 in Evan Charteris, *John Sargent* (London: William Heinemann, 1927), 217.

8. 12 May 1920: Evan Charteris, *John Sargent* (London: William Heinemann, 1927), 217.

9. *The Times* (7 February 1910).

10. *Westminster Gazette* (10 February 1910).

11. Clive Bell, 'The English Group' in *Second Post-Impressionist Exhibition*, 5 October – 31 December 1912, Grafton Galleries, exhibition catalogue (London, 1912), 9.

12. Quoted in Tom Cross, *Artists and Bohemians: 100 Years with the Chelsea Arts Club* (Quiller Press, 1992), 38.

13. Meirion & Susie Harries, *The War Artists* (London: Imperial War Museum and Tate Gallery, 1983), 87.

14. Siegfried Sassoon, *Siegfried's Journey, 1916–1920* (London: Faber & Faber, 1946), 50.

15. Ibid., 49.

16. Ibid., 51.

17. Ibid., 50.

18. Ibid., 51.

19. Letter to Thomas Lowinsky, April 1918, in Rupert Hart-Davies (ed.) *Siegfried Sassoon, Sassoon Diaries 1915–18*

(London: Faber and Faber, 1983), 294.

20. Nicola D'Inverno, 'The Real John Singer Sargent' in *Boston Sunday Advertiser* (1926).

21. Charles Ricketts, R.A., in *Self-portraits*, ed. Cecil Lewis (London, 1939).

22. Adrian Stokes, 'John Singer Sargent, RA, RWS' in Randall Davies (ed.) *The Old Water-Colour Society's Club*, volume 3 (London, 1926).

Chapter 26. Last of the Titans

1. Quoted in William Downes, *John S. Sargent: His Life and Work* (London: Thornton Butterworth, 1925), 100.

2. Amanda B. Waterman, 'Frank Cadogan Cowper: The Last Pre-Raphaelite' (Thesis: University of Washington, 2008).

3. Philip Heseltine to Edith Buckley Jones, 5 September 1930, Barry Smith (ed.), *The Collected Letters of Peter Warlock* (Woodbridge: Boydell Press, 2005), 280.

4. Ibid.

5. Philip Heseltine to Frederick Delius, 22 April 1916, Barry Smith (ed.), *The Collected Letters of Peter Warlock: Volume 3* (Woodbridge: Boydell Press, 2005), 512.

6. Philip Heseltine to Olivia Smith, 27 February 1914, Barry Smith (ed.), *The Collected Letters of Peter Warlock: Volume II* (Woodbridge: Boydell Press, 2005), 271.

7. D.H. Lawrence to Robert Nichols, 17 November 1915, *The Selected Letters of D.H. Lawrence* (Cambridge: Cambridge University Press, 2000), 109.

8. Cecil Gray, *Warlock: A Memoir of Philip Heseltine* (London: Jonathan Cape, 1934), 119.

9. Augustus John, *Chiaroscuro: Fragments of Autobiography* (London: Pellegrini & Cudahy, 1952), 80.

10. Ibid., 56.

11. Barry Smith, *Peter Warlock: The Life of Philip Heseltine* (Oxford: Oxford University Press, 1994), 220–6.

12. Denis Ivor, 'Philip Heseltine: A Psychological Study', *Music Review*, 46 (1985), 118–32.

13. Peter Warlock to Edith Buckley Jones, 5 September 1930, Barry Smith (ed.), *The Collected Letters of Peter Warlock* (Woodbridge: Boydell Press, 2005), 280.

14. 16 August 1881 letter to Violet, quoted in Richard Ormond, "John Singer Sargent and Vernon Lee" in Colby Quarterly, Volume 9, Issue 3, September 1970.

15. John Postle Heseltine to Whistler, 27 November 1878, Library of Congress, Manuscript Division, Pennell-

Whistler Collection, PWC; GUW 08920.

16. Whistler to John Postle Heseltine, [27/30] November 1878, GUL H232; GUW 02131.

17. Full account of inquest in Cecil Gray, *Warlock: A Memoir of Philip Heseltine* (London: Jonathan Cape, 1934), 290-5.

18. *New Chronicle* (18 December 1930).

19. Full account of inquest in Cecil Gray, *Warlock: A Memoir of Philip Heseltine* (London: Jonathan Cape, 1934), 290-5.

20. Augustus John, *Chiaroscuro: Fragments of Autobiography* (London: Pellegrini & Cudahy, 1952), 81.

21. Mark Girouard, 'Chelsea's Bohemian Studio Houses', *Country Life* (23 November 1972), 1370.

22. Cyril Connolly, *The Modern Movement* (London: Deutsch/Hamilton, 1965), 67.

23. Michael Holroyd, *Augustus John* (revised edition: London: Pimlico, 2011), 523.

24. *Horizon*, volume III, 18 June 1941, 400.

25. Oscar Wilde to William Rothenstein, 4 October 1899, Merlin Holland & Rupert Hart-Davis (eds), *The Complete Letters of Oscar Wilde* (London: Fourth Estate, 2000), 1166.

26. Augustus John, *Chiaroscuro: Fragments of Autobiography* (London: Pellegrini & Cudahy, 1952), 53.

27. Evan Charteris, *John Sargent* (London: William Heinemann, 1927), 215.

28. Cyril Clemens, *My Chats with Thomas Hardy* (London: T Werner Laurie, 1944).

29. Michael Holroyd, *Augustus John* (revised edition: London, Pimlico, 2011), 563.

30. Ibid., 561–2.

31. Nancy Cunard, *Grand Man: Memoirs of Norman Douglas* (London: Secker & Warburg, 1954), 195.

32. Michael Holroyd, *Augustus John* (revised edition: London, Pimlico, 2011), 562.

33. Ibid.

34. Michael Holroyd, *Augustus John* (Harmondsworth: Penguin Books, 1976), 679.

35. Galina Gorokhoff (ed.), *Love Locked Out: The Memoirs of Anna Lea Merritt with a checklist of her works* (Boston: Museum of Fine Art, 1982), 201.

36. Michael Holroyd, *Augustus John* (revised edition: London: Pimlico, 2011), 559.

37. Alan Moorehead unpublished monograph 'Augustus John' quoted in Michael Holroyd, Augustus John (revised edition: London: Pimlico, 2011), 559.

38. Michael Holroyd, *Augustus John* (revised edition: London: Pimlico, 2011), 559.

39. *Sunday Times* (22 July 1973), 34.

40. Augustus John to Mavis Wheeler; Michael Holroyd, *Augustus John* (revised edition: London: Pimlico, 2011), 559.

41. George Bernard Shaw to Augustus John, 26 February 1944; see Alan Moorehead, *Montgomery: A Biography* (London: Hamish Hamilton, 1946), 187–90.

42. Michael Holroyd, *Augustus John* (revised edition: London: Pimlico, 2011), 560.

43. Peregrine Worsthorne, *Tricks of Memory* (London: Weidenfeld & Nicolson, 1993), 56.

44. An inventory of the house is held at the Kensington Central Library.

45. Peregrine Worsthorne, *Tricks of Memory* (London: Weidenfeld & Nicolson, 1993), 56.

46. Ibid.

47. Ibid.

48. Herbert Read, *Burlington Magazine* (December 1940), 28.

49. John to Cyril Connolly, 5 November 1949. McFarlin Library, University of Tulsa.

50. Augustus John, *Chiaroscuro: Fragments of Autobiography* (London: Pellegrini & Cudahy, 1952), 264.

51. Michael Holroyd, *Augustus John* (revised edition: London: Pimlico, 2011), 562.

52. Jacqueline Hope-Nicholson, *Life Amongst the Troubridges: Journals of a Young Victorian 1873–1884* (London: Tite Street Press, 1999, revised edition), 152.

53. Michael Holroyd, *Augustus John* (revised edition: London: Pimlico, 2011), 562.

Pink Note – the Novelette by James Abbott McNeill Whistler, 1883–4

SELECT BIBLIOGRAPHY

Anderson, Ronald, and Anne Koval. *James McNeill Whistler: Beyond the Myth*. London: John Murray, 1994.

Baker, Michael. *Our Three Selves: A Life of Radclyffe Hall*. London: Hamish Hamilton, 1985.

Baron, Wendy. *Sickert: Paintings and Drawings*. New Haven: Yale University Press, 2006.

Birnbaum, Martin. *John Singer Sargent, A Conversation Piece*. New York: W. E. Rudge's Sons, 1941.

Blanche, Jacques-Emile. *Portraits of a Lifetime*. London: J.M. Dent and Sons, 1937.

Blunt, Reginald. *Paradise Row*. London: Macmillan and Company, 1906.

Brooks, Romaine. *No Pleasant Memories*. Unpublished manuscript, 1926.

Burlington Fine Arts Club. *Illustrated Memoir of Charles Wellington Furse, A.R.A*. London, 1908.

Calloway, Stephen, and Lynn Federle Orr, editors. *The Cult of Beauty: The Aesthetic Movement 1860-1900*. London: Victoria and Albert Museum, 2011.

Cannadine, David. 'The British Aristocracy in the Age of Sargent' in *Portrait of a Lady: Sargent and Lady Agnew*. Edinburgh: National Gallery of Scotland, 1997.

—— *The Decline and Fall of the British Aristocracy*. London: Yale University Press, 1990.

Chadwick, Whitney. *Amazons in the Drawing Room: The Art of Romaine Brooks*. Berkeley: University of California Press, 2000.

Charteris, Evan. *John Sargent*. London: William Heinemann, 1927.

Collier, The Hon. John. *A Primer of Art*. London: Macmillan and Co., 1882.

—— *A Manual of Oil Painting*. London: Cassell and Co., 1887.

—— *The Art of Portrait Painting*. London: Cassell and Co., 1910.

—— *The Religion of an Artist*. London: Watts, 1926.

Comyns Carr, Joseph. *Some Eminent Victorians*. London: Duckworth, 1908.

Cross, Tom. *Artists and Bohemians: 100 Years with the Chelsea Arts Club*. London: Quiller Press, 1992.

D'Inverno, Nicola. 'The Real John Singer Sargent' in *Boston Sunday Advertiser*, 1926.

Delaney, J.G.P. *Glyn Philpot: His Life and Art*. Aldershot: Ashgate, 1999.

Dellamora, Richard. *Radclyffe Hall: A Life in Writing*. Philadelphia: University of Pennsylvania Press, 2011.

Dorment, Richard and Margaret MacDonald, editors. *James McNeill Whistler*. London: Tate Gallery Publications, 1994.

Downes, William Howe. *John Singer Sargent: His Life and Work*. London: Thornton Butterworth, 1926.

Duret, Theodore. *Whistler*. London: Grant Richards, 1917.

Easton, Malcolm and Michael Holroyd, editors. *The Art of Augustus John*. London: Secker & Warburg, 1974.

Ellman, Richard. *Oscar Wilde*. London: First Vintage Books, 1988.

—— editor. *The Artist as Critic: Critical Writings of Oscar Wilde*. London: W.H. Allen, 1970.

Felberman, Heinrich. *The Memoirs of a Cosmopolitan*. London: Chapman Hall, 1936.

Fletcher, Pamela M. *Narrating Modernity: The British Problem Picture, 1895-1914*. Aldershot: Ashgate, 2003.

Frith, William Powell. *My Autobiography and Reminiscences*. London: Richard Bentley & Son, 1888.

Fryer, Jonathan. *Robbie Ross: Oscar Wilde's Devoted Friend*. New York: Carroll and Graf, 2000.

Gere, Charlotte. *The House Beautiful: Oscar Wilde and the Aesthetic Interior*. London: Lund Humphries, 2000.

Gibson, Robin. *Glyn Philpot, 1884-1937: Edwardian Aesthete to Thirties Modernist*. London: National Portrait Gallery, 1984.

Gillett, Paula. *The Victorian Painter's World*. Gloucester: Sutton, 1990.

Girouard, Mark. 'Chelsea's Bohemian Studio Houses: The Victorian Artist at Home II' in *Country Life*. 23 November 1972, 1370–4.

Gorokhoff, Galina, editor. *Love Locked Out: The Memoirs of Anna Lea Merritt*. Boston: Museum of Fine Arts, 1982.

Graham Robertson, W. *Time Was*. London: Hamish Hamilton, 1945.

Gray, Cecil. *Peter Warlock: A Memoir of Philip Heseltine*. London: Jonathan Cape, 1934.

Hamilton, James. *The Misses Vickers: The Centenary of the Painting by John Singer Sargent*. Sheffield: Sheffield Arts Department, 1984.

Hamilton, Walter. *The Aesthetic Movement in England*. London: Reeves and Turner, 1882.

Harbron, Dudley. *The Conscious Stone: The Life of Edward William Godwin*. London: Latimer House Ltd., 1949.

Harris, Frank. *Oscar Wilde: His Life and Confessions*. New York: printed and published by the author, 1916.

Hatcher, John. *Laurence Binyon: Poet, Scholar of East and West*. Oxford: Clarendon Press, 1995.

Heseltine, Nigel. *Capriol for Mother: A Memoir of Philip Heseltine (Peter Warlock)*. London: Thames, 1992.

Holland, Merlin and Rupert Hart-Davis, editors. *The Complete Letters of Oscar Wilde*. London: Fourth Estate, 2000.

Holland, Vyvyan. *Son of Oscar Wilde*. London: Penguin, 1957.

Holme, Thea. *Chelsea*. London: Hamilton, 1972.

Holroyd, Michael. *Augustus John*. London: Pimlico, 2011.

Jacomb-Hood, George Percy. *With Brush and Pencil*. London: John Murray, 1925.

Jenkins, David Fraser. *Whistler, Sargent, and Steer: Impressionists in London from Tate Collection*. Nashville Tennessee: First Center for Visual Arts, 2002.

John, Augustus. *Chiaroscuro: Fragments of Autobiography*. London: Jonathan Cape, 1952.

—— *Finishing Touches*. Edited by Daniel George, London: Jonathan Cape, 1966.

Kilmurray, Elaine and Richard Ormond. *John Singer Sargent: Complete Paintings Volumes 1–7*. New Haven, London: Published for the Paul Mellon Centre for Studies in British Art by Yale University Press, *c*.1998–2012.

Kinchin, Juliet and Paul Stirton. *Is Mr Ruskin Living Too Long? Selected Writings of E. W. Godwin on Victorian Architecture, Design and Culture*. Oxford: White Cockade, 2005.

Lancaster, Marie-Jaqueline, editor. *Letters of Engagement 1884–1884: The Love Letters of Adrian Hope and Laura Troubridge*. London: Tite Street Press, 2002.

Langtry, Lillie. *The Days I Knew*. London: Hutchinson, 1925.

Lomax, James and Richard Ormond. *John Singer Sargent and the Edwardian Age*. Leeds Art Gallery, 1979.

Lucas, Edward Verrall. *Edwimr Austin Abbey: The Record of His Life and Work*. London: Methuen and Co., 1921.

MacDonald, Margaret. *Beatrice Whistler: Artist and Designer*. Glasgow: Hunterian Art Gallery, 1997.

—— editor. *Whistler, Women and Fashion*. London: Yale University Press, 2003.

——, Patricia de Montfort and Nigel Thorp. *The Correspondence of James McNeill Whistler, 1855–1903*; including *The Correspondence of Anna McNeill Whistler, 1855–1880*, edited by Georgia Toutziari. On-line edition, University of Glasgow, 2003–2010.

—— and Patricia de Montfort. *An American in London: Whistler and the Thames*. London: Philip Wilson, 2013.

McConkey, Kenneth. *Edwardian Portraits: Images of an Age of Opulence*. Woodbridge: Antique Collector's Club, 1987.

—— *The New English: A History of the New English Arts Club*. London: Royal Academy of Arts, 2006.

McKenna, Neil. *The Secret Life of Oscar Wilde*. London: Arrow Books, 2004.

—— *Fanny and Stella: The Young Men Who Shocked Victorian England*. London: Faber and Faber, 2013.

Menpes, Mortimer. *Whistler As I Knew Him*. London: Adam and Charles Black, 1904.

Merrill-Mount, Charles. *John Singer Sargent: A Biography*. London: Cresset Press, 1957.

Morgan, Gary. *The Etched Works of Mortimer Menpes, 1855–1938*. Crafers West, South Australia: Stuart Galleries, 2012.

Moyle, Franny. *Constance: The Tragic and Scandalous Life of Mrs Oscar Wilde*. London: John Murray, 2011.

Olson, Stanley. *John Singer Sargent: His Portrait*. London: Macmillan, 1986.

Ormond, Richard. *John Singer Sargent: Paintings, Drawings, Watercolours*. London: Phaidon, 1970.

Pearsall, Phyllis. *Fleet Street, Tite Street, Queer Street*. London: Phyllis Pearsall, 1983.

Pearson, Hesketh. *Oscar Wilde: His Life and Wit*. London: Harpers, 1946.

—— *The Man Whistler*. London: Macdonald and Jane's, 1978.

Pennell, Elizabeth and Joseph. *The Whistler Journal*. Philadelphia: Lippincott, 1921.

—— *The Life of James McNeill Whistler*. London: William Heinemann, 1925.

Preston, Kerrison, editor. *Letters of W. Graham Robertson*. London: Hamish Hamilton, 1953.

Prettejohn, Elizabeth, editor. *After the Pre-Raphaelites: Art and Aestheticism in Victorian England*. Manchester: Manchester University Press, 1999.

—— *Art for Art's Sake: Aestheticism in Victorian Painting*. New Haven: Yale University Press, 2007.

Ransome, Arthur. *Bohemia in London*. London: Chapman and Hall, 1907.

Rossetti, Helen Maria Madox. *Pre-Raphaelite Twilight: The Story of Charles Augustus Howell*. London: Richards Press, 1954.

Rothenstein, William. *Men and Memories 1872–1900*. London: Faber and Faber, 1931.

Sassoon, Siegfried. *Siegfried's Journey: 1916–1920*. London: Faber, 1945.

Secrest, Meryle. *Between Me and Life: A Biography of Romaine Brooks*. London: Macdonald and Jane's, 1976.

Smith, Barry. *Peter Warlock: The Life of Philip Heseltine*. Oxford: Oxford University Press, 1994.

—— editor. *The Collected Letters of Peter Warlock*. Woodbridge: Boydell Press, 2005.

Souhami, Diana. *Gluck: Her Biography*. London: Pandora, 1988.

Staley, Allen. *The New Painting of the 1860s: Between the Pre-Raphaelites and the Aesthetic Movement*. New Haven: Yale University Press, 2011.

Stedman, Jane. *W.S. Gilbert: A Classic Victorian and His Theatre*. Oxford: Oxford University Press, 1996.

Strong, Roy. *The Spirit of Britain: A Narrative History of the Arts*. London: Hutchinson, 1999.

Sturgis, Matthew. *Passionate Attitudes: The English Decadence of the 1890s*. London: Macmillan, 1995.

—— *Walter Sickert: A Life*. London: Harper Perennial, 2005.

Surtees, Virginia. *The Actress and the Brewer's Wife: Two Victorian Vignettes*. Wilby, Norwich: Michael Russell, 1997.

Sutherland, Daniel E., *Whistler: A Life for Art's Sake*. London, Yale University Press, 2014.

Sweet, Frederick. *Sargent, Whistler and Mary Cassatt*. Chicago: Art Institute of Chicago, 1954.

Terry, Ellen. *The Story of My Life*. London: Victor Gollancz, 1933.

Tickner, Lisa. *The Spectacle of Women: Imagery of the Suffrage Campaign 1907–1914*. London: Chatto and Windus, 1987.

Troubridge, Laura. *Life Amongst the Troubridges: Journals of a Young Victorian 1873–1884*. Edited by Jacqueline Hope-Nicholson, London: Tite Street Press, 1999.

Troubridge, Una. *The Life and Death of Radclyffe Hall*. London: Hammond and Hammond, 1961.

Walkley, Giles. *Artists Houses in London 1764–1914*. Aldershot: Scolar Press, 1994.

Waterman, Amanda. *Frank Cadogan Cowper: The Last Pre-Raphaelite*. Thesis: University of Washington, 2008.

Way, Thomas. *Memories of James McNeill Whistler: The Artist*. London: John Lane, 1912.

Wedd, Kit. *Artists' London: Holbein to Hirst*. London: Merrell, 2001.

Weintraub, Stanley. *The London Yankees: Portraits of American Writers and Artists in England, 1894-1914*. London: W.H. Allen, 1979.

—— *Whistler: A Biography*. London: Collins, 1974.

Whistler, James McNeill. *The Gentle Art of Making Enemies*. London: William Heinemann Ltd., reprinted 1994.

Whittington-Egan, Molly. *Frank Miles and Oscar Wilde: Such White Lillies*. High Wycombe, Rivendale Press, 2008.

Wilde v Whistler: Being an Acrimonious Correspondence on Art between Oscar Wilde and James A. McNeill Whistler. London: privately printed by Leonard Smithers, 1906.

INDEX

Note: page numbers in *italic* type refer to the captions to the illustrations; houses in Tite Street listed by number (e.g. No. 44 Tite Street) and also by house name where it exists

PICTURE CREDITS

Every care has been taken to trace copyright holders. Any copyright holders we have been unable to reach are invited to contact the publishers so that a full acknowledgment may be given in subsequent editions.

P.2 *The Acheson Sisters* by John Singer Sargent, 1902, oil on canvas, 273 x 200 cm, Chatsworth House, Derbyshire © Devonshire Collection, Chatsworth, reproduced by permission of Chatsworth Settlement Trustees / Bridgeman Images **P.6** *A View of Tite Street* by Joseph Pennell, 1889 from *Old Chelsea* by Benjamin Martin Ellis **P.13** Library of Congress, Washington D.C., image LC-USZ62-61275 **P.14** *Symphony in White, No. 1: The White Girl* by James Abbott McNeill Whistler, 1862, oil on canvas, 213 x 108 cm, National Gallery of Art, Washington, Harris Whittemore Collection **P.15** *Symphony in White, No. 2: The Little White Girl* by James Abbott McNeill Whistler, 1864, oil on canvas, 76.5 x 51 cm © Tate, London **P.19** *Arrangement in Grey and Black, No. 1: Portrait of the Artist's Mother* by James Abbott McNeill Whistler, 1871, oil on canvas, 144 x 162.5 cm, Musée d'Orsay, Paris **P.22** Kensington Central Library image SB02 CM1922 **P.23** Kensington Central Library **P.25** *Nocturne: Blue and Silver – Chelsea* by James Abbott McNeill Whistler, 1871, oil on wood, 50 x 61 cm © Tate, London **P.26** Entrance of the Grosvenor Gallery, New Bond Street, London from *The Graphic*, 19 May 1877, engraving, private collection © Look and Learn / Peter Jackson Collection / Bridgeman Images **P.31** James Abbott McNeill Whistler by unknown photographer, 1885, platinum print, 18 x 12 cm © National Portrait Gallery, London **P.32** Freer Gallery of Art, Smithsonian Institution / Bridgeman Images **P.34** © Victoria and Albert Museum, London **P.37** Kensington Central Library **P.40 LEFT** Carlo 'Ape' Pellegrini by Arthur Marks in *Vanity Fair*, April 1889 **P.40 RIGHT** Archibald Stuart-Wortley by Leslie 'Spy' Ward in *Vanity Fair*, January 1890, colour litho, private collection © Look and Learn / Peter Jackson Collection / Bridgeman Images **P.43** Benjamin Disraeli, Earl of Beaconsfield by Carlo Pellegrini in *Vanity Fair*, January 1869, chromolithograph, 34 x 21 cm © National Portrait Gallery, London

P.46 *Miss Maud Franklin* by James Abbott McNeill Whistler, *c.*1872–3, oil on canvas, 63 x 41 cm, Harvard Museums, Fogg Museum, bequest of Grenville L. Winthrop 1943.164, Photo: Imaging Department © President and Fellows of Harvard College **P.50** *Arrangement in Brown and Black: Portrait of Miss Rosa Corder* by James Abbott McNeill Whistler, 1876–8, oil on canvas, 192 x 92 cm, Frick Collection, New York, Henry Clay Frick Bequest 1914.1.134 © Frick Collection, New York **P.51** *Mr__ and Miss__ Nervously Perpetuating the Touch of the Vanished Hand* by Max Beerbohm, 1918, pencil and watercolour on paper, 32 x 39 cm © The estate of Max Beerbohm **P.52** RIBA 105085 **P.55** *Nocturne in Black and Gold: The Falling Rocket* by James Abbott McNeill Whistler, 1875, oil on panel, 60 x 47 cm, Detroit Institute of Arts **P.58** *The Gold Scab: Eruption in Frilthy Lucre (The Creditor)* by James Abbott McNeill Whistler, 1879, oil on canvas, 187 x 140 cm, Fine Art Museums of San Francisco 1997.11 **P.62** © Victoria and Albert Museum, London **P.63** RIBA 105087 **P.67** *Elaine* by Frank Miles, *c.*1872–4, Michael Seeney Collection **P.70** RIBA 105086 **P.73** *The Sleep of an Acorn* by Archibald Stuart-Wortley, 1884, oil on canvas, 139 x 160 cm, The Collection: Art and Archeology in Lincolnshire (Usher Gallery, Lincoln) **P.77** RIBA 16811 **P.81** *The Yellow Room* by James Abbott McNeill Whistler, *c.*1885, watercolour on paper, 50 x 30.5 cm, extended anonymous loan, Museum of Fine Arts, St. Petersburg, Florida TR 1981.4386.1. **P.82** Library of Congress, Washington D.C., image LC-DIG-ds-04747 **P.83** Library of Congress, Washington D.C. **P.84** *A Little Shop in Chelsea* by Mortimer Menpes, 1884–7, oil on canvas, 20 x 16 cm, The Hunterian, University of Glasgow / Bridgeman Images **P.87** *The Grey Dress* by Walter Sickert, 1884, oil on canvas, 51 x 30 cm, Manchester Art Gallery / Bridgeman Images **P.91 LEFT** © Victoria and Albert Museum, London **P.92** *A Private View at the Royal Academy* by William Powell Frith, 1881, oil on canvas, 102 x 193 cm, private collection **P.94** Library of Congress, Washington D.C., image LC-DIG-ppmsca-07756 **P.99** *'Whistler's Lady Meux'* attributed to Mortimer Menpes or Charles Brookfield, pen, ink, watercolour and pencil, 13 x 19 cm, Rosenbach Museum and Library, Philadelphia **P.100** *Arrangement in Black: Lady Meux* by James Abbott McNeill Whistler, 1881, oil on canvas, 194 x 130 cm, Honolulu Academy of Arts **P.101** *Harmony in Pink and Grey: Portrait of Lady Meux* by James Abbott McNeill Whistler, 1881–2, oil on canvas, 194 x 93 cm, The Frick Collection, New York 18.1.132 **P.103** *Arrangement in Black: La Dame au brodequin jaune – Portrait of Lady Archibald Campbell* by James Abbott McNeill Whistler, 1882, oil on canvas, 218 x 110 cm, Philadelphia Museum of Art **P.104** *Note in Green and Brown: Orlando at Coombe* by James Abbott McNeill Whistler, c.1884–5, oil on panel, 15 x 9 cm, The Hunterian, University of Glasgow / Bridgeman Images **P.109** Theatrical cartoon by Sir Percy Shelley, MS. Abinger c.83, fol. 46r, Bodleian Libraries, University of Oxford **P.114** *John Collier* by Marian Collier, c.1882–3, oil on canvas, 127 x 108 cm, © National Portrait Gallery, London **P.116** *Clytemnestra* by John Collier, 1882, oil on canvas, 239 x 143 cm © Guildhall Art Gallery, City of London **P.118** *Marian Collier (née Huxley)* by John Collier, 1882–3, oil on canvas, 62 x 49 cm © National Portrait Gallery, London **P.121** *Love Locked Out* by Anna Lea Merritt, 1890, oil on canvas, 116 x 64 cm © Tate, London **P.125** *Ellen Terry as Ophelia* by Anna Lea Merritt, 1880, etching, 23 x 16 cm plate size; 28 x 19 cm paper size © National Portrait Gallery, London **P.126** *War* by Anna Lea Merritt, 1883, oil on canvas © Bury Art Gallery and Museum, Lancashire / Bridgeman Images **P.130** Sketch of an interior, possibly Oscar Wilde's drawing room by Beatrice Godwin, c.1884, pen and ink on paper, 23 x 36 cm, The Hunterian, University of Glasgow / Bridgeman Images **P.134** courtesy Merlin Holland **P.140** *Madame X (Madame Pierre Gautreau)* by John Singer Sargent, 1883–4, oil on canvas, 208 x 110 cm, The Metropolitan Museum of Art, New York **P.144** *Ellen Terry as Lady Macbeth* by John Singer Sargent, 1889, oil on canvas, 221 x 114 cm © Tate, London **P.147** *Carmencita* by John Singer Sargent, 1889, oil on canvas, 232 x 142 cm, Musee d'Orsay, Paris / Bridgeman Images **P.149** *Lady Agnew of Lochnaw* by John Singer Sargent, 1892–3,

oil on canvas, 124 x 100 cm © Scottish National Gallery, Edinburgh / Bridgeman Images **P.152** *Harmony in Red: Lamplight* by James Abbott McNeill Whistler, 1884, oil on canvas, 190 x 89 cm, The Hunterian, University of Glasgow, Scotland / Bridgeman Images **P.157** Illustration from Oscar Wilde's *The Remarkable Rocket* by Walter Crane, 1888, engraving, private collection © Look and Learn / Bridgeman Images **P.162** *The Picture of Dorian Gray* by Oscar Wilde in *Lippincott's Monthly Magazine*, July 1890 **P.166** *W. Graham Robertson* by John Singer Sargent, 1894, oil on canvas, 230 x 119 cm © Tate, London **P.167** *Arrangement in Black and Gold: Comte Robert de Montesquiou-Fezensac* by James Abbott McNeill Whistler, 1891–2, oil on canvas, 208 x 92 cm, Henry Clay Frick Bequest 1914.1.131 © Frick Collection, New York **P.173** *William Rothenstein* by John Singer Sargent, 1897, lithograph, 57 x 44 cm © National Portrait Gallery, London **P.174** *The Climax*, illustration from Oscar Wilde's *Salomé* by Aubrey Beardsley, 1893, line block print, the Stapleton Collection / Bridgeman Images **P.176** *Diana of the Uplands* by Charles Wellington Furse, 1903–4, oil on canvas, 237 x 179 cm © Tate, London **P.179** *The Doll's House* by William Rothenstein, 1899–1900, oil on canvas, 89 x 61 cm © Tate, London / The estate of Sir William Rothenstein. All Rights Reserved 2010 / Bridgeman Images **P.180** *Group Portrait* by William Rothenstein, 1894, oil on canvas, 113 x 87 cm, private collection © The estate of Sir William Rothenstein. All Rights Reserved 2010 / Bridgeman Images. Photo © Crane Kalman, London / Bridgeman Images **P.184** courtesy Merlin Holland **P.189** © Sotheby's Images **P.194** LEFT Michael Seeney Collection **P.194** RIGHT Robert Walker Macbeth by E. H. Mills, bromide print on card mount, c.1900, 19 x 14.5 cm © National Portrait Gallery, London **P.106** *Richard, Duke of Gloucester, and the Lady Anne* by Edwin A. Abbey, 1897, oil on canvas, 134 x 265 cm, Yale University Art Gallery **P.198** *The Coronation of King Edward VII* by Edwin A. Abbey, 1902–7, oil on canvas, 275 x 458 cm, Royal Collection Trust © Her Majesty Queen Elizabeth II / Bridgeman Images **P.202** *Lord Ribblesdale* by John Singer Sargent, 1902, oil on canvas, 258 x 143.5 cm, National Gallery, London, De Agostini Picture Library / Bridgeman Images **P.205** Courtesy Richard Ormond **P.206** *John S. Sargent, R.A.*

by George Percy Jacomb-Hood, *c.*1895, pencil, brush and indian ink, 40 x 25 cm, image courtesy Abbott and Holder Ltd, London **P.209** *Fantaisie en Folie* by Robert Brough, 1897, oil on canvas, 102 x 126 cm © Tate, London **P.211** *31 Tite Street* by Max Beerbohm, *c.*1908 © The estate of Max Beerbohm **P.212** *Mr Sargent at Work* by Max Beerbohm, 1907 © The estate of Max Beerbohm **P.216** *Self-portrait* by Romaine Brooks, 1923, oil on canvas, 117.5 x 68 cm, Smithsonian American Art Museum 1966.49.1, Gift of the artist **P.219** *Mrs George Batten Singing* by John Singer Sargent, 1897, oil on canvas, 89 x 43 cm, Glasgow Museums / Bridgeman Images **P.221** © Museum of London **P.222** © Museum of London **P.225** *Gluck* by Gluck (Hannah Gluckstein), 1942, oil on canvas, 30.5 x 25 cm © National Portrait Gallery, London / The estate of Hannah Gluckstein **P.227** *Peter, A Young English Girl* by Romaine Brooks, 1923–4, oil on canvas, 92 x 62 cm, Smithsonian American Art Museum 1970.70, Gift of the artist **P.229** *Medallion (YouWe)* by Gluck (Hannah Gluckstein), 1936, oil on canvas, 29 x 34 cm, Private Collection, photo © Christie's Images / Bridgeman Images / The estate of Hannah Gluckstein **P.233** *General Officers of World War I* by John Singer Sargent, 1922 oil on canvas, 300 x 528 cm © National Portrait Gallery, London **P.235** *La Zarzarosa* by Glyn Philpot, 1910, oil on canvas, 260.5 x 184 cm, Fitzwilliam Museum, University of Cambridge / Bridgeman Images **P.236** *Siegfried Sassoon* by Glyn Philpot, 1917, oil on canvas, 61 x 51 cm, Fitzwilliam Museum, University of Cambridge / Bridgeman Images **P.238** *Melampus and the Centaur* by Glyn Philpot, 1919, oil on canvas, 122 x 204 cm, Glasgow Museums / Bridgeman Images **P.241** Hasan Shahid Suhrawardy; Philip Arnold Heseltine (Peter Warlock); D.H. Lawrence by Lady Ottoline Morrell, 29 November 1915, vintage snapshot print, 10 x 6 cm © National Portrait Gallery, London **P.247** *Field Marshall Lord Montgomery* by Augustus John, 1944, oil on canvas, 77 x 62 cm, The Hunterian, University of Glasgow / Bridgeman Images © The estate of Augustus John **P.272** *Pink Note – the Novelette* by James Abbott McNeill Whistler, 1883–4, watercolour on paper, 25 x 15 cm, Freer Gallery of Art, Smithsonian Institution, Washington D.C., Gift of Charles Lang Freer, F1902.158

ACKNOWLEDGEMENTS

In memory of Julian Barrow (1939–2013)

This book has been greatly enriched by advice and support from a number of readers including Katherine Astbury, David Boyd-Haycock, Tracy Bryson, David Coates, Erin Griffey, Katherine Hambridge, Michael Hatt, Merlin Holland, John de Holland, Sir Michael Holroyd, Pamela Fletcher, Elaine Kilmurray, David Le Lay, Linda Merrill, Naomi Paxton, Margaret Poplak, Malcolm Rutland, Ros Savile, Samuel Shaw, Clare Siviter, Barry Smith, John Stokes, James Stourton, Matthew Sturgis, Daniel E. Sutherland, Lisa Tickner and Simon Wartanby.

For invaluable background information and guidance in writing the book I would like to thank Brian Allen, Nigel Boardman, David Boyd Haycock, Stephen Calloway, Nicholas Coleridge, Nicholas Courtenay, Mark Girouard, Lady Anne Glenconner, Patrick Jephson, Margaret Macdonald, Gillian Malpass, Andrew Roberts, Meryle Secrest, Nelson Shanks, Asa Tillman, Susan Weber, Miranda Welby and Sir Peregrine Worsthorne.

Special thanks are owed to Dave Walker and the excellent team at the Local Studies of the Royal Borough of Kensington and Chelsea. I am grateful for research support from the British Library, the Chelsea Society, the Peter Warlock Society, the Whistler Society and the Oscar Wilde Society.

I am incredibly grateful to Richard Ormond for all his guidance with John Singer Sargent material and to Michael Seeney for his assistance with all things Oscar Wilde.

For their generous financial contributions towards research costs and the reproduction of images for the book I would like to acknowledge David Harding and Winton Capital and the Humanities Research Fund at the University of Warwick as well as the Society of Authors' K. Blundell Trust Awards for their kind assistance.

Julian and Serena Barrow provided early guidance for the book along with fascinating details of the street's history. The entire project has had the continued interest and support from Alex and Elinor Sainsbury as well as Sir Evelyn and Lady de Rothschild who have all kept the 'wonderful possibilities' of Tite Street alive.

My agent, Duncan McAra, was a strong believer in the project and invaluable in making it into a book. My editor, Nicki Davis at Frances Lincoln, was absolutely everything a publisher should be!

Above all I would like to thank my family and my partner, James Drury. Although I wrote the book, James lived it!